CURRENT ISSUES
IN FINANCIAL SERVICES

CURRENT ISSUES IN FINANCIAL SERVICES

Edited by

Brian Anderton

First published 1995 by
MACMILLAN PRESS LTD
Houndmills, Basingstoke, Hampshire RG21 2XS
and London
Companies and representatives
throughout the world

ISBN 0–333–56794–3 hardcover
ISBN 0–333–56799–4 paperback

A catalogue record for this book is available
from the British Library.

10   9   8   7   6   5   4   3   2   1
04   03   02   01   00   99   98   97   96   95

Printed in Great Britain by
Antony Rowe Ltd, Chippenham, Wiltshire

Contents

List of Tables   viii
List of Figures   x
Notes on the Contributors   xi
Acknowledgements   xvii
Preface   xviii

1 Introduction   *Brian Anderton*   **1**

   1   The growth and significance of the financial
      services sector   2
   2   Significance of financial services in the economy   3
   3   The pace of change   7

**2 The Framework of Financial Regulation – Fundamentally
Flawed?**   *Stephen Curry and Howard Jarman*   **13**

   1   Introduction   13
   2   The present system   14
   3   A cumbersome system   16
   4   Compensation costs   20
   5   Commission   21
   6   Self-regulation or self-delusion?   22
   7   Competence?   24
   8   Investor choice and investor information – both lacking 25
   9   Crime pays   25
  10   Recommendation – piecemeal change   26
  11   Recommendations – wholesale change   27

3 Regulation in Practice
Patrick Bentley, Howard Jarman and David Winstone   **31**

   1   Introduction   31
   2   Bank supervision and regulation   31

3   The Basle Accord   33
4   The supervision of building societies   36
5   The supervision and state regulation of insurance   41

4 The Macroeconomic Environment   *David Ramsay*   **48**

1   Introduction   48
2   Macroeconomic developments   49
3   Banks and other financial institutions   55
4   Conclusions   64

**5 The Impact of Information Technology on the Financial
Services Sector**   *Brian Anderton, John Davis, Guhlum
Hussain and Alan Staley*   **67**

1   Introduction   67
2   The impact of information technology: an overview   68
3   Operational issues   73
4   Relational databases   75
5   The database approach   77
6   Conclusions   78

6 The Tax Environment   *Pandora Hancock*   **80**

1   Introduction   80
2   An initial look at taxation in the UK   81
3   Taxation: the historical perspective   82
4   Fiscal neutrality   83
5   Taxation today   83
6   Recent developments in UK tax legislation   88
7   Conclusions   93

7 Institutional Investment – Theory and Practice
Stephen Curry   **95**

1   Growth of institutional investment   95
2   Institutional investment – the theory   100
3   Problems in applying modern portfolio theory   104
4   Asset allocation by type of fund   110
5   Summary and conclusions   118

8 Corporate Credit Analysis   *Tony Sawyer and Ken Andrews*   **122**

1   Introduction   122
2   Bank lending – a traditional approach   122

3	**Case Study**: John James Precision Engineering	126
4	Corporate credit analysis – a modern approach	133
5	Conclusions	140

9 The Problem of Costs and Cost Identification   *John Davis*   **142**

1	Introduction	142
2	The significant rise in consumer credit	142
3	The complicated business of retail banking and the diverse financial services industry	143
4	Low bank profitability and the problem of the financial service industry's cost structure	145
5	Retail branch banking is very expensive	147
6	The problem of costing intangible products	151
7	Conclusions	155

10 Marketing and Corporate Strategy for Financial Institutions
David Deakins and Stephen MacKay   **157**

1	Introduction	157
2	Corporate strategy	158
3	Market structure	158
4	Some applications of theory	159
5	The competitive environment	161
6	Strategy decisions	164
7	The marketing environment	168
8	Marketing decisions	173
9	Conclusions	176

11 A Unified European Market for Financial Services
Diane Walker   **178**

1	Introduction	178
2	Free movement of capital	178
3	The single licence	178
4	Achievements towards harmonisation	180
5	Problem areas	181
6	Reactions to a unified market	184
7	UK strengths and weaknesses	186
8	Conclusions	188

Index   191

List of Tables

1.1	Changing structure of employment, UK, 1971–93	2
1.2	Proportion of total UK employment, Banking/Finance/Insurance, 1971–93	3
1.3	Components of M4, 1993:4	4
1.4	Households, Great Britain, 1961–91	12
2.1	Costs of the regulatory system	19
2.2	Compensation and allocation to SROs, 1988–90 to 1991–2	21
2.3	Compensation caps on SROs	21
3.1	Varying requirements for capital under the Basle Accord	34
3.2	Progressive increases in Class 2 and 3 limits, 1986–93	38
4.1	The UK macroeconomy, 1950–92	50
4.2	Large British banks, sources of income, 1987–92	56
4.3	UK real growth rates, 1971–92	56
4.4	UK banks, lending to UK residents, 1987/8–1992	58
4.5	UK banks' sterling deposits and interest rates, 1981–92	60
4.6	Domestic net interest spread and margins, 1980–92	61
7.1	Percentage of total market value of UK listed ordinary shares held by different groups, 1963–92	96
7.2	Personal sector, acquisition and sale of financial assets, 1988–92	97
7.3	Selected asset holdings of self-administered pension funds, 1978 and 1990	111
7.4	Selected asset holdings of long-term insurance funds, 1978 and 1990	113
7.5	Selected asset holdings of UK authorised unit trusts, 1978 and 1993	114
7.6	Selected asset holdings of UK approved investment trusts, 1978 and 1993	117
9.1	The rise in UK consumer credit, 1982–92	143
9.2	Domestic bank spreads, 1986 and 1990	146
9.3	Post-tax percentage return on average total assets, 1986–92	146
9.4	British banks and building society branch size, 1982 and 1992	148

9.5	UK consumer credit, new advances, 1982 and 1992	149
9.6	Comparative staff costs, 1992	149
9.7	Operating costs as a percentage of operating income, 1992	150
9.8	Midland Bank, service delivery costs, 1989 and 1992	152
10.1	The growth in shares and deposits with building societies, 1979–90	162
10.2	Banks' and building societies' advances compared, 1980–90	163
10.3	Financial assets of the UK personal sector, 1981, 1989 and 1993	170
10.4	Financial liabilities of the UK personal sector, 1981 and 1990	170
10.5	Top 10 brands, 1990, by advertising spend	174

List of Figures

1.1	Credit creation in the banking system	5
2.1	The framework of investor protection	16
2.2	The fragmented nature of investor protection	17
2.3	Regulatory structure framework	18
2.4	Suggested new regulatory framework	29
4.1	Net interest margins for banks and building societies, 1980–92	62
4.2	The net interest spread	63
5.1	File-based approach to data storage	75
5.2	Account-based data	76
5.3	Database approach to data storage	77
5.4	Relational data tables	78
7.1	The utility of wealth	101
7.2	Efficient portfolios	102
7.3	The capital market line	103
8.1	The traditional approach to risk–credit appraisal	124
8.2	Lending with knowledge of the past and the future	124
8.3	Traditional lending model	125
8.4	John James Precision Engineering Ltd: company data	128
8.5	John James Precision Engineering Ltd: Balance Sheets	128
8.6	John James Precision Engineering Ltd: budgeted cash flow statement	130
8.7	John James Precision Engineering Ltd : itemised working capital calculations	132
8.8	Financial ratios: categoric framework	134
8.9	Comparing the performance of firms	136
8.10	z-score for discriminant analysis	138
10.1	The kinked demand model	160
10.2	The Cournot duopoly model	161

Notes on the Contributors

Brian Anderton is the Head of the Department of Financial Services, one of the five academic departments in the University of Central England Business School. After leaving school, he worked for a period with Westminster Bank (later National Westminster Bank). Brian took time out from banking to read economic geography at the London School of Economics, after which he resumed his banking career with Lloyds Bank. He has an extensive list of publications, mainly in the area of law relating to banking and banking law and practice. Brian has been very active in the area of professional education for bankers, writing textbooks, developing and running short courses for banking organisations, and examining for the Chartered Institute of Bankers. During the period 1990–2, he was Chairman of the Association of Banking Teachers, and he is currently Vice-President of the Association. In 1987 Brian was elected a Fellow of the Chartered Institute of Bankers in recognition of his services to banking education. More recently, Brian has taken an interest in banking education in central and eastern Europe. This has involved working with the newly emerging banking communities in both Hungary and the Ukraine.

Ken Andrews is Emeritus Senior Lecturer in the Department of Financial Services, University of Central England Business School. He specialises in the application of quantitative techniques to the solution of business problems. He has extensive teaching experience on programmes ranging from BTEC Higher National through to specialist masters' programmes. In addition, he is an experienced supervisor of postgraduate research students. Ken has extensive research experience in the area of corporate failure prediction, particularly as applied to the construction industry. He obtained an MSc in industrial and business studies by research from Warwick University in 1988 for a thesis on failure prediction models. He has continued research in this area, in part with research funding from the Chartered Institute of Management Accountants. Developments have included construction of a research database of failed companies, and the application of new predictive techniques. Although his work has tended to be 'leading-edge' research, Ken has ensured that its results have reached a wider audience. This has included papers presented to the British Accounting Association, seminars for practioners from the construction industry, and legal and accounting professions, and incorporation of his work into teaching programmes at both masters and undergraduate levels.

Patrick Bentley had a career in insurance stretching back nearly twenty years before he moved into higher education. His experience included underwriting and training activities in the life assurance sector. Although moving into higher education as a senior lecturer, Patrick has retained his interest in insurance with his teaching programme split between preparing insurance staff for the professional examinations of the Chartered Insurance Institute, and teaching specialist insurance options to undergraduate students. Patrick is a Fellow of the Chartered Insurance Institute, and takes an active role in the affairs of the Society of Fellows in the West Midlands. He is also a Member of the Society of Financial Advisers. In the area of research, Patrick has collaborated with other colleagues in the Enterprise Research Centre at UCEBS, on a project investigating risk, insurance and high technology small firms. The results of this research have formed the basis of a seminar for entrepreneurs and insurance professionals, and also the basis of an academic paper delivered at the High Technology Small Firms Conference in 1994. The work has also attracted national press coverage. In addition, Patrick co-authored a standard text *UK Financial Institutions and Markets* (Macmillan, 1991) with other colleagues in the university.

Stephen Curry is Principal Lecturer in Finance in the Department of Financial Services in the University of Central England Business School. After undergraduate and postgraduate studies in economics at Reading University, Stephen ('Bob') spent a period as an investment analyst with a major insurance company before moving into higher education. His teaching concentrates on investment topics and the stock market, and he teaches on professional, undergraduate and postgraduate programmes. Bob has a range of publications to his credit, notably *Success in Investment* (John Murray) which he co-authored with Roderick Winfield, and which has become the standard investment text on both professional and undergraduate programmes. He is also actively involved in the area of professional qualification for practitioners in banking and the securities industry. He is an examiner for the Chartered Institute of Bankers, and has worked closely with the Securities Institute in connection with professional examinations for practitioners. His current research interests include an investigation of the working practices of UK equity analysts. A paper based on this research, entitled 'New Directions in UK Financial Reporting and their Relevance to UK Equity Analysis', was presented to the British Accounting Association National Conference in 1994.

John Davis is Senior Lecturer in Accounting and Information Technology in the Department of Financial Services, University of Central England Business School. He qualified as an Associate of the Chartered Institute of Cost and Management Accountants, and pursued a career as a cost and management accountant with a number of private and public sector organisations. In the later 1980s, John completed the MA accounting and finance programme at Birmingham Polytechnic (now University of Central England) as a part-time student. Subsequently, he joined the university as a full-time member of staff. John's MA dissertation was a case study of financial planning in the public sector. This led to a conference paper given to the British Accounting Association Northern Accounting Group in 1991, and an invitation to join the CIMA working party investigating the 'Impact of Delegated Budgets on GP Practice'. John's current research focus has shifted to securitisation and its impact within banking. In addition, John has a strong interest in applied information technology, particularly the use of expert systems and neural networks. He has authored the standard user-guide to the crystal expert systems software used at UCE, and he has pioneered the integration of expert systems into undergraduate teaching in the Business School.

David Deakins is the Renfrewshire Enterprise Professor of Enterprise Development at the University of Paisley, prior to which he was a Senior Lecturer in Economics and Director of the Enterprise Research Centre in the University of Central England Business School. David has first degrees in economics and in business studies, and a master's in business economics. David began his career in higher education in mainstream economics, and he retains a strong teaching interest in microeconomics, industrial economics and labour economics. However, his research interests increasingly carried him into the area of small business, initially from the standpoint of support agencies for small business development, and more recently in connection with bank finance for small businesses and ethnic small businesses. As Director of the Enterprise Research Centre, David not only conducted his own research, but also facilitated the work of other colleagues. The Enterprise Research Centre, under David's direction, has been responsible for running a considerable number of conferences and seminars, bringing together both practitioners and academics, and for numerous publications. The work of the Enterprise Research Centre has received significant national media coverage. David is now continuing his research in the Paisley Enterprise Centre, holding a Chair sponsored by the Renfrewshire Enterprise Agency.

Pandora Hancock is Principal Lecturer in Finance at Leeds Metropolitan University, and she was formerly Senior Lecturer in Taxation in the Department of Financial Services, University of Central England Business School. She has a first degree in mathematics, and qualified as a Chartered Accountant with Peat Marwick Mitchell & Co. She has research experience, particularly in the area of taxation, and investment and financial decision-making in multinational corporations. She has authored a number of books and articles on taxation issues.

Guhlum Hussain is Senior Lecturer in Economics in the Department of Financial Services, University of Central England Business School. He has a first degree in economics and a master's degree in money, banking and finance from the University of Birmingham. He has held posts in finance in both public and private sector organisations. Before joining the staff of the University of Central England, he was a financial analyst with the Forward Trust Group. In this position, Guhlum gained substantial experience in the application of information technology in a financial services context. Guhlum's main teaching interests lie in the area of the economics of finance, and he is currently undertaking doctoral research on the prediction of stock market returns. He has also conducted collaborative research on ethnic small businesses, and on bank financing for small businesses with colleagues in the Enterprise Research Centre at UCE. This research has culminated in a series of seminars for academics and practioners, and to publications in small business and accountancy journals.

Howard Jarman is Senior Lecturer in Finance in the Department of Financial Services, University of Central England Business School. He holds a first degree in economics, and a master's degree in financial economics. Howard's principal area of interest is financial institutions and markets, and in particular building societies. He has recently completed a doctoral thesis at Loughborough University in the area of supervision of building societies. In addition, he has extensive teaching experience in finance-related topics on professional, undergraduate and postgraduate programmes.

Stephen MacKay is Principal Lecturer in the Marketing of Financial Services in the Department of Financial Services, University of Central England Business School. He has a fist degree in sociology, and an MBA from Manchester Business School. In addition, he is an Associate of the Chartered Insurance Institute, and a member of the Chartered Institute of Marketing. Stephen held marketing posts with a number of insurance companies during the 1980s, and gained substantial practical experience in the marketing of insurance and pension products. In 1987 he moved into higher education, taking up a post as a Senior Lecturer in Marketing at Bolton Institute of Higher Education. He has also been a visiting lecturer at UMIST

School of Management. Stephen has substantial research experience in the area of financial services marketing, and regularly presents papers at national and international conferences. In the last three years, he has supervised the work of a research assistant in the Department of Financial Services at UCE, investigating product deletion strategies in the financial services sector. Stephen has extensive experience as a teacher of marketing at professional, undergraduate and postgraduate levels.

David Ramsay is Senior Lecturer in Economics and Director of Economics in the Department of Financial Services, University of Central England Business School. He holds a first degree in economics and a master's degree in social sciences from the University of Birmingham. In addition, David is a Fellow of the Chartered Insurance Institute. David's early career was in insurance, and he held posts with both Legal & General and Sun Alliance. Subsequently, he held posts as a lecturer in economics both in the UK and at the University of Zimbabwe. He was also, for a time, a research assistant with the National Economic Development Organisation (NEDO), and had a period of secondment with the World Bank. David's teaching and research interests lie in the area of macroeconomics, and more particularly the economics of money and banking. He has extensive under-graduate and postgraduate teaching experience in this area, and a number of publications.

Tony Sawyer is Senior Lecturer in Banking in the Department of Financial Services, University of Central England. He is a Fellow of the Chartered Institute of Bankers. Tony's career was initially in clearing banking, and he held a number of posts with Lloyds Bank. Latterly, Tony became an account-ant in an industrial company, gaining valuable experience in the operation of the accounting function within a business. Tony has written a substantial number of textbooks and study aids for students undertaking the professional banking examinations. His area of specialism is accounting and lending tech-niques. In addition, he regularly provides training inputs for lending man-agers in several major banking organisations.

Alan Staley is Senior Lecturer in Applied Information Technology in the Department of Financial Services, University of Central England Business School. He holds a first degree in biological sciences, and a master's degree in information technology. Before moving into higher education, Alan held a number of posts with manufacturing companies, and these gave him a partic-ular insight into the application of information technology to the accounting function in a business. Alan teaches applied information technology on a range of professional and undergraduate programmes. He is also an examiner and revision course tutor for the Chartered Institute of Bankers. Alan's partic-ular interests lie in the strategic management of information technology, and the way information technology may be used by a business to gain commercial advantage.

Diane Walker holds the Birmingham Insurance Lectureship in the Department of Financial Services, University of Central England Business School. Her post is sponsored in a unique way by a consortium of insurance companies, insurance brokers and loss adjusters. Diane is a Fellow of the Chartered Insurance Institute and holds a Diploma in Business Administration from Aston University. She has a particular interest in the development of a unified European market for financial services. Diane had a varied career in the insurance industry before moving into the higher education. She has experience of underwriting in several large composite insurance companies. Latterly, she ran her own insurance broking business in the West Midlands. Diane has a major commitment to the effective education of insurance professionals. She has been a past president of both the Worcester and the Birmingham Insurance Institutes, as well as playing an active role in the Chartered Insurance Institute at a national level. Diane has considerable teaching experience preparing insurance staff for the professional examinations of the Chartered Insurance Institute, and on specialist insurance units on undergraduate courses.

David Winstone is Senior Lecturer in Finance in the Department of Financial Services, University of Central England Business School. He has first degrees in both modern history and applied economics, and a master's degree in industrial relations from Warwick University. Before moving into higher education, David held a number of positions in companies based in the motor industry. Latterly, David was director of his own company, running a distributorship for Bosch GmbH. This gave David a good insight into business finance, and particularly a practical knowledge of issues relating to the finance of international trade and international payments. David's main teaching interests lie in the area of financial institutions and markets, and he delivers programmes of study to both professional and undergraduate students. He is co-author of a standard text *UK Financial Institutions and Markets* (Macmillan, 1991) with other colleagues in the Department of Financial Services. More recently, David has developed a particular interest in financial derivatives (futures, options, swaps) and their use in corporate treasury management. He has delivered training programmes on derivatives to staff in an international bank based in London, and he is also a visiting lecturer on the MBA programme at Exeter University, providing specialist inputs on treasury management. He is currently involved in the development of a new master's programme in finance in the University of Central England Business School; and he is also involved in a TEMPUS (TACIS) project to develop a banking faculty at the Kiev State University of Trade and Economics.

Acknowledgements

The editor and publishers wish to thank the following for permission to reproduce copyright material.

Journal of Business, Finance and Accounting, for Figure 8.8, adapted from J.K. Courtis, 'Modelling a Financial Ratios Categoric Framework' (1978). Media Expenditure Analysis Ltd, for Table 10.3.

A special thank-you is due to Mrs Lynn Mellington for her skill and patience in typing and retyping the manuscript.

BRIAN ANDERTON

Preface

(Financial services has become a popular area for study over the last decade or
so with the treatment of the sector as part of business studies programmes,
and the development of whole undergraduate degrees devoted to the study of
financial services.

The problem is that financial services is not an academic discipline, but
rather a functional area and, moreover, a highly diverse functional area. The
study of financial services requires a degree of competence and knowledge in
a wide range of relevant disciplines. In addition, there will be issues relating
to one branch of financial services which will not be relevant to another.)

In this text, we make no claim to comprehensive coverage of such a wide-
ranging field of study. Rather, we have chosen to focus on a number of key
topic areas which we believe are significant to the way the modern financial
services sector has evolved and now operates. Equally, we make no pretence
to providing discussion of the latest 'twist' in the ever-changing story of
financial services. Interested readers are referred to the quality press and
trade/professional periodicals for this.

There is a loose organisational framework to the way the topics are presented. The early chapters examine some of the major environmental factors
which have played a role in shaping the financial services sector in recent
years: the regulatory framework; macroeconomic policy; the information
technology revolution; the tax environment; and the dominance of institutional investment in the decision-making process. The later chapters pick up
important operational issues: developments in techniques used to appraise
credit risk; problems in deriving a sound basis for the allocation of costs in a
multi-product financial institution; and response to the market.

The contributions are primarily set within the context of UK financial institutions and markets. However, the final chapter widens the discussion, and
provides a summary of the difficult journey towards a unified European
market for financial services.

Each chapter seeks to provide the reader with an overview of the main
issues, and with a framework within which to gain a perspective on these
issues. The further reading, at the conclusion of each chapter, is designed to
enable the reader to develop a deeper understanding of the topic under con-

sideration. In nearly all cases, the further reading has been chosen to be readily accessible to undergraduate students.

The financial services sector is, perhaps, the most dynamic and significant part of post-industrial western economies. It is interesting to note that, in the restructuring of the economies of central and eastern Europe, high priority has been given to the creation of an effective financial infrastructure. The contributors to this text have collectively had many years working in, teaching, researching and writing about financial services. We hope some of our enthusiasm for study of the sector will communicate itself to the reader.

BRIAN ANDERTON

Introduction

Brian Anderton

This book takes as its focus what has become known, in the last 15 years or so, as the financial services sector. The meaning of the term 'financial services', as it is applied in the UK, is broadly understood to include banking, insurance, building societies, stockbroking and investment services.

However, precise definition of the sector is by no means straightforward. For example, in the UK, the Standard Industrial Classification (1980 version) defines a broad category of Banking/Finance/Insurance which brings together activities classified under SIC headings 81–85. This does, indeed, include banking, insurance and investment services. But it also includes a wide range of other business and professional services, including legal services, accountants, estate agency, architects and advertising. For comparative purposes, this chapter and later chapters in the book make use of statistics presented under the broad SIC 81–85 heading. However, for the purposes of discussion within the book, the meaning of 'financial services' is more closely circumscribed to focus on core activities like banking (including building societies), insurance, and investment services.

The question remains: why should there need to be a book dealing with Current Issues in Financial Services, any more than with any other sector in the economy? Three main reasons may be adduced to justify the focus of this book.

1. In the UK, as in other developed western economies, the financial services sector has grown rapidly over the post-war period, and now represents a significant proportion of total economic activity in most western economies.
2. Institutions and markets within the financial services play a major role in the operation of the economic system.
3. The financial services sector has been, arguably, the most dynamic sector in developed western economies over the last 25 years, showing an amazing capacity for change, innovation and adaptation.

These three factors are discussed in more detail in the rest of this chapter, partly to provide a 'thumb-nail sketch' of the financial services sector, and partly to set the scene for succeeding chapters.

1. The growth and significance of the financial services sector

Although the discussion, here, concentrates on the financial services sector of the UK, the trends would be mirrored for most other developed western economies, albeit the scale and timing of trends will not be identical.

When one examines the structure of most western developed economies over the last 25 years, perhaps the most striking feature is the growth of the service sector and the concomitant relative, if not absolute, decline of the manufacturing sector. This is well reflected in the employment statistics shown for the UK in Table 1.1.

These changes should not come as any surprise. While employment is only one measure of the significance of each group of activities within the economy as a whole and while it may be true that labour-saving technology may have had a somewhat earlier and stronger effect in manufacturing than in services, there are other more profound reasons, for regarding this shift in employment as unexceptionable.

1. In post-industrial economies, the market for manufactured goods will tend towards saturation, while many services will experience an acceleration in demand for their products as income and wealth grow (i.e. they will have an income elasticity greater than plus one).
2. The manufacture of more standard goods, will tend to migrate away from high wage economies towards those developing economies with lower labour costs.

Table 1.1   Changing structure of employment, UK, 1971–93

Year	% of total employment	
	Service sector employment %	*Manufacturing and construction industry employment* %
1971	53	36
1979	59	32
1983	64	27
1986	67	26
1989	69	25
1991	71	21
1993	73	20

Sources: *Social Trends, 1990–1994* (London: CSO).

*Table 1.2   Proportion of total UK employment,
Banking/Finance/Insurance (SIC 1980 categories 81–85),
1971–93*

Year	% of total employment
1971	6.03
1979	7.11
1981	7.94
1983	8.90
1986	10.13
1988	11.10
1990	11.96
1993	12.39

Source: 1971–90: *Social Trends, 1990*; 1993: *Monthly Digest of Statistics* (January 1994) (London: CSO).

The fortunes of the financial services sector have mirrored and, indeed, outperformed the growth of the service sector as a whole. Thus, at the beginning of the 1970s, in the UK, Banking/Finance/Insurance (as measured by SIC 1980 categories 81–85) represented around 11% of total employment within the service sector; but, by the beginning of the 1990s, this had risen to over 17% of total employment in the service sector. Looked at from the point of view of overall employment trends, as Table 1.2 shows, employment in Banking/Finance/Insurance in the UK has more than doubled as a proportion of total employment in the economy between the beginning of the 1970s and the early 1990s.

The rate of growth and the size of the financial services sector as a proportion of the overall economy is good reason to single out the sector for special consideration.

2.   Significance of financial services in the economy

Financial intermediation

At the centre of the financial services sector of any economy is the process of financial intermediation. Financial institutions act as a channel through which the financial surpluses of some groups in society (for example, households) are collected and then redistributed to other groups in society (for example, firms) which have a financial deficit. In other words, financial institutions have traditionally acted to mobilise the savings within an economy, and to direct them into productive investment.

This may be seen in the role of banks, which take in deposits from customers and convert them into loans for other customers; or in the traditional role of building societies taking deposits from some of their members and relending them to other members of the society wishing to invest in residential property. In a similar fashion the insurance companies, notably those involved in long-term life assurance business, have collected premiums from policyholders, and invested these surpluses in industrial/commercial activity via the stockmarket.

On the face of it, there would be a logic in those with financial surpluses (savings) lending them directly to those with a financial deficit (borrowing/investment requirement), thereby 'cutting out the middleman'. In fact, there have been very good reasons why funds should be channelled via a financial intermediary such as a bank, building society or insurance company. These are well detailed in the literature on financial intermediation! Suffice to say that, in the development of complex modern economies, the financial intermediation role played by the financial services sector has been crucially important in mobilising savings for investment purposes.

Credit creation

Within the financial services sector, the banks have a particular importance to the operation of the economy and to the conduct of government economic policy. This arises since the principal liability of banks, customer deposits, is the most significant element in a country's money supply. For example, Table 1.3 shows the composition of the UK monetary aggregate M4 and, in particular, the dominance of bank (and building society) deposits.

Table 1.3   Components of M4, 1993: 4

M4 private sector holdings of:	£ million	%
Notes and coin	17,992	3.3
Bank deposits (retail and wholesale)	316,734	57.6
Building society shares and deposits	214,981	39.1
	549,707	100.0

Source: *Bank of England Quarterly Bulletin* (February 1994).

The particular importance of banks is that, through their lending activities, they are able to create new bank deposits and hence increase the country's money supply. This is summarised in the old proposition: 'every loan creates a deposit'. A very simplified version of this process is illustrated in Figure 1.1, which charts the effect of lending on the balance sheet of the banking system.

From the simple example in Figure 1.1, it may be seen that the banking system has increased its deposits (and hence the money supply) to 250% of its initial level.

This process of deposit creation through lending could continue indefinitely (assuming cash advances are always repaid into the banking system as fresh deposits); but, in practice, it will be constrained by the need of the bank to retain a reasonable percentage of its deposits in cash (or other liquid assets) in order to meet the demand for repayment by some of its depositors. Without this ability to repay the small proportion of depositors wishing to withdraw cash in any given time period, there would be a loss of confidence in the banking system leading to a 'run on the bank', that is a

	Liabilities	Assets	Cash to deposits ratio %
Stage 1	Bank customer *A* deposits £10,000 of cash		
↓	Deposits 10,000	Cash 10,000	100
Stage 2	Bank lends to customer *B* £5,000 by way of a cash advance		
↓	Deposits 10,000	Cash 5,000	50
Stage 3	Customer *B* spends his cash advance with customer *C* who deposits it with the banking system		
↓	Deposits 15,000	Cash 10,000	66 $^2/_3$
		Loans 5,000	
Stage 4	Bank lends £10,000 to customer *D* by making a loan, and crediting customer *D*'s current account		
↓	Deposits 25,000	Cash 10,000	40
		Loans 15,000	
Stage 5	Customer *D* writes a cheque for £10,000 on his account in favour of Customer *E* who pays the cheque into his own account		
↓	Deposits 25,000	Cash 10,000	40
		Loans 15,000	

(i.e. no change in the overall banking system balance sheet, but the banking system now owes *E* rather than *D* £10,000).

Figure 1.1   Credit creation in the banking system

very large-scale withdrawal of funds by depositors. If, for example, the banking system deems it prudent to hold 10% of its deposit liabilities as a cash reserve, then it may easily be calculated that an injection of £1,000 of new cash into the banking system could finance an increase in lending and of deposits up to tenfold the original cash deposit (i.e. £10,000).

Given the central role which many economists have ascribed to the rate of growth in money supply as a major factor in the expansion of aggregate demand and concomitant inflation, it is not surprising that the activities of the banking system have been a continuing focus for government monetary policy. This is examined in much greater detail and from a more contemporary perspective in Chapter 4.

Distinctiveness of product

The products of the financial services sector share many of the features of the products of other service industries. In particular, they are intangible and perishable.

However, in some respects, they have features which make them significantly different from the products of other service industries. First, financial services are often technically sophisticated, and the consumer may lack both the information and understanding necessary to make meaningful comparisons between the products of different suppliers. Moreover, a number of financial services are long-term in nature. This is especially so in the investment sector with such products as life assurance and pensions. The consumer will not be in a position to know, with certainty, whether he chose the best investment product until many years after its purchase. This is compounded by the fact that choice of the right financial services product is frequently a decision of major importance to the well-being of the consumer, for example the choice of mortgage or pensions product.

Given the lack of information and understanding about many financial services products by consumers, and the importance to the consumer of the decision to buy a particular financial services product, it is not surprising that the consumer should seek external advice. However, much of this advice on product suitability, quality and price comes from the seller of the service, either directly or via an agent/broker who is paid a commission by the seller of the service. Clearly, this is a situation in which there are strong temptations to make purchasing recommendations to the consumer which are not the most appropriate, but which maximise the profits of the seller. Recent criticisms, in this regard, have included high-pressure selling of endowment mortgages, where the mortgage-lender benefits from commission on the sale of the endowment life policy; and suspect advice to employees to leave in-company pension schemes, and to take out personal pension plans. It is for these reasons that the financial services sector has traditionally been subject to regulation. The present regulatory framework and some of its inadequacies are discussed in Chapters 2 and 3.

3. The pace of change

Throughout the western developed economies, the pace of change in the financial services sector has been at least as rapid as in any other sector of the economy and, in most cases, appreciably faster. The rate of change and innovation has been, in part, a reaction to changes in the environment in which the sector operates. But the sector has also been proactive in exploiting new opportunities and new markets. Space, here, precludes discussion of many of the important changes in financial services in the last 25 years, but some of the more significant changes are summarised below.

Changing structure of financial services

Up to the late 1970s, in the UK, the financial services sector presented a picture of a highly structured and stratified industry. Different types of institution specialised in a particular type of activity, and there were clear demarcation lines between the functions of different institutions within the financial system. Though there was some rationalisation within the sector through mergers and takeovers, there were few new entrants to the industry. In part, this was a result of restrictions in the regulatory framework within which institutions operated, but it was also a function of technical and economic barriers to entry. For example, in banking, the need to offer customers a local branch network and a cheque payment service inhibited the entry of new players.

The 1980s was a decade of deregulation. This was true not only for financial services but also for many other sectors of the economy, and it was true not only for the UK but also for the majority of western developed economies. Taking the UK as an example, such statutory changes as the Financial Services Act 1986 (which ushered in the so called 'Big Bang' in the investment industry), and the Building Societies Act 1986 (which liberalised the range of activities in which building societies could engage), coupled with less formal policy relaxations, brought a dramatic change in the mode of operation of the UK financial services sector. However, it would also be true to say that such legislative changes were purely permissive. They required the financial institutions to be proactive in exploiting the changes in the regulatory regime and, to some extent, this was already happening ahead of the legislative changes. Towards the end of the 1970s, the UK clearing banks had already begun to make inroads into the house mortgage market, the traditional preserve of the building societies. This had little to do with changes in the regulatory framework, and much to do with the perception of the banks that lending to home-buyers was a preferable alternative to lending to companies in a recession, or lending to high-risk less developed countries.

Structural deregulation in the UK had two contrasted effects. It led to a marked blurring of the boundaries between financial institutions. Thus, building societies became increasingly important players in the provision of retail banking services, providing current accounts, loans for purposes other than house purchase, credit cards, ATM. facilities, etc. As well as making inroads into home loans, banks have expanded into stockbroking and, with the building societies, become a major force in the sale of insurance products. Thus, in many ways, the sector as a whole has become more homogeneous, with decreasing differentiation between different types of institution.

By contrast, the effect of deregulation has been to cause greater variation in the activities of similar types of financial institution. Within the building societies sector, a sharp divide has opened up between the larger societies able to exploit the potential of the Building Societies Act for the diversification of their activities, and the smaller societies unable because of their size to have the same degree of diversification. But, even among the largest societies, there has been considerable variation in the pattern of diversification. Some societies have seen it as important to offer their customers current account facilities with cheque books while others have preferred to avoid the high costs associated with paper-based payments systems, and to offer more restricted payments services based on plastic cards and ATMs. Some societies have seen advantages in diversifying into estate agency, as a natural adjunct of their traditional mortgage business and less traditional insurance broking business; while others, perhaps wisely, have eschewed investment in over-priced estate agency assets. Only one society to date, Abbey National, has gone to the limit of the Building Societies Act, and transformed itself into a public limited company (thereby transforming itself from a building society into a bank). In other words, as the financial services sector as a whole has become more homogeneous, particular types of financial institution have become more heterogeneous.

Deregulation has also permitted the entry of wholly new players in to the financial services sector. For example, major retailing firms are often well placed to provide retail financial services. Perhaps the best example of this is Marks & Spencer plc whose financial services arm provides a growing range of personal financial services including credit facilities, plastic payment cards, unit trust investments and pension products. Other significant players of the future are likely to include the major telecommunications companies, while large industrial–commercial conglomerates such as British American Tobacco have acquired a stake in the financial services sector by acquiring existing companies such as Eagle Star Insurance.

The entry of new, non-financial, institutions to the sector is a reflection of the reduced barriers to entry. Apart from the liberalisation of the regulatory framework, there have been significant reductions in the technical and economic barriers. For example, it was a long-held view that new competitors were precluded from retail banking by the very high cost of acquiring the requisite branch network. However, the advent of new delivery systems for retail banking services, particularly those based on the application of information technology, has revolutionised the position (see Chapter 5). Thus, the success of branchless retail banking is now well established, and the success of organisations such as First Direct (albeit owned by Midland Bank) seems certain to be emulated by others. In fact, something of an asymmetry has developed in retail banking. While the barriers to entry have come down, permitting new and highly effective competitors to enter the industry, the barriers to exit on the part of traditional banks remain very high. Chief amongst these barriers to exit, ironically enough, is the very branch network which for so long protected the banks from external competition. The branch network is very expensive to operate and a substantial part of it is unremunerative. Moreover, the excess profits, which in earlier days allowed the banks to cross-subsidise less remunerative parts of the network, are likely to be competed away by the new entrants. Yet an orderly disinvestment from the branch network is likely to be a slow and painful process and the problem of overcapacity is likely to persist for some years (see Chapter 9 for more discussion of the problem of costs in the banking sector).

Globalisation

'Globalisation' is a term which has been coined to cover the linking together of the financial markets of individual countries to form a world-wide market. Thus, it is possible to trade the major currencies 24 hours each working day, moving from the Far Eastern to the European and on to the North American markets. In a similar way, a global market in lending and borrowing Eurocurrencies has also developed. It is also possible to trade in the new financial derivatives markets, such as financial futures and options, moving from the Far East via London or other European exchanges to North America.

The factors which have underpinned globalisation of financial markets are various.

- Deregulation, and in particular the relaxation of exchange controls, has been a major impetus.
- The growth of multinational corporations has created a demand for the linking together of financial markets, as corporations seek finance on an international scale. This is, in part, a convenience where corporations seek to raise finance in the currency of the country in which they intend to invest. But it also reflects the scale on which such companies wish to

borrow, requiring the international pooling of financial resources and the spreading of risk across more than one market.

● Developments in information technology and telecommunications have allowed much greater access to information between markets, so that information from one market is readily communicated to other markets in the global network.

The significance of globalisation lies in the fact that markets will closely track one another. If prices in one market move out of line with those in other markets, traders will take a position which gains advantage from this (a process known as arbitrage). For example, if the cost of borrowing dollars is lower in one market than in other markets, traders will borrow dollars in the cheap market and re-lend them on other markets where dollar interest rates are higher. The very act of increasing the amount of dollar borrowing in the cheap market will drive up dollar interest rates in this market, until they come into alignment with rates in other markets.

The process of globalisation, and the associated development of international banking and finance groups, has been restricted to the wholesale financial markets. Developments in the internationalisation of retail financial services have been very much more limited, even within groups of countries with close economic ties, such as the European Community countries (see Chapter 11).

Changing markets

Corporate financial services

Within the market for corporate financial services, perhaps the most significant development of the last 10–15 years has been the growth of financial disintermediation and the associated growth of debt securitisation. What this means is that large corporations go directly to the market to raise finance, rather than borrowing in a more conventional way via their banks. They do so by the issue of marketable debt instruments or securities such as bonds and commercial paper.

Debt securitisation simulates the main advantages of financial intermediation. Maturity transformation is achieved since the company issuing the debt instrument is guaranteed the funds until the bond is due for redemption, but the investor gains liquidity since the bond can be sold at any time to a new investor through the secondary market. Risk transformation is achieved, since such debt instruments are only issued by the largest and most reputable companies, while their financial soundness is subject to independent scrutiny by the credit-rating agencies whose findings are made public.

The drive towards disintermediation in corporate finance derives from a number of influences. Primarily, it is now possible for some of the largest corporations to borrow funds in the market more cheaply than is possible for their bankers who would, in any case, need to add a 'mark-up' to their lending rates to cover their costs and create a profit. This state of affairs has arisen since some large industrial and commercial corporations have a better credit-rating than their bankers, whose financial standing has been damaged over the last two decades by bad-debt problems in both international and national markets.

However, the banks themselves have been active in promoting the development of disintermediation by corporate customers. This is, in part, because traditional lending to such large corporate customers has become unprofitable, with the interest rate spreads between deposit and lending rates being inadequate to cover the bank's costs. This is particularly so since banks have to provide capital cover for loans to customers at the same rate, irrespective of the customer's financial standing (see Chapter 3). In addition, banks have placed an increasing emphasis on developing their non-interest income (i.e. income from sources other than the interest charged on loans). Banks are able to generate substantial fees from assisting corporations in the raising of finance through the issue of debt securities.

Retail financial services

There continues to be several interesting trends in the market for retail financial services. First, as society becomes richer, in terms both of income and wealth, there is a more than proportionate increase in demand for personal financial services (i.e. demand for many personal financial services will be income elastic). Moreover, there is a growing financial sophistication amongst consumers, with a rising demand for bespoke or customised financial services.

This trend, and the response of the financial services sector, is well illustrated in the growth of so-called 'bank assurance'. The UK clearing banks have become major players in the insurance market, selling both life and general insurance products. The Financial Services Act 1986 requires organisations selling investment insurance products to observe the principle of polarisation (see Chapter 2). Either the organisation must be a tied agent, selling only the products of one company; or the organisation must be an independent financial intermediary, in which case it may only recommend its own insurance products where these are superior to alternative products from other companies. All the major UK clearing banks, and nearly all the building societies have elected to follow the tied agent route. Thus, customers will be sold insurance products from only one company, sometimes a captive company owned by the bank. The product is likely to be safe but not particularly price-competitive. However, for the more financially sophisticated customer, the bank is likely to refer him or her to another subsidiary of the banking group, which will be an independent financial intermediary. This

Table 1.4   Households, Great Britain, 1961–91

Household size %	1961	1971	1981	1991
1 person	14	18	22	27
2 persons	30	32	32	34
3 persons	23	19	17	16
4 or more persons	34	31	29	23
Average household size (persons)	3.1	2.9	2.7	2.5
Total number of households (000)	16.2	18.2	19.5	21.9

Source: *Social Trends, 1994* (London: CSO).

will ensure the customer is sold a product which is likely to be more customised to his or her personal needs, and which will probably be more price-competitive.

The market for personal financial services is also influenced by changing social structure. Thus, in the UK and in many other European and North American markets, there has been a significant increase in the number of households; but, at the same time, the average household size has declined (see Table 1.4). The decision to purchase a particular financial service, whether choice of bank or life assurance product or unit trust, has traditionally been a male orientated activity. However, the growing financial independence of women and, indeed, the increasing number of households where the head of the household is female, means that today this assumption can no longer be so readily made. At the very least, this is likely to have a significant impact on the way personal financial services are marketed in the future (see Chapter 10).

CHAPTER 2

The Framework of Financial Regulation – Fundamentally Flawed?

Stephen Curry and Howard Jarman

1. Introduction

Why should financial firms be regulated? Are they different from non-financial firms? A financial service cannot generally be tested at the time of purchase, and much of the rationale for financial regulation stems from the problems of market failure that exist in the financial system, particularly in relation to investors. 'Market failure' here refers to a variety of events that can imperil the safety of investors' funds – fraud, misfeasance, collapse of an institution (either through fraud or mismanagement, for example).

Financial failures are not new, and nor can they be completely eliminated. Financial institutions have been collapsing ever since they were first introduced. The secondary banking crisis in 1973–5 showed how easy it is for a whole subsection of financial institutions to hit problems (most of them through poor management – over-exposure to the property market which then collapsed, and funding fixed rate assets with floating rate liabilities). Fraud has also been to the fore with funds being misappropriated for example at Grays Building Society, and the affair of Barlow Clowes leading to fraudulent misappropriation of investors' funds. Nor has the insurance sector escaped, with the spectacular collapse of Vehicle and General in the 1970s. More recently, British and Commonwealth Bank collapsed because of the failure of one of its subsidiaries, Atlantic Computers.

Also, there has recently been the collapse of BCCI and the misappropriation of the Maxwell pension funds. It is generally argued that because fraud or the failure of an institution or intermediary can potentially lead to the loss of life-savings for many investors, then some form of regulation is necessary. The nature of the large volume of funds involved in financial collapse and fraud makes the situation quite different from such occurrences in non-financial companies.

The main questions to be addressed are these:

1. Given that some form of financial regulation is deemed to be necessary, has the present system shown itself to be adequate?
2. Are there improvements that could be made to the present system of regulation?

2.   The present system

It is possible to divide financial regulation into three main types, although clearly it is difficult in practice precisely to delineate between them: *structural regulation*, which covers the main types of activities that different forms of institution are permitted to engage in; *prudential regulation*, which covers the internal management of financial institutions in relation to capital adequacy, liquidity and solvency; and *investor protection regulation* which is designed to shield investors from malpractice, fraud and collapse. There is some degree of overlap because investors, for example, are also protected by prudential regulation from insolvency of institutions, which prevents under-capitalisation of financial firms and excessive risk-taking, and protected by structural regulation from conflicts of interest that could occur if types of business were not separated.

Structural regulation involves demarcation lines between the activities of financial institutions, many of which have in fact been eroding in recent years, largely through the desire of the regulatory authorities to create greater competition. This erosion of structural demarcation lines has had a significant impact on the overall manner in which regulation is carried out, as shown later.

Prudential regulation refers to the internal aspects of the management of financial institutions. The regulations set down minimum ratios which the institutions must comply with, although of course the institutions would themselves monitor these relationships very closely even if prudential regulations did not exist (but the argument is that some would inevitably overstep the mark if the ratios were not mandatory). Capital is merely proof of reserves that are available to cushion investor confidence, whilst liquidity is the ability to meet liabilities as and when they come due. These are the bedrocks of prudential regulation, and are examined in greater detail in Chapter 3.

The main emphasis here is on investor protection. There is a large information asymmetry between what an investor knows about a particular financial intermediary or institution and what the institution itself knows, because of the complicated nature of finance. This market failure means that most investors are totally unaware, for example, of the soundness or probity of intermediaries or institutions or, moreover, are unable easily to gain redress on an individual basis if they are wronged. It is therefore argued that because of information asymmetries and the large amounts of money involved, some form of regulation of financial institutions is desirable.

The three types of regulation – structural, prudential and investor – ought to have as their objectives the soundness and safety of financial institutions (and hence stability of the system), the maintenance of the efficiency of the provision of financial services and products (in terms of both pricing and investor choice), the maintenance of the integrity of the transmission mechanism (the payments system) and the protection of the consumers of financial services.

The system of regulation thus needs to take into account both macro and micro aspects. Macro aspects relate to the interest of the financial system as a whole – systemic interest. A major objective of regulation is the control of system risks, which could threaten the stability of the financial systems as a whole. Systemic risk can be explained as the domino effect – if one financial institution fails many others will topple over with it. There is some evidence that systemic risk has been increasing in recent years, particularly with the rise of financial conglomerates and financial innovation. The growth of financial conglomerates has introduced a greater interdependency amongst financial institutions. The possibility that one section of a large financial services group might pull down the rest of the group has increased with the number of conglomerates emerging. Micro aspects relate to the interests of the producer and the consumer – particularly the latter.

Regulation can be carried out through formal statute, informal self-imposed rules (or self-regulation) or some hybrid of these. The current system of investor regulation in the UK is one of self-regulation within a statutory framework. The Securities and Investments Board (SIB) authorises and oversees four self-regulatory organisations (SROs) which are responsible for the authorisation and regulation of their members. Overall regulation is overseen by the Treasury, which has now taken over this role from the Department of Trade and Industry (DTI) (see Figure 2.1).

The SROs cover both retail and wholesale financial markets and services. The SROs are financed by industry levies, and anybody who wants to carry out investment business has to register with the SIB or the appropriate SRO(s). The SROs have created detailed codes of practice, each guided by 10 broad principles and 40 core rules set out by the SIB (see Pawley, 1991). The SROs have the right to levy fines and withdraw licences. By the end of 1994, LAUTRO for example had levied fines totalling £3.5 million. The largest single fine was £300,000 imposed on each of Irish Life, Norwich Union and Premium Life.

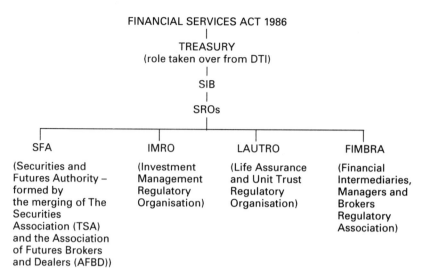

Figure 2.1   The framework of investor protection

3.   A cumbersome system

One of the main difficulties with the current system lies with the fragmented nature of the regulatory process. The emphasis is on functional rather than institutional regulation, which is generally agreed to be necessary because of the growth of multi-product financial institutions. But alongside this functional approach are the unwieldy and overlapping SROs. Figure 2.2 shows the extent to which the SROs are linked, and the problems this causes for intermediaries.

This regulatory structure is both complicated and far too fragmented, particularly if the other parts of the regulatory system are taken into consideration (see Figure 2.3). There are a whole range of overlapping jurisdictions, which allows for the possibility of both over-regulation of functions and under-regulation of functions, where poor harmonisation and co-operation exists amongst the regulators. Partly in response to this criticism, FIMBRA and LAUTRO will be superseded in 1995 by the Personal Investment Authority (PIA).

A prime example of diffused responsibility is that of insider dealing (effectively a crime against the market itself – investors will instinctively stay away from a market in which they are unfairly treated through second-hand access to price-sensitive information), where the SIB, the Department of Trade and Industry, the Treasury, the Bank of England and the London Stock Exchange may all be involved. This reduces investigations to the speed of a crawl, and complicates agreement amongst the parties on best how to

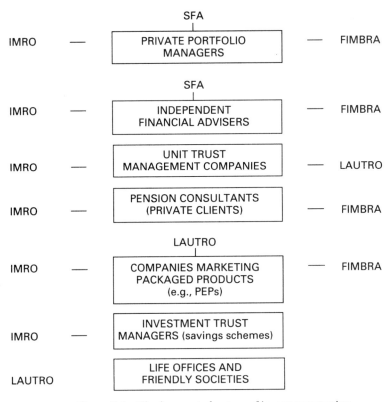

Figure 2.2   The fragmented nature of investor protection

proceed. From 1987 to the end of 1992 only 12 convictions had taken place out of over 100 cases of suspected insider dealing referred by the London Stock Exchange to the Department of Trade and Industry.

There is a great deal of concern that the complex and fragmented system of regulation in the UK is not cost-effective. The main costs involved with the regulatory system can be broadly divided into direct costs and indirect costs (see Table 2.1).

The setting up costs for financial institutions needed to comply with the wide range of regulations written or re-written in the 1980s and 1990s – the Financial Services Act 1986, the Building Societies Act 1986, the Banking Act 1987, the Lloyd's of London Act 1982, the Insurance Companies Act 1982, the Friendly Societies Act 1992 and the Criminal Justice Act 1993 (which included provisions against insider dealing) – have never been thoroughly researched, but they are likely to have run into thousands of millions of pounds. Financial institutions will of course have had some systems already in place in order to comply with previous regulations, but the nature

18

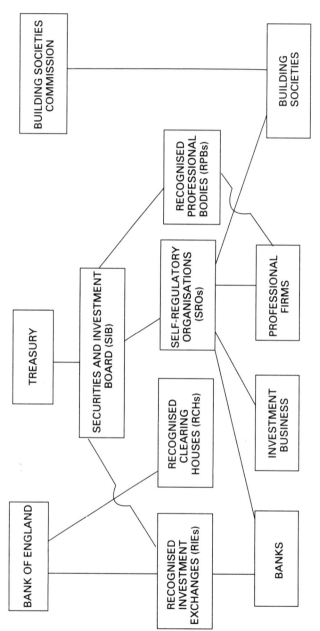

Figure 2.3 Regulatory framework (simplified)

Table 2.1   Costs of the regulatory system

Direct costs	(1)	Cost to financial institutions of setting up compliance systems
	(2)	Cost to financial institutions of running day-to-day compliance and controls
	(3)	Cost of setting up regulatory bodies
	(4)	Cost of running regulatory bodies
	(5)	Cost of refunding investors.
Indirect costs	(1)	Barriers to entry
	(2)	Reduced competition
	(3)	Cost of a deposit protection scheme
	(4)	Potential costs of moral hazard
	(5)	Restraint on growth
	(6)	Lower profitability
	(7)	Reduced financial innovation
	(8)	Reduced efficiency of financial institutions
	(9)	Poor allocative efficiency in the economy
	(10)	Costs of non-neutral competition with respect to overseas institutions.

of the overhaul of the regulatory framework in the 1980s meant that many had to start again more or less from scratch.

Direct costs would have included the employment of compliance officers, training of staff on the new regulations, setting up computer systems for reporting requirements and to record transactions with customers. Annual running costs were estimated to be around £100 million per year, although this is likely to be a conservative estimate. The smaller financial institutions are likely to have been the worst hit in terms of both set up and annual running costs. The direct costs of setting up regulatory bodies include office premises, hiring of staff, consultation with institutions, installation of computer hardware and software, writing and distributing regulatory manuals, etc. Of course, many of these direct costs are paid by the financial institutions themselves through their membership fees to the regulatory bodies.

It is argued by many that the complex regulations regarding the setting up of a financial institution and subsequent costs of compliance deter new firms from entering the financial services industry, and are therefore an effective barrier to entry. This acts as an indirect cost because barriers to entry will tend to reduce the competitiveness of the incumbent financial institutions, possibly leading to over-pricing to the detriment of the consumer, and inefficient allocation of financial resources in the economy. Even without barriers to entry, it must be recognised that there is a fine dividing line between a suitable level of regulation and a suitable level of competition. Over-regulation could lead to a stifling of competition, whilst a lack of regulation could in turn lead to over-competition. It is important (but difficult) to ensure that there is a satisfactory mix of regulation and competition.

What happens when there is under-regulation? The answer is failure of financial institutions. In the early 1970s, for example, the large banks were suitably regulated by the Bank of England, but the secondary (smaller) banks effectively slipped through the supervisory net, and ultimately failed. What happens if there is over-regulation? An inefficient market. The cartel run by the building societies up until the 1980s (a form of self-regulation) led to a lack of competition and the inefficient pricing of mortgages.

The main question is whether or not the costs of a particular form of regulatory framework are justified by the magnitude of consumer protection that ensues, and the gains in efficiency and allocation that evolve from a properly regulated, competitive financial system. One of the greatest direct costs of regulation has turned out to be the payments made to investors through the compensation schemes for failed and/or fraudulent institutions. Indeed, one self-regulatory organisation (FIMBRA) almost became insolvent through experiencing so many problems of this kind.

4. Compensation costs

One of the major problems and costs facing the SROs is that of investor compensation. Compensation is paid by the Investors Compensation Scheme (ICS) when a firm or intermediary is unable to meet its obligations or has failed. FIMBRA has borne the brunt of failures, as can be seen from Table 2.2. During 1988–92 FIMBRA members accounted for over £34 million of compensation, around 76% of the total. The compensation paid by each individual SRO has been capped, as shown in Table 2.3. For FIMBRA, for example, the compensation cap was £19 million, the additional costs are spread out amongst all of the other SROs. In fact, members of LAUTRO (which relied on FIMBRA members to sell their products) reduced FIMBRA's compensation costs to only £5 million, the life companies making up any difference between £5 million and £19 million. For 1991–92 insurance was taken out by the SROs to cover compensation costs over and above £25 million per year, but the premiums have been escalating rapidly, and given the size of the claims involved, it is likely that the cost of insurance in future years will be so great as to make it unacceptable to the SROs; this would mean the SROs being responsible for the whole sum of investor compensation claims. The whole issue of compensation is thus becoming extremely important for the survival of the SROs. Either a new mechanism needs to be found to share out the burden of compensation costs or, more satisfactorily, steps need to be taken to ensure that there is a reduction in failures and hence in compensation payments.

Table 2.2   Compensation and allocation to SROs, 1988–90 to 1991–2

SRO	1988–90 £ million	1990–1 £ million	1991–2 £ million	Total £ million
FIMBRA†	3.38	9.49	21.25	34.12
LAUTRO†	–	0.26	0.28	0.54
IMRO	0.32	0.16	2.33	2.81
AFBD*	0.24	0.03	–	0.27
TSA*	3.12	1.43	2.41	6.96
SIB	0.02	0.05	0.05	0.12
Total	7.08	11.42	26.32	44.82

*AFBD and TSA merged now into SFA.
†FIMBRA and LAUTRO to be replaced by PIA in 1995.
Source: Investors Compensation Scheme Ltd and Clucas Report (1992) Figures rounded.

Table 2.3   Compensation caps on SROs

SRO	£ million
FIMBRA	19
LAUTRO	27
SFA	51
IMRO	18
SIB	5

Source: Clucas Report (1992).

5.   Moral Hazard

The SIB has set up training initiatives to enhance the competence of members and LAUTRO even suspended staff from some companies until adequate retraining was completed. Whilst this may improve the advice given to investors, it is unlikely to stem the tide of failures.

In many countries there has been a great deal of debate as to the effectiveness of investor compensation schemes. These schemes are intended to bolster and maintain confidence in the financial system and ensure stability. In theory, however, it is possible that these schemes have exactly the opposite effect. This damaging effect may occur because of what is termed 'moral hazard'. This is the possibility that financial institutions might take on more risk than is strictly necessary, knowing that depositors are going to be protected if these risks are crystallised. Investor compensation schemes, therefore, interfere with the risk–return trade-off that underlies much of institutions' financial activities. Ordinarily, with no such schemes, investors would shy away from those institutions seen to be taking on excessive risk (at least in theory, but remember that information asymmetries mean that many personal depositors would be unaware of excessive risk-taking). With these schemes available, however, financial institutions that actually seek out greater risk for a marginal return over their competitors will be *rewarded* by depositors placing their funds with the institution.

There are still serious problems with the Investors Compensation Scheme (ICS). The ICS has never really got to grips with the 'moral hazard' problem, because the riskiness of particular types of business has never adequately been linked with contributions to the compensation fund. The ICS needs to look much more closely at quantifying risk and return. At present, there is an arbitrary apportioning of potential liabilities (up to a value of £100 million) amongst the SROs, with no regard to risk and return.

6.   Self-regulation or self-delusion?

There are a variety of ways in which the three main forms of regulation – structural, prudential and investor – can be carried out. The polar opposites are complete self-regulation or complete, formal legal rules. Within the span of these two poles there are combinations of the self-regulation/formal rules mix. Proponents of self-regulation argue that the practitioners involved in a particular financial business are the best placed to carry out the regulatory function, because they have the highest level of necessary expertise and inside knowledge. This experience can be harnessed to carry out effective self-regulation. The main point of self-regulation is that it is in the interest of all those in finance that the profession's image is not ruined by individual examples of fraud or sharp practice. Self-regulation is driven by the fear that investors will shun a market if it is felt to be improperly run in some way. One rotten apple, in other words, could mean a whole barrel of rotten apples.

There is thus reasonable justification for the existence of self-regulation, but it was unclear whether such informal 'clubs' could ever be rigorous enough to fully regulate their members in an increasingly sophisticated market place. The London Stock Exchange, for example, had long been used to complete freedom in determining its working practices. In fact, one leading stockbroker wrote in a letter to the Times in June 1971 that 'the Exchange was a private gentleman's club and not an institution which exists to perform a public service'.[1] Prior to Big Bang in 1986, the Exchange had become outmoded with its traditional dealing practices, barriers to entry, and fixed scale commissions. There were a declining number of market-makers (at the time known as 'jobbers'), which led to difficulties in dealing in large amounts of shares with narrow bid-offer spreads. There was a danger that the Exchange would lose institutional business to more dynamic markets such as New York. Unless it agreed to voluntary reform, the Exchange was threatened by the DTI with a possible referral to the Restrictive Practices Court.

The Exchange did reform itself with 'Big Bang' and dealing became much more competitive. The Exchange also came under external scrutiny. As a Recognised Investment Exchange ('RIE') its rule book is reviewed by SIB, and its members must abide by Conduct of Business Rules set by their self-regulatory body, the Securities and Futures Authority ('SFA'), also under the auspices of SIB.

The stimulus behind the move from self-regulation to more formal external regulation was the desire for a greater level of competition in the financial services market. As mentioned earlier, structural regulation, which refers to the lines of business that institutions are allowed to enter, has been greatly relaxed in the 1980s and 1990s in order to promote competition amongst financial institutions. Building societies are now able to offer cheque books (money transmission) and unsecured personal loans in their own names, both in competition with the retail banks, and many institutions are able to offer insurance products. With this greater freedom of provision of services and increased competition came the fear that self-regulation could not cope, and the need for a more rigorous framework of regulation. Structural deregulation was thus contained within a more legalistic approach to supervision and regulation. The system is still one of self-regulation by practitioners, but it now operates within a (limited) statutory framework. The system has not been successful, however.

The question here is not whether practitioners ought to be involved in the regulatory system (*all* forms of regulation need the experience and expertise of practitioners), but the extent to which regulation should lean towards a statutory or non-statutory basis. One of the main problems of SROs (which operate self-regulation within a limited statutory framework) is that they have all too often acted like trade associations, acting on behalf of their members, and so reverting back to a cosy club-type system, rather than acting in the interests of investors. Practitioners have a vested interest in the status quo, and shambolic episodes such as the Maxwell pensions fiasco (over which the IMRO chairman resigned) only serve to show that the SROs do not have enough bite. This is compounded by the SROs being in some degree affected by 'regulatory capture'.

Whilst it is clear that self-regulation under the FSA has not been satisfactory, it is also clear that financial markets outside of the scope of the FSA have fared no better in protecting investors. One of the most surprising omissions of the Financial Services Act 1986 was that of Lloyd's of London. The scope of the FSA does not reach as far as the Lloyd's insurance market, which is instead regulated under the Lloyd's of London Act 1982. Lloyd's has often fallen foul of regulatory standards and failed to protect the interests of Names. Sir David Walker's report on Lloyd's in 1992 commented that market professionals did not carry out due care and diligence and that 'some members' agents took a very lax view of their fiduciary duties'. A report into the governing of Lloyd's by Sir Jeremy Morse, also in 1992, suggested that regulation should be the responsibility of a regulatory board and be separate from the business planning and day-to-day administration of the market, whilst at the same time maintaining the system of self-regulation set up under the Lloyd's of London Act 1982. These comments could lead to Lloyd's eventually coming under the umbrella of the FSA, but it is not at all clear as to whether or not this will restore the confidence of present Names or future capital providers. Self-regulation has not worked in the past for Lloyd's, and there is no reason it will work simply because it is codified under the FSA, which itself is a flawed framework for investor protection.

7.   Competence and disclosure

The Financial Services Act 1986 widened the net of investor protection regulation to include the *competence* of the suppliers of financial services (a recommendation from the 1982 Gower Report), as well as their honesty. Suppliers of financial services must be 'fit and proper' persons, and must be granted authorisation by an SRO or the SIB in order to carry out investment business.

Despite the preponderance of costly regulations and complex rule books, it was obvious that both the competence and integrity of financial advisers was unsatisfactory. A study by SIB found that one in four endowment life assurance policies were encashed within two years, which suggested that either investors were entering into inappropriate investments at the outset (i.e. receiving poor advice), or were being persuaded to cash in one policy for another (poor advice bordering on dishonesty). This was a combination of incompetence, poor training and lack of integrity at work, and it was exacerbated by commission-based rewards rather than fee income, which encouraged unscrupulous advisers to persuade customers to change policies (sometimes called 'churning') or to push them towards the more highly-commissioned policies.

These problems were not properly addressed until 1994. Prior to this date, the self regulatory bodies seemed to act more like trade associations. Despite complaints from the Consumers' Association, only minimal ('soft') disclosure was required when selling life assurance and personal pensions. Commission and other charges were largely hidden, usually only being given in cash terms when specifically requested. Surrender sums were not fully disclosed, concealing the fact that in some cases the 'break-even year', when the sum recovered equalled the premiums paid, was not until near the end of the policy term.

Mounting criticism as a result of increasing evidence of mis-selling of packaged products resulted in a change in policy. 'Hard' disclosure became mandatory for life assurance and personal pensions from 1 January 1995. This imposed a greater degree of transparency of charges and much fuller disclosure of surrender values. Furthermore, more stringent training requirements were imposed on companies, with sales staff being suspended in some cases until retraining had taken place. One feature of the PIA as compared with its predecessors, FIMBRA and LAUTRO, is a greater degree of consumer representation.

8. Investor choice

One of the stated rationales of regulation was that the provision of financial services and products should be carried out efficiently – in terms both of low cost and investor choice. The SIB's rules on polarisation and disclosure have, however, increased costs and reduced investor choice. The polarisation rules require institutions selling 'packaged products' such as life assurance, personal pensions and unit trusts either to become tied agents (selling only the products of the company to which they are tied – i.e. company representatives), or to become independent intermediaries (selling a whole range of products except their own). The main lending institutions (banks and building societies), have preferred to become tied agents, selling to their customers either their own 'packaged products', or those of a single life assurance company. Interestingly, some of the major banks have set up subsidiaries which act as independent intermediaries. The result is that 'ordinary' customers are sold the tied agent product, but high net-worth and more sophisticated customers are referred to the independent-intermediary subsidiary of the bank. Thus, for 'normal' customers at least, the result of polarisation has been a marked reduction in consumer choice.

9. Crime pays

It is evident that the regulatory system has been unable to show an ability to prevent fraud, nor to successfully prosecute the alleged offenders. The Blue Arrow case, for example, was the longest and most costly fraud trial ever in the UK, but failed to end in any prosecutions. Moreover, in the second Guinness trial there were no convictions, and the third Guinness trial was abandoned. Out of 29 charges brought in the Blue Arrow, Guinness and Barlow Clowes trials only six convictions resulted. The Serious Fraud Office (SFO) was criticised for bringing charges to court that were too complex and took too much time to cover, and the situation can only have been exacerbated by the number of regulators involved in the information-gathering process for the prosecution.

If future fraudsters are to be deterred, then there is clearly a need for changes to the law and to the overall system of regulation. Take insider dealing, for example. Around 50% of defendants in insider dealing trials brought by the DTI have been acquitted out of the 28 trials between 1987 and 1993 (and more than 60% of those convicted actually pleaded guilty). Moreover, only a very small percentage of suspected cases reach court. This can be contrasted with the Securities and Exchange Commission (SEC) in the USA, where around 35 successful prosecutions are made each year. One answer might be to deal with securities offences through civil rather than criminal law, as the former requires lower standards of proof. Civil Law requires a case to be established on the balance of probabilities, rather than beyond reasonable doubt, as currently exists under criminal proceedings. It would also make sense if, as in the US example of the SEC, the UK had a sole regulator, investigator and prosecutor. In the UK these tasks are inadequately shared amongst a disarray of institutions – the DTI, the London Stock Exchange, the Takeover Panel, the SFA, the SFO, and the Director of Public Prosecutions (DPP).

10. Recommendations – piecemeal change

The Clucas Report (1992) was set up to examine the feasibility and appropriateness of setting up a self-regulatory organisation solely for the retail sector. This stemmed from the view that the requirements for investor protection at the retail level are somewhat different from those at the wholesale level. In particular, it is a common view that the wholesale sector may have suffered unnecessarily harsh regulation as a result of the wish of the authorities to protect the retail investor. It would therefore seem sensible to separate out the different markets for regulatory purposes, particularly as the wholesale markets are likely to involve better-informed, more financially sophisticated professional players.

The Clucas Report recommended that a retail SRO should be set up, to be called the Personal Investment Authority (PIA), to regulate the entire retail sector. The PIA would include members of both LAUTRO and FIMBRA (i.e. these SROs would be merged into the PIA), along with other retail financial institutions that are currently regulated elsewhere, such as banks and building societies which are regulated by IMRO. This would leave only three SROs – PIA, IMRO, and SFA. So, two SROs are being merged to produce a single retail SRO, with a new constitution and new set of rules to be written and then digested and acted upon by the institutions involved in retail business. Unfortunately, this new SRO, whilst being set up for the most laudable of reasons, will still not greatly simplify the fragmented nature of regulation in the UK. Banks, for example, will be accountable to the PIA, IMRO, SFA and the Bank of England: hardly a great leap in the right direction.

One of the aims of establishing the PIA was to apportion more fairly the costs of regulation in the retail sector. FIMBRA was being particularly damaged by falling membership (and hence financing) and rising compensation costs, which is affecting the independent financial advice sector. One of FIMBRA's main problems was that its members found it difficult to pass on compensation costs to their customers because their earnings are commission- rather than fee-based. To maintain independent advice, the outcome was to merge LAUTRO and FIMBRA into the PIA. The Clucas Report stated that major changes to the legislation were out of the question, but it is unlikely that piecemeal changes to the SROs are likely to stem the tide of failures, bad advice, and spiralling costs (both direct and indirect).

A further area of regulation that has undergone piecemeal change is the insider dealing legislation. The Criminal Justice Act 1993 widened the definition of insider dealers to anybody who picks up information in the course of his work. It also shifts the burden of proof away from prosecution towards defence as to whether or not a suspect did or did not intend to profit from inside information. Most lawyers, however, argue that this is unlikely significantly to improve enforcement, or the success rate of prosecutions.

11. Recommendations – wholesale change

Why bother with the whole plethora of SROs that currently exist (or, indeed, with the proposed PIA), each with their own rulebooks, their own premises, computer systems and professional staff, each duplicating many of the activities of the others? Why should financial institutions and intermediaries gain authorisation and follow the rules of more than one self-regulatory authority? It is difficult to see the benefits of such a system, particularly when the events of BCCI, Maxwell and Barlow Clowes have shown the inadequacies of the SROs in preventing fraud and maintaining investor confidence. Would it not be far better to abolish the SROs and the SIB and set up a new government organisation, let's call it the Securities and Exchange Board (SEB), to carry out investor protection? The SEB could maintain the emphasis on regulation of financial functions rather than financial institutions, and indeed could set up different systems for retail business and wholesale business – as recommended by the Clucas Report. The most far-reaching change, however, would be the move closer towards statutory regulation and away from the present system, which is one of self-regulation through a limited statutory framework. This is not in fact as revolutionary as it sounds. The Prudential has called for the statutory regulation of investment business by a government body, and the National Westminster Bank has put forward arguments for a single statutory regulator with separate retail and wholesale divisions.

The International Securities Market Association (ISMA) report, 'Towards a Single European Securities Trading Market' (1995) enforces the view that retail trade needs to be separated from wholesale and that in retail markets *caveat emptor* cannot be the basis of the transaction. It also makes the statement that 'It is our view that without a statutory regulator supervising the self-regulators, over time, self-regulation is liable to become less effective'.

Indeed, there is some precedent for the idea of greater statutory regulation. Professor Jim Gower, the author of the 'Review of Investor Protection' (1984), which set out the creation of the SIB and the SROs, is widely thought to have preferred a statutory government body similar to the US Securities and Exchange Commission (SEC). He took the route of SROs, however, when the pressure for such a system was felt from financial practitioners.

The SEB, with greater statutory backing and enforcement powers, could be supervised by the Bank of England, thus allowing the regulators to present a more united front in setting rules and enforcing them, preventing overlapping of jurisdictional functions, allowing a more straightforward system of authorisation for financial institutions, and reducing the likelihood of 'regulatory capture' as can happen with smaller less powerful SROs. The new regulatory framework could be as shown in Figure 2.4.

The SEB could also regulate Lloyd's which should be brought under the aegis of the Financial Services Act 1986 (from which it is currently exempt). This would go further than the recommendations of Sir Jeremy Morse (1992) in that regulation would become more statutory, and would be seen to be less under the control of Lloyd's itself (i.e. less self-regulatory and less open to abuse). This would reinforce the integrity of Lloyd's and help to attract more investors and a more stable capital base. Lloyd's would also be seen by potential investors as simply another financial institution, rather than some curious survival that operates outside of the mainstream umbrella of UK regulation.

There is also no logical or economic reason for continuing with separate regulators for building societies and banks. If the rest of the regulatory system is based on functional areas of business, why should bank and building society prudential regulation and supervision be separate (i.e. the Bank of England for banks and the Building Societies Commission for building societies), given that they operate in many of the same business areas? The Building Societies Act 1986 is anachronistic, particularly with respect to changes in EC regulation, where a single European Market for credit business is being set up, but which the building societies will not be able to take advantage of because of the restrictions of the Act on their overseas operations. The Building Societies Commission (BSC) should be wound down and the regulation of building societies brought under the supervision of the Bank of England.

Finally, if the SEB were to take over the role of regulator, investigator and prosecutor (as the SEC in the USA), with the ability to prosecute under civil rather than criminal law, a united regulatory front would be shown to both

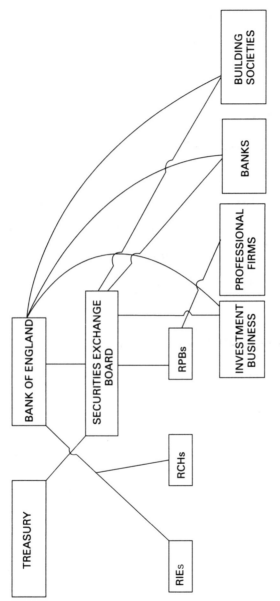

Figure 2.4 Suggested new regulatory framework

investors and professionals alike, with reduced costs and a greater chance of successful prosecutions.

Note

1. Quoted in McRae, H. and Cairncross. F. *Capital City* (Eyre Methuen, 1974) p. 102.

Further reading

1. General Principles of Regulation

Pawley, M., Winstone, D., and Bentley, P., *UK Financial Institutions and Markets* (Macmillan, 1991).

Davies, E.P., 'Theories of Intermediation, Financial Innovation and Regulation', *National Westminster Bank Quarterly Review,* May 1993, pp. 41–53.

Gardener, E.P.M., *UK Banking Supervision: Evolution, Practice and Issues* (Allen & Unwin, 1986).

Gowland, D., *The Regulation of Financial Markets in the 1990s' (Edward Elgar, 1990).*

Quinn, T., 'The Economics of Financial Regulation – a Survey', *Central Bank of Ireland Quarterly Bulletin,* Winter 1992, pp. 55–70.

2. Regulation of the Investment Industry

Abrams, C., Ferran, E. and Rider, B.A.K., *Guide to the Financial Services Act, 1986,* 2nd edn. (CCH Editions, 1989).

Blair, M., *Financial Services: the New Core Rules* (Blackstone Press, 1991).

Blair, M., *et al. Banking and the Financial Services Act* (Butterworths, 1993).

Cobham, D. (ed.) *Markets and Dealers: the Economics of the London Financial Markets* (Longman, 1992).

Franks, J. and Mayer, C. *Risk Regulation and Investor Protection: the Case of Investment Management* (Oxford University Press, 1989).

Hall, M.J.B., *The City Revolution – Causes and Consequences* (Macmillan, 1987).

Page, A.C. and Ferguson, R.B., *Investor Protection* (Weidenfeld & Nicolson, 1992).

White, J., *Regulation of Securities and Futures Dealing* (Sweet & Maxwell, 1992).

CHAPTER 3

Regulation in Practice

Patrick Bentley, Howard Jarman and David Winstone

1. Introduction

In Chapter 2, the reader was introduced to the issues and principles of regulation of the financial system. By way of exemplification, this was illustrated by reference to the investment sector of the financial services industry. The present chapter builds on this by examining the practice of regulation in three other sectors of the financial services industry: banking, building societies and insurance.

2. Bank supervision and regulation

Banks, in common with other financial institutions, are subject to three types of regulation.

1. There are limits to the level of activities they may pursue – **structural** regulation.
2. There are constraints with regard to their own internal finance, principally in relation to capital adequacy, liquidity and solvency – **prudential** regulation.
3. There are regulations designed to protect their clients from fraud and dubious practices – **investor** protection.

It is aspects of prudential regulation which will be detailed here.

UK banks must comply with relevant sections of the Banking Act 1987 and EC Banking Directives, principally the Own Funds and Solvency Ratio directives, which follow the recommendations of the Basle Committee on Banking Regulations and Supervisory Practices (the Basle Accord).

Bank prudential regulation focuses upon a minimum acceptable level of capital relative to a bank's actual activities, and pays particular attention to the amount and type of assets which the bank holds. Amount and type of assets are the factors which determine the amount of capital which must be held.

The requirement that banks should have 'capital adequacy' is so that they may continue to conduct banking business by absorbing losses arising from falls in asset values. Even if asset values fall, there will still be sufficient value to repay depositors. Conversely, a demonstration of adequate capital ensures that deposits continue to be made, that continuous net withdrawal of deposits does not occur, thus threatening the stability of an individual bank, and the stability of the banking system as a whole.

The purposes for which capital is required are often summarised as:

1. A cushion against losses.
2. A demonstration to depositors that the owners of the bank, the shareholders, are prepared to put their own funds at risk on a permanent basis.
3. To provide resources free of the obligation to pay fixed interest.
4. To provide the infrastructure of the business, the fixed assets, such as premises.

Capital adequacy is a separate issue to that of the regulation of bank liquidity. A bank with adequate capital will still find itself in difficulty should its liquidity be insufficient, that is, having insufficient cash to fund its operations 'today' leading, therefore, to collapse. Having a surplus asset value over liabilities will not save it. Of course such a situation is common to any business. A business which cannot meet its obligations on a day to day basis will be pressed by its creditors, even if it has large value net assets. In turn this will cause its liquidity position to deteriorate even further.

A simple numerical example follows to demonstrate why adequate capital is necessary to protect depositors' funds. A bank has raised funds by:

	£m
Selling shares	5
Retaining past profits (reserves) and	10
attracting deposits	50
Total:	**65**

These funds have been used to create the following assets:

	£m
Premises	3
Commercial and personal loans	50
Treasury bills, CDs, bills	10
Cash	2
	65

If the loans were not fully repaid by the borrowers so that their value became £30m then this would require the writing off of reserves and share capital, there would be insufficient asset value (£45m) to repay deposits of £50m.

Clearly a fall in asset values is relative to risk. Bank A might well have low risk loans of the same nominal value as Bank B, but Bank B may have a less conservative lending policy so that risk of default is greater. Taking balance sheet asset value is therefore not necessarily the correct approach when deciding how much capital (shares and reserves) are needed to protect depositors. A risk weighted approach is needed, like that taken by the Basle Accord.

3. Details of the Basle Accord

The Basle proposals are designed to achieve convergence in that institutions should not be at a competitive disadvantage as would be the case if different levels of capital were allowed to cover the same type of business. In addition they are designed to ensure that they strengthen the soundness and stability of the international banking system.

A common measure of capital was necessary. A method of weighting risk in relation to assets was also necessary. Having decided upon these weights it was decided to set capital related to risk-weighted asset values to a minimum of 8%.

Capital is classified as Tier 1, Core Capital and Tier 2, supplementary capital, each is required to be at a minimum of 4% related to risk weighted values.

Example of risk weighting to common assets.

0%   Cash
20%   Deposits with discount houses
50%   Loans fully secured on residential property
100% All loans to the non bank private sector

Now consider the simple set of examples shown in Table 3.1.

Both banks have the same balance sheet asset values, but because Bank A has a higher proportion of high risk assets it required more capital than Bank B to support those assets. Bank A needs 8% of £1026.5K capital, £82.12K. Bank B needs 8% of £933K capital, £74.64K.

Risks which are off-balance sheet are also captured by the risk-weighting process. Off-balance sheet risks are converted to an on-balance sheet amount, then risk-weighted. Examples would be bank acceptances and standby letters of credit being 100% risk-weighted.

In summary, the more risky the assets, the greater the amount of capital is needed relative to balance sheet value. It necessarily follows that what constitutes 'capital' has to be carefully decided. There are various ways of raising capital – ordinary and preference shares – as well as types of 'loan capital' –

Table 3.1   Varying requirements for capital under the Basle Accord

Bank A	Assets £000 (balance sheet values)	Risk-weighting %	Risk-weighted value £000
Cash	10	0	0
Treasury bills	15	10	1.5
Mortgages	500	50	250
Loans	760	100	760
Fixed assets	15	100	15
	1,300	Total risk-weighted value	1,026.5

Bank B	Assets £000 (balance sheet values)	Risk-weighting %	Risk-weighted value £000
Cash	15	0	0
Treasury bills	30	10	3.0
Mortgages	650	50	325
Loans	585	100	585
Fixed assets	20	100	20
	1,300	Total risk-weighted value	933

bonds, notes, debentures. The features of these instruments need to be examined to assess what it is about them which should or should not qualify them as capital.

Some assets will need more capital than others to support them. It means that banks have to arrange their activities carefully so that the impact upon their capital requirements is minimised. Some assets will absorb more capital than others.

Capital adequacy has always been a bank supervision issue. It is only of late that it has been subjected to a *systematic* approach, that of the Basle Accord and EC Directives. The traditional way to measure the adequacy of bank capital was by the 'free resources test', similar to the 'gearing test'. The free resources test comprises the ratio of available capital resources (reduced by the value of fixed assets) to other liabilities. In essence, this largely relates capital to the banks' deposit base. The gearing test often relates capital (adjusted for goodwill and fixed assets) to current account deposits. This test is still used with a risk-weighted assets test by the Bank of England in bank regulation.

The Basle Accord (1988) compares with the EC Own Funds Directive (adopted 1988) and the Solvency Ratio Directive (1989): they are broadly similar in approach and differ only in detail.

There are financial risks to which banks are subjected which are not covered by the Basle Accord and EC Directives.
   They are:

- Exchange risk
- Liquidity/Funding risk
- Concentration risk

1. *Exchange risk*: there may be a bank mismatch of assets and liabilities in a particular currency.
2. *Liquidity/funding risk*: a bank may not have sufficient liquid funds to meet its obligations, yet have sufficient net asset worth.
3. *Concentration risk*: a bank may have lent a high proportion it its funds to one economic sector or firm.

In the case of the UK, the Bank of England takes these factors into account when supervising banks. However, in other countries the Basle Accord minimum may be implemented and not adjusted for any of these factors.
   The main criticism of the Basle Accord is that the same risk-weighting is given to a highly diverse group of assets. The weighting given to all unsecured non-bank private sector debts is the same (50%). Thus top-rated AAA corporate debt is deemed to have the same risk as that of a personal loan to a student. This means that the loan to the AAA-rated corporate will absorb per unit of the loan as much capital as the personal loan. As the interest rate spread on the AAA rated loan may be very narrow, it may not be able to be justified in terms of its capital adequacy requirement. There is thus every incentive, in relation to capital adequacy management, to take on higher risk, higher return loans.
   Other criticisms focus upon the classification of what can be counted as 'capital' for the purposes of the capital adequacy calculation. Many new forms of capital are not allowed, owing to perceived risk or lack of liquidity. As a result, banks are effectively prevented from using them. This affects their competitive ability, as other financial institutions can operate without such effective restrictions on sources of capital.
   The Second Banking Directive from the EC (adopted December 1989) enables a bank authorised, for example, in the UK to be able to operate in other EC States without needing to apply for additional authorisation. This is known as a 'single licence' or 'passport'. It means that banks can operate in EC countries other than their own and also carry out activities specifically prohibited to domestic banks.

The EC Own Funds Directive and Solvency Directive are based on the Basle Accord approach to capital adequacy requirements, capital of course equates here to 'own funds', and if these are adequate then the bank can be judged solvent. The Basle Accord uses Tier 1 and Tier 2 capital, the EC Directive uses 'original own funds' and 'additional' own funds.

The Solvency Ratio Directive works as follows. Own funds are calculated using the formula in the Own Funds Directive; this figure is then divided by the value of its risk-weighted assets, including off-balance sheet. This is then expressed as a percentage, with a minimum allowable value of 8%. The solvency ratio must be calculated at least twice per year.

It should be noted that the Directives do not carry the force of law, they merely direct EC Members to implement legislation to enforce at least minimum standards. In the case of the UK the relevant legislation is the Banking Act 1987. Schedule 3 to the Act sets out a requirement of minimum net assets of £1million, i.e. paid-up capital plus reserves. There should be ongoing compliance and authorisation can be revoked, and has been.

4. The supervision of building societies

Introduction

It has been a characteristic of the history of building society regulation that safeguards and powers have been added piecemeal to the framework set by the original Building Societies Act 1874 as the more notable failures showed them to be necessary. (HMSO, 1980, para 1247)

The above statement from the 1980 Wilson Report exemplifies the unstructured approach to prudential supervision in the UK, and several additional factors emerged in the 1980s:

1. the disintegration of the building society cartel;
2. the banks being freed from monetary policy constraints;
3. moves towards fiscal neutrality; and
4. pressure for competitive neutrality and wider powers for building societies.

The result was the Building Societies Act 1986, which is basically designed to construct an overall framework within which building societies are allowed to operate. Much of the day-to-day supervisory detail and revisions are therefore covered by secondary legislation and Prudential Notes, the latter being issued by the Building Societies Commission (BSC).

Authorisation

The Building Societies Act requires societies to be authorised before they can raise funds or borrow money, and the minimum qualifying capital was set at £100,000. However, the European Community's Second Directive on Credit Institutions defines a minimum capital of ECU5million (approximately £3.5million), although the UK authorities are permitted to reduce this to ECU1million (approximately £0.7million) for new institutions. Even so, the first hurdle may deter most potential newcomers.

The BSC can remove a director or other officers of the society, obtain information and documents from the society and possesses quite extensive powers in order to protect investors and to control the likelihood and extent of institutional failure. For instance, if it is concerned about a society's conduct of business, it can impose conditions on the current authorisation of a society or it can require a society to apply for renewal of its authorisation, where there is concern about the investments of members and depositors, as happened with the Peckham Society, where the board of the society quickly recommended a merger with the Cheltenham & Gloucester. One function which the BSC is still unable to perform is that it cannot on its own enforce the winding-up of a society.

Activity restrictions

There are four principal aspects of building society activity restrictions:

1. geography;
2. commercial assets;
3. financial services; and
4. the Schedule 8 Review.

With reference to geography, societies are empowered to lend directly in the Channel Islands, the Isle of Man and Gibraltar. 'Commercial assets' represent total assets *less* the sum of liquid and fixed assets, and are divided into three classes with limits being placed on Class 2 and 3 assets (see Table 3.2). Class 1 assets are those secured on first mortgages to owner-occupiers of residential property. Class 2 is composed of non-Class 1 assets (e.g. loans to corporate bodies), while Class 3 comprises unsecured lending, property and land ownership, investment in estate agencies and insurance brokers, etc. and other subsidiary activities. Individual unsecured loans could not initially exceed £5,000, which was increased to £10,000 after the Schedule 8 Review and more recently to £25,000.

Financial services or investment business must be carried out exclusively by authorised institutions and, rather surprisingly, the Financial Services Act (FSA) did not create a super-agency. Instead, powers are delegated to a

Table 3.2   Progressive increases in Class 2 and 3 limits, 1986–93

Class	1986 Act	Maximum % Jan. 1990	Jan. 1991	Jan. 1993
2	10	17.5	20	25
3	of which:			
	5	7.5	10	15

Source: Compiled from *Economic Progress Report*, 184 (February 1988), p. 11.

designated body, basically the Securities and Investments Board (SIB), which can 'subcontract' the power to a number of trade associations, known as self-regulatory organisations (SROs), as we saw in Chapter 2. Drafting errors and Building Societies Association (BSA) lobbying resulted in a Review of Schedule 8 of the Building Societies Act 1986 (see Table 3.2), involving the Treasury and the Commission, and its conclusions led to a gradual extension of powers into fund management, equity stakes in life and general insurance companies and a wider range of banking and housing services, e.g. stockbroking.

Capital

Building societies need capital for a variety of reasons, for example as a cushion against mortgage arrears and default, and capital has traditionally stemmed from retained profits, now supplemented by subordinated debt and permanent interest bearing shares (PIBS), the latter being the approximate equivalent of company preference shares.

The 'public measure' of capital equals:

$$\frac{\text{Free capital}}{\text{Total liabilities}} \tag{1}$$

where Free capital represents Gross reserves *plus* general bad debt provisions *less* fixed assets.

This is published in the *Annual Accounts*, and can be dismissed as largely cosmetic or irrelevant because no account is taken of differences in risk within a society.

The more important unpublished 'operational measure' takes account of these risks and was initially contained in the calculus. By attributing a capital requirement to each specific group of assets or activities, the calculus represented a systematic attempt to link capital to risk, the Commission sought to establish and agree two measures of the capital required with each society:

1. The minimum acceptable capital (MAC) – related to the current business of the society and below which the society would be at risk; and
2. The desired capital (DC) – the basis for planning and budgeting, etc. This was at least 0.5 per cent above the minimum, i.e.

$$DC = MAC + \text{at least } 0.5\% \qquad (2)$$

This approach merely constituted a ranking of risk rather an absolute measure of risk, and it is therefore questionable whether the calculus included the appropriate categories of risk, whether the capital requirement attached thereto was appropriate, and whether at least a 0.5 per cent differential over the minimum in determining the target level was also appropriate.

However, there has been a move towards competitive neutrality, which may be illustrated by the BSC running the (old) calculus and the (new) risk asset ratio systems (see section 2 above on banking supervision) in parallel in 1993 and then allowing the calculus quietly to fade away.

Liquidity

The Act indicates a maximum liquidity ratio of one-third of total assets, but no minimum is specified in section 21(1) of the Act, merely 'such a proportion, as will at all times enable the society to meet its liabilities'. The permitted liquid assets include cash, bank deposits/Certificates of Deposit (CDs), Treasury bills, gilts, local authority loans/securities, certain building society CDs and certain foreign currency instruments. As indicated above, there is strangely a capital requirement for liquid assets but no specific minimum cash requirement. Liquidity targets are set separately for each society, and there is no lender of last resort facility.

Treasury risk management

Retail funds – or savings 'coming across the counter' – have traditionally constituted the backbone of any building society but the wholesale markets often, though not necessarily, appear to be an attractive source of lower cost finance. The initial limit on their use was 20% of a society's total funds. Privatisation and an upsurge of interest in the stock market were starting to bite into the societies' retail base so that, in November 1987, the BSA made a formal submission for an increase to 30% and was rewarded with the limit being raised to the statutory maximum of 40%. Hedging represents the techniques which can provide protection by exchanging fixed rate commitments for variable ones (or vice versa) or by guaranteeing a predetermined exchange rate, e.g. swaps, futures and options, and the associated rules on hedging are contained in a series of Prudential Notes which preclude speculation.

Reporting

The reporting requirements exist to provide information for the Commission and society members. The BSC carries out inspections and receives monthly monitoring returns, primarily directed to cash flow and margins, quarterly returns related to revenue budgets and outturns, the annual return and the annual capital monitoring return. Peer group comparisons via a database should continue to enable the early identification of a markedly out of line society. The *Annual Accounts*, the *Annual Business Statement*, a Directors' Report, a Summary Financial Statement and an Auditors' Report must be produced for members.

Management and systems

There are rules with respect to the system of internal control within a building society and these comprise guidelines governing, *inter alia*, directors, management information systems and human resources. The BSC emphasises the importance of a society possessing a clearly defined and documented organisational structure. Management information systems must contain appropriate and accurate information with reference to key areas such as capital, liquidity, treasury management, balance sheet ratios and profits. Fully tested contingency plans are required for such things as computer failure.

Investor protection

The Building Societies Investor Protection Fund (BSIPF) provides protection for 90% of the first £20,000, and is not a standing scheme, like the scheme applicable to banks. Instead, section 26(10) of the Act allows for a call on a society's resources, on an ad hoc basis, of up to 0.3% of the society's share and deposit base, i.e. there is no annual levy such as that imposed upon banks. Should it become necessary, a problem society can engage in temporary borrowing and section 31 permits two or more societies to provide a voluntary deposit protection scheme. The BSIPF has not been used, and mergers (with or without assistance from other societies) have been the favoured solution for troubled institutions. Investors are more aware of investor protection since the BCCI collapse in 1991.

Mergers and conversion

With reference to mergers the Commission is keen to examine, first, whether members are in favour of a merger and, secondly, the resultant soundness of the new financial intermediary. The voting regulations, outlined in the Act and the associated Guidance Note, demand a Special Resolution (minimum 75% vote of qualifying shareholders voting) and a borrowing members' resolution (minimum 50% of qualifying members voting).

There are two principal reasons for conversion into a company (effectively a bank): avoiding the constraints of the Act and raising more capital, the latter becoming less of a problem since the advent of subordinated debt and PIBS. The regulations call for a 20% turnout of shareholders (with a 75% majority in favour) and a majority of borrowers in favour.

Voting is costly and time-consuming, and problems can arise with mergers or conversion if there is public disagreement between board members, between different factions of members or between the members and the board, e.g. Abbey Members Against Flotation (AMAF). A 'run' on the society becomes a distinct possibility, as dissenters may vote with their feet.

Conclusions

The post-1986 supervisory environment has meant more freedom and power, and may result in exposure to different types of risk. The degree of supervision has been intensified and auditors, concerned about a society, may breach the principle of confidentiality and reveal information to the BSC. Notwithstanding the improvements, there are some unresolved issues, such as the future role of mutuality and whether a merger between the Commission and the Bank of England is appropriate. The Act has been stretched in many cases to its full extent, new forms of capital have been introduced, and the once apparently overwhelming attractions of conversion have faded.

5.   The supervision and state regulation of insurance

Introduction

Government supervision began in the UK with the enactment of the Life Assurance Companies Act 1870 following the collapse of two large life insurance companies. This pattern of collapse, followed by a tightening and extension of supervision or regulation, has continued to the present day. This legislation has been primarily concerned with the protection of policyholders from insolvent or fraudulent insurers. In addition, modern developments have set about modifying the contractual relationship between suppliers and consumers, reflecting the trend in other areas such as consumer credit, hire purchase and the passing of the Unfair Contract Terms Act 1977.

The prudential regulation of insurance companies is the responsibility of the Insurance Division of the Department of Trade and Industry (DTI). It remains responsible for authorising new life and general insurers and for monitoring the activity and solvency of the business which is transacted. The primary legislation in this field is the Insurance Companies Act 1982 which has been considerably supplemented and amended by Regulations.

The UK approach to regulation has been to state what insurers must not do, rather than prescribe what they must do. Insurers are in addition required to provide information which is publicly available. The aim is to balance security with opportunity and to avoid regulation which may prevent policyholders from enjoying high levels of profit or cheap non-profit premiums.

The problems of maintaining solvency in insurance

Successive governments in the UK have gradually extended the scope and type of regulation to ensure that insurers have sufficient assets to pay claims. Claims payments are the single biggest cost faced by an insurer. They are subject to significant fluctuation from year to year, depending upon the type of risk or risks insured.

The potential claims of an insurer represented by the 'sums at risk' are many times greater than its assets. However, only risks where the probability of the insured event occurring is relatively small are insurable. The estimated maximum probable losses must be met from the premiums received. Predicting the proportion of maximum probable losses is a difficult process, and at best produces an inexact calculation of the exposure to risk. When the actual loss exceeds the estimates then problems of solvency can arise unless the insurer has maintained sufficient reserves for such eventualities.

Since competition will tend to force premiums down the market will, unless checked, lead to some insurers trading when they are unlikely to be able to meet all future claims. Government legislation has tried to cope in a variety of ways to protect policyholders. However, in trying to solve this problem Government has to try and reconcile two conflicting needs. These are on the one hand the security of the policyholder and on the other the opportunity of the insurer to develop better and more competitive services in the market place. In the mid-1960s a company called Fire Auto and Marine Insurance was liquidated leaving many policyholders without cover. This led to substantial amendment of the original legislation by Part II of the Companies Act 1967, which doubled the size of the minimum paid-up share capital and increased the solvency margin to the greater of £50,000 or

20% of the previous year's premium income up to £2.5 million and 10% thereafter.

Two further events led to the growth of additional regulation in the form of the 1974 Insurance Companies Act. In 1971, the disastrous failure of the cut-price motor insurer the Vehicle and General Insurance Company left 1 million motorists without cover. The government also set up the Scott committee to investigate property bonds and equity linked life assurance, and it reported in 1973.

The growth of pressure for legislation to regulate life companies was increased by the failure of Nation Life in 1974. This company was the subsidiary of a property company and made substantial loans to it, and also invested substantial amounts of its policyholders' funds in one illiquid asset. When the parent company failed in the secondary banking and property collapse of the 1970s, the subsidiary became insolvent. As a result of the public outcry over the many policyholders who lost their savings, the Policyholders Protection Act 1975 was passed. This created a fund by a levy on insurance companies to compensate policyholders and to ensure they were not left out of pocket as result of insurance insolvencies.

An additional factor which promoted the growth of insurance legislation was membership of the EC. Non-life Directive 73/239/EEC was passed in 1973 followed by Life Directive 79/267/EEC which sought to harmonise legislation of Member States on the solvency requirements of insurers. This led to UK legislation, culminating in the Insurance Companies Act of 1982.

Insurance Companies Act 1982

The Insurance Companies Act 1982, together with the related Statutory instruments, are the primary source of insurance legislation:

- Insurance Companies Regulations 1981
- Insurance Companies (Accounts and Statements) Regulations 1983
- Insurance (Lloyd's) Regulations 1983.

The scope of 'prudential regulation' consists of three areas. These are conditions which have to be met prior to authorisation, conditions which have to be met to maintain authorisation, and conditions which have to be met on the termination of the insurance enterprise due to winding-up or bankruptcy.

The extent of control varies in a continuum from supervision through to regulation. At one end it begins with the requirement to provide adequate public information before, during and on winding-up, through checking and inspection to prescribed margins of solvency which have to be maintained. The detailed description of these requirements will be seen later.

No insurance company may carry on insurance business in the UK unless authorised by the DTI. Each insurer must be authorised for a specific class of business. The EC Directives introduced 17 classes of general business and seven classes of life (long-term business). These are included in the 1982 Act and the applicant for authorisation must state which of these classes of business it intends to transact; the authorisation will be restricted to those classes for which it is granted.

The applicant must submit its business proposals under section 5. The Act lays down three classes of applicants, and each is subject to differing requirements:

1. An applicant in the UK must be a registered company.
2. A Community company, one with its head office in an EC country other than the UK, having an agency or branch in the UK, and must be licensed in its own country to carry on insurance business and nominate a general representative in their country.
3. An external company, one with its head office outside the EC, must in addition possess a minimum of assets in the UK and lodge a prescribed deposit.

Before authorisation, the Secretary of State for the DTI will require certain information according to the status of the applicant and the types of business to be transacted. Basically, the information required will cover the following headings:

- *The company itself*: date of formation, objects, auditors, bankers, names of key personnel
- *Scheme of operations*: source of business, premium tariffs, reinsurance, assets, costs of installing administrative systems, etc.
- *Projections*: estimates over the first three financial years of management expenses, premiums, claims, balance sheet
- *Other*: Nature of investments, copies of reinsurance treaties, agreements with brokers, etc.

Once granted, an authorisation can be revoked by the Secretary of State for one of four reasons:

- if it appears to have failed to satisfy its obligations
- if there are grounds on which it would be refused authorisation (e.g. fit and proper person basis)
- if it is an insurer from another EC state and that state has withdrawn authorisation
- if it has ceased to carry on insurance business or failed to commence business within a year of authorisation.

New minimum solvency margins were introduced from 1 January 1982, varying according to the status of the insurer and the class of business being transacted. The 'solvency margin' is the minimum amount by which assets are required to exceed liabilities measured in ECU, and it must be reached within four years following authorisation. For non-life business solvency margin, by which assets exceed liabilities, has to be maintained by law equal to the greater of either the Guarantee Fund (a minimum related to the class of business), a percentage of the premiums or a percentage of the claims. This ensures that companies showing adverse results or a declining account maintain adequate reserves. Adjustments are made to allow for reinsurance.

The DTI lays down rules on the valuation of assets and liabilities. Assets must be valued on a break-up basis and limits are set on the admissibility of certain types of asset for the purposes of demonstrating the required solvency margins. Long-term business, where premium rates are fixed for periods longer than one year, has a formula for calculating the required solvency margin based on mathematical reserves and the capital at risk. 'Mathematical reserves' are assets set aside to meet future liabilities which will arise in future years. Since level premiums are charged for an increasing risk which may last from one to 40 years based on the mortality of human life, these reserves are used up in the future when the risk premium would exceed the actual premium being charged. Capital at risk is the sums insured *less* the mathematical reserves. The required margin is the greater of the Guarantee Fund and an aggregate of the specified percentages by class of business of the mathematical reserves and capital at risk. This amount is adjusted for reinsurance.

The assets and liabilities must be valued in accordance with the DTI rules. For the assets this means a break-up basis. There are rules on the admissibility of certain types of assets and restrictions as to the extent to which individual holdings of assets may be taken into account for the purposes of demonstrating solvency.

Valuation of assets

The stages involved in valuing assets for the purpose of inclusion in the DTI return of an insurance company are as follows:

- valuation
- admissibility
- matching
- localisation

1. *Valuation*

   The regulations set out rules requiring assets to be valued in a specific way which is intended to give break-up values. This contrasts with valuation in financial statements which assumes a going-concern basis. Assets not referred to in the Regulations cannot be included in the Returns; goodwill would be valueless in this context. The rules for each class of asset are set out in the Regulations.

2. *Admissibility*

   When completing returns these regulations limit the proportion of total assets which can be held in individual funds. These restrictions are related to the volume of general and long-term business. Amounts held in excess of these amounts will be ignored in the Returns.

3. *Matching and localisation rules*

   Regulations prescribe that, whenever liabilities of an insurance company in any particular currency exceed 5% of that company's liabilities, then the company must hold assets capable of realisation into that currency without exchange rate risk to cover at least 80% of the liabilities in that currency.

Where the company carries on life and non-life business, the requirement applies to the assets to each kind of business separately.

The location of these matching assets is also restricted, which basically means that:

- sterling liabilities must be matched by assets in the UK
- liabilities in any other currency must be matched by assets in the UK or in the country of that currency.

Further reading

Bank of England Papers, BSD/1990/2, BSD 1990/3.

Birds, J., *Modern Insurance Law*, 3rd edn (Sweet & Maxwell).

Boléat, M., *Building Societies: The Regulatory Framework*, 3rd edn (Building Societies Association).

Building Societies Association and Council of Mortgage Lenders, *Building Societies Year Books* (Franey & Co.).

Building Societies Commission, *Annual Reports* (HMSO).

Building Societies Commission, *Prudential Notes* (BSC).

Drake, L., *The Building Society Industry in Transition* (Macmillan, 1989).

Ellis, T.H. and Wiltshire, J.A. (eds), *The Regulation of Insurance in the United Kingdom and Ireland*, Issue 38 (December 1993).

Goacher, D.J., Curwen, P.J., Apps, R., Boocock, J.G., Cowdell, P.F. and Drake, L., *British Non-Bank Financial Intermediaries (Allen & Unwin, 1987)*.

Hall, M., '*Banking Regulation and Supervision*' (Edward Elgar, 1993).

Hall, M., 'Deregulation of Building Societies: The Prudential Issues', *Royal Bank of Scotland Review*, 156 (December 1987), pp. 11–27.

HMSO, *Insurance Annual Report 1992* (HMSO).

HMSO, *Report of the Committee to Review the Functioning of Financial Institutions* (Wilson Report), Cmnd 7937 (HMSO, 1980).

Murray-Stone, A. and Gamble, A., *Managing Capital Adequacy* (Woodhead Faulkner, 1991).

Norton, J.J. (ed.), *Bank Regulation and Supervision in the 1990's* (Lloyds of London Press, 1991).
Pawley, M., Winstone, D. and Bentley, P., *UK Financial Institutions and Markets* (Macmillan, 1991).
Price Waterhouse, *A Guide to the UK Insurance Industry* (Graham & Trotman, 1990).
Rose, F.D. (ed.), *New Foundations for Insurance Law* (Stevens & Sons, 1987).

CHAPTER 4

The Macroeconomic Environment

David Ramsay

1. Introduction

This chapter opens with an account of developments in macroeconomic thought and policy analysis to place in context the contemporary economic environment in which financial services operate. The final section analyses the recent behaviour of banks and other financial institutions, emphasising the linkages which are evident between the financial sector and the macroeconomy. If there is perhaps some noticeable bias towards banking institutions in this chapter, this may be explained by the monetary nature of their activities and the importance of money in the economy. This, however, should not necessarily make us 'monetarists'. The relationship between the stock of money in the economy and aggregate monetary expenditure is by no means fixed and unchanging over time because, during a boom or on the upswing of the business cycle, monetary expenditures may run ahead of the supply of money, whilst during a recession quite the opposite might happen. However, as observed by Joseph Schumpeter, this expansion and contraction of bank credit might not be the cause of the economic cycle but without banks these booms and slumps might not be what they are![1]

The view expressed in this chapter is that there is a significant degree of interdependence between activities in the financial sector and in the macroeconomy but the pace of change of such activities, illustrated for example by variations in output and employment, might not always exhibit as strong an association as might be expected. In particular, the effects of deregulation and technical change are not evenly and simultaneously spread across the whole economy.

2. Macroeconomic developments

The very significant changes in macroeconomics over the previous two decades have been described in such terms as a shift either from Keynesian to Monetarist thinking, or from demand-siders to supply-siders, or from interventionist to non-interventionist, or from a control economy to the free play of markets. Whilst these terms can be helpful and are often unavoidable it should be recognised that they over-simplify the theory, the policy and the reality. There are (or were!) Keynesians who thought money important; there are supply-siders who accept the need for some demand management in the economy, and there is many a compromise between the advocates of market intervention *vis-à-vis* the free play of market forces.

The ideological revolution initiated in 1936 by J.M. Keynes[2] dominated economic thought and policy-making until the end of 1960s. It was virtually unquestioned that calculated intervention by government on prevailing and planned revenues and expenditures (budgetary policy) would so influence the level of aggregate demand in the economy as to achieve generally agreed policy objectives. There was a broad consensus between the main political parties in the UK that budgetary policy could maintain full employment and economic growth without inflationary pressure. Government demand management was both fundamental and foremost in determining the level of economic activity.

The international economy was then a stabilising force. The Bretton Woods (1944) pegged exchange rate regime, with the US dollar as the key currency tied to a gold value of $US 35 an ounce, provided a global system of fairly stable exchange rates and low inflation with little inter-country variation. Monetary policy in the UK was externally directed towards the balance of payments and stabilising the exchange rate through variations in short-term interest rates aimed at the international money and capital markets.

With UK budgetary policy occupied with domestic employment and growth objectives and monetary policy directed to the external objectives of balance of payments equilibrium and a pegged exchange rate, there remained the problem of dealing with persistent inflationary pressures. These first arose from domestic sources and then later from an over-extended and over-valued US dollar. Whilst the latter required a change in US foreign policy, in Vietnam for example, or an international solution (a realignment of currencies) the former was tackled by a succession of price and income controls and other ad hoc measures. A cursory examination of the data suggests that Keynesian macroeconomic theory and policy appeared reasonably equipped to manage conflicting macroeconomic objectives.

Table 4.1 summarises the performance of four macroeconomic target variables by decades since 1950. Until the early 1970s government demand management looks broadly successful, but both unemployment and inflation were tending to rise together in the late 1960s and early 1970s. It can be argued that unemployment was maintained at too low a level

Table 4.1   The UK macroeconomy, 1950–92, average annual % changes

	GDP % p.a.	Inflation % p.a.	Unemployment % p.a.	BOP % of GDP
1950–9	2.5	4.3	1.7	+0.6
1960–9	3.3	3.5	2.0	−0.1
1970–9	2.3	12.6	3.2	−0.3
1980–9	3.3	5.5	9.9	+0.2
1980–2	*2.3*	*7.4*	*9.0*	*+0.0*
1983–9	*3.7*	*4.7*	*10.3*	*+0.3*
1990–2	*−0.8*	*6.3*	*7.8*	*−2.1*

Sources: *Economic Trends* (London: CSO) and *Department of Employment Gazette*, various issues.

between 1950 and 1970, thus exacerbating inflationary pressure. Lord Beveridge, who earlier in 1944 had laid the post-Second World War foundations for employment and social policy, had suggested 3% as a feasible unemployment target given the structure of the labour force at the time.[3] In fact it was not until 1975 that the figures show unemployment reaching as high as 3%, but by then inflation had soared to 24.2%! Unemployment deepens in each successive decade and appears less related in the longer term to either output growth or inflation than orthodox Keynesian theory would have us believe. Other factors become significant; for example, 'hidden' unemployment and employment, social and technological causes including education and training, innovation and industrial change, demographic changes and, not least, the issue of the appropriate statistics with which to record the number of unemployed persons.

It was the coincidence of rising inflation and unemployment in both the USA and the UK, illustrated and explained by the 'expectations augmented Phillips curve,[4] which launched a counter-revolution in monetary and macroeconomic thought. Although this new economic condition was the catalyst for a radical rethink in macroeconomic policy, there were a number of other significant developments in the argument leading to the policy transition during the 1970s and 1980s. In particular, the following areas can be noted.

Monetary theory and policy

Foremost was the ascendancy of the new counter-revolutionary view about the long-run importance of monetary growth which in theory and evidence is regarded as a determinant of the price level and money incomes, but little else. This is known as the 'Modern Quantity Theory' and had been developed by Milton Friedman and the 'Chicago School' as a reaction to Keynesian economic theory and policy. Essential to the predictions of the theory was the historical evidence regarding the stability of the money demand function, which was seen to confirm that price stability would result only from monetary stability. The optimal role for monetary policy would be to facilitate the growth of money GDP, providing for real growth within a nation's productive capacity and a tolerable rate of inflation. Any significant variation would bring only undesired deflation or inflation. Thus was derived the argument for a monetary rule rather than discretion. The monetary rule or 'target' should be 'credible', so as to favourably influence inflationary 'expectations'.[5]

Broad money targets were first publicly introduced by the UK in 1976 and target 'ranges' in the following year. Because direct controls and prices and incomes policies continued to be in evidence until 1979 this policy period has been aptly described as 'monetarily constrained Keynesianism'.[6]

In 1979–80, following the election of a radical Conservative government, monetary targets and the anti-inflationary strategy immediately became central to macroeconomic policy. There was a clear shift away from direct and quantitative controls, which were rapidly abolished between 1979 and 1981, towards market-based mechanisms resulting in the Bank of England's monetary instruments being effectively restricted to the setting of short-term interest rates and, when appropriate, intervention in the gilt-edged and foreign exchange markets. It has been estimated by Britton[7] that the level of interest rates during the 1980s was higher than in the 1970s by a significant margin of about 3% points. This may have resulted from the increased reliance upon interest rates or changed international circumstances, or perhaps the consequences of deregulating the financial system.

The budget constraint

This is the recognition that monetary and budgetary policies are interdependent in their use. Decisions about the level of government expenditures and taxes over a particular period determine the extent to which the government must borrow to finance its activities. The extent of government borrowing and the way in which it is financed impinges upon monetary variables. Borrowing from the private sector raises interest rates and 'crowds out' private investment and consumption, whereas borrowing from the banking system will increase the stock of money and ease monetary conditions. The point is well made in the following extract of evidence given to the Expenditure Committee of the House of Commons in 1974:

> The influence of monetary variables on aggregate demand has been, and continues to be, greatly underestimated in the conduct of economic policy

in this country. As a corollary the indirect effects of fiscal policy have been and continue systematically to be ignored. This is an error in economic analysis which lies at the root of many of our present difficulties and continues to lay up future trouble for us. (D.E.W. Laidler[8])

It is this view about the monetary nature of the overall fiscal stance (the 'budget constraint'), together with the importance of monetary growth and monetary controls, which later, as the Medium Term Financial Strategy (MTFS), underpinned UK macroeconomic policy in the 1980s.

Supply-side strategy

This is the view that state intervention, regulation and fiscal policies create and foster adverse supply-side effects discouraging investment, productivity change, competition and the 'enterprise' culture. Budget deficits raise the national debt, putting upward pressure on government borrowing and the level of interest rates, and increase the interest burden of servicing the debt.[9] This process is described as 'crowding out' the private sector, and was a further argument for the reduction of public sector expenditure. Supply-side policies included a wide range of fiscal reforms and market liberalisation measures throughout the 1980s in addition to the privatisation programme which returned a large number of public sector enterprises to the private sector. By the end of the financial year 1992/3 approaching 70% of the nationalised sector in 1979, representing 47 companies, had been privatised, transferring more than 900,000 jobs to the private sector and £50 billion to the public purse.[10]

Some microeconomic aspects of fiscal policy were thought to restrict opportunities for economic growth. In particular, high and progressive tax rates provided a disincentive to work effort for both individual and corporate activity. This reasoning provided a foundation for fiscal reform, for example switching from direct to indirect taxes and simplifications to the tax system.[11]

Perhaps the most significant of the major supply-side reforms in the financial sector has been the drive towards increased competition and economic efficiency, identified by the active intervention of government in the deregulation and liberalisation of markets. In financial markets, this has been evident with a number of far-reaching changes starting with the abolition of exchange controls in 1979 and later measures affecting the operations of banks, building societies, insurance companies (see Chapters 2 and 3), the stock exchange and security houses. These measures are thought to have had a considerable impact upon the availability of credit and the rise in personal debt during the 1980s.

The international economy and exchange rate policy

The breakdown of the Bretton Woods international monetary system during the years 1971–3 brought about more flexible exchange rates, predominately market determined for many of the industrial countries. This allowed the UK monetary authorities to use short-term interest rates towards domestic rather than external objectives. Earlier, the balance of payments had been seen as a constraint towards achieving economic growth and full employment. Monetary policy was then directed by changes in the Central Bank's discount rate (then called the Bank Rate) to influence the movement of short-term capital flows: 'hot money'. Such capital movements were expected to stabilise the exchange rate.

In the years leading up to 1970 the increasing size and volatility of these capital movements, and the failure of central bank reserves to grow in line with demand, produced the opposite of the desired effects and led to instability and the eventual collapse of the Bretton Woods system. Rising interest rates and capital flows were but symptoms; the root causes were international differentials in productivity, economic growth, inflation and the inadequacies of the US dollar as the reserve currency in the international monetary system. The UK economy was characterised by 'stop-go' policies which impeded longer-term investment and economic growth.

It has been noted that the discipline of the Bretton Woods pegged exchange rate system was 'irksome'.[12] With inflation and unemployment both rising but economic growth faltering and averaging only 2% in 1969–71 there was a widespread feeling in (Conservative) government circles that investment and growth should not be subordinated to a fixed exchange rate. Further, interest rates could then either be placed under domestic control or permitted to move with the markets. However as Table 4.1 shows, the performance of the UK economy in the decade 1970–9 was disappointing: economic growth did not substantially improve whilst inflation and unemployment further deteriorated. It would be too simplistic to attribute this performance only to floating exchange rates and/or the loose conduct of monetary policy. The oil 'shocks' in 1973–4 and again in 1979 contributed to world-wide inflation and recession, but the effect of the international economy and the operation of the business cycle and technical change may also have been significant. The deep recession of 1980–2 was followed by an exceptional upturn in the UK between 1983–9. Unemployment, however, remained higher than at any stage since the 1930s until it began to decline rapidly after 1986. The improvement in the unemployment rate, down from 11.6% to 5.9% by the end of 1989, was accompanied by a rise in inflation, up from 3.3% to 10.0% by 1990.

European monetary integration

The UK government joined the European Monetary System (EMS) in March 1979, but not its most significant feature, the Exchange Rate Mechanism (ERM). The 'petro-currency' argument was thought to be one compelling reason for deferring the decision to enter the ERM. The relatively favourable performance of other industrial countries, especially West Germany, and the political and economic initiatives towards closer European economic integration during the 1980s, increased the pressures on the UK to join the ERM. The abandonment of broad domestic monetary targets in 1985–6 and again in 1986–7 led to an increased role for the exchange rate as a clear and unambiguous monetary target. The path was thus laid towards UK membership of the ERM.

By 1990, the UK was suffering from rapidly rising inflation, historically high real interest rates and clear signs of recession. The entry of sterling into the ERM in October 1990 was expected to reduce both inflation and interest rates without depreciating sterling which might otherwise have added to inflationary pressure. Inflation did decline gradually in line with the European average, but interest rates did not fall quickly enough to significantly reduce the domestic burden of high real interest rates. Consequently the recession deepened, and it became evident that the initial central value for sterling in the ERM (£1=DM2.95) represented a significant over-valuation of the UK currency.

On 15 September 1992 ('Black Wednesday') the international speculative selling of sterling forced the UK government to withdraw from the ERM. Paradoxically it was the German economy which had indirectly and inadvertently created widespread currency instability in the ERM through its own domestic costs of the unification of East and West Germany. The inflation resulting from the Germany unification necessitated a very different monetary policy for Germany than was appropriate for most other countries. Since sterling's withdrawal from the ERM, the UK government has restated its ultimate objective of sustainable non-inflationary economic growth, but without any foreseeable prospect of rejoining the ERM or entertaining full-scale European Monetary Union (EMU). The ERM discipline upon the level of UK interest rates has been replaced by a range of indicators including narrow and broad monetary aggregates, asset prices and the exchange rate. No targets for these indicators are published, but there is now an official target range for inflation of 1–4% with the objective that inflation should drop to 2% or below by the mid-1990s.[13]

In summary, during the 1980s we have noted a marked change of emphasis towards the role of government in the economic management of the economy. This has not been a peculiarly British phenomenon as is evidenced by the USA, France, Australia, New Zealand, the economic reforms in the newly emergent East European market economies and the IMF/World Bank programmes for macroeconomic adjustment in both middle income and low income developing countries. The rationale is that post-Second World War government intervention with market mechanisms had proved counter-productive, distorting resource allocation and fostering inefficiencies instead of furthering economic and social efficiency. The creation of free, or freer, markets to foster competitive forces has become a priority. This also involves the exposure of public utilities and services to market forces where complete privatisation has not already taken place. The most significant switch has been the use of a supply-side strategy rather than the post-1945 consensus of demand management to reduce unemployment and stimulate economic growth.

This leaves the macroeconomic role of fiscal policy with a fairly passive 'balanced budget' strategy, whilst monetary policy has been directed more actively towards macroeconomic stabilisation, in particular the anti-inflation objectives, via the adoption of monetary rules and the use of short-term interest rates. There is perhaps a danger that monetary policy may have become 'over-burdened' because the other policy instruments have proved relatively rigid in practice. It remains the 'official' view, however, that monetary policy has a comparative advantage in promoting price stability which should continue to be its prime responsibility.[14]

3. Banks and other financial institutions

running in parallel

The period since 1970 has seen two decades of rapid growth in financial services concurrent with unprecedented structural change. The breakdown of previously segmented markets – for retail deposits, payments services, home mortgages, insurance and securities – has blurred those earlier boundaries or 'functional divisions' between different classes of financial intermediaries which had comfortably existed for a century or more.

Banks have not only diversified their lending into the longer term, with home mortgage loans in competition with the building societies and some insurance companies, but they now engage in the provision of extensive retail services in insurance, money markets and in real estate. These activities increase the banks' non-interest income, now considered more important as their traditional business has itself become more competitive and less profitable (see Table 4.2).

'Financial and business services have been the most successful sector of the UK economy in the 1980s, in terms of employment creation and output growth'.[15] Between June 1979 and June 1990 employment growth in financial services – more narrowly defined but including banking, building societies, insurance, securities and commodity broking – increased by an average of 4.2% p.a. compared to 0.03% p.a. for the economy as a whole and a decline of -3.3% p.a. in manufacturing industry.

Table 4.2   Large British banks, sources of income, 1987–92, £ billion

Source	1987	1988	1989	1990	1991	1992
Net interest	11.06	12.32	13.92	13.97	14.45	14.82
Non-interest	6.02	7.02	8.44	8.95	10.42	11.54
Total income	17.08	19.34	22.36	22.92	24.87	26.36
Non-interest income as % of total income	35.3	36.3	37.7	39.1	41.9	43.8

Source: *Bank of England Banking Act Reports* (various years).

Table 4.3   UK real growth rates, 1971–92, % p.a., average

Period	Financial services	GDP	Financial services as % share of nominal GDP
1971–3	6.2	3.4	11.5
1974–6	2.0	–0.6	11.4
1977–9	5.4	3.1	11.2
1980–2	4.5	–0.7	11.7
1983–9	8.1	3.6	15.5
1990–2	–0.7	–0.7	17.9*

*Includes an estimate for 1992.
Sources: *National Income and Expenditure 'Blue Books'* (various years).

Table 4.3 summarises the actual extent of financial sector growth over recent years, including the more significant cyclical downturns in 1974–6, 1980–2 and 1990–2. The observed trend and cyclical movements, which are quite dramatic, require some explanation.

The growth in financial and business services is higher than GDP in every period except 1990–2 and for the period as a whole, raising its share in nominal GDP from 7.1% in 1970 to 17.7% in 1991. However the increase was more significant during the 1980s, when between 1983 and the end of 1990 the share of financial services had risen from 13.0% to 18.8%. The cyclical behaviour of financial services appears more in tune with GDP than does the trend, but whereas in 1974–6 the percentage declines were of the same order (about 4%), there appear to be significant differences in both 1980–2 and 1990–2. In the former period deregulation and liberalisation in the financial sector accompanied by a buoyant housing market acted as a substantial buttress against a significant decline in GDP. In 1990–2 the relatively more pronounced decline in the growth rate of financial services may be explained by adjustments to the 'over-shooting' from previous years, in lending and debt accumulation in general, and to the housing and property markets in particular.

Structural change has not only accompanied the growth but has itself played a significant part in the determination of this exceptional period of growth and development in the financial sector. The financial services 'revolution' of the 1980s was activated by two separate but interdependent forces: first, the UK government's policy of market liberalisation through deregulation and, second, the prevailing wind of financial innovation accompanied by advances in information technology (see Chapter 5).[16]

Deregulation may be considered to have commenced earlier, with the Bank of England's document 'Competition and Credit Control' (CCC) issued in May 1971. This, however, was not fully implemented and was at least partially rendered ineffective before the end of 1973 when direct controls were reintroduced in the form of supplementary special deposits (the 'corset'). CCC applied only to the banking system. The removal of UK exchange controls in 1979 rendered the 'corset' ineffective, and it was abolished later in 1980. Innovation may proceed unevenly but it is a continuous activity; no less with financial innovation and the application of information technology. The implementation of innovatory practices, however, required the incentives derived from participation in a more freely competitive environment than existed in the UK financial sector before 1980. Such innovation, competition and initiatives through the introduction of new products than existed prior to 1980 related more to international banking and finance and perhaps also in wholesale transactions where generally markets had been relatively unregulated. Indeed it could be argued that it was largely the impact of the growth of the monetarily unregulated sectors, such as Euromarkets, parallel markets and the building societies during the 1960s and 1970s, which later influenced domestic official opinion towards a more 'level playing field' as regards both the acceptance of deposits and the provision of loans.

Financial sector deregulation has been a significant supply-side measure of successive UK governments in the 1980s. Alongside similar policy strategies in the labour and goods markets, legislation was introduced to reduce price and quantity distortions in the financial markets thereby improving allocative efficiency in the economy as a whole. 'The 1980s. experienced one of the fastest growth rates of lending to the personal sector of any decade this century.'[17] In the banking sector, this increase more than outpaced a decline in the relative importance of lending to industrial and commercial companies despite the rapid growth in the 1987/9 takeover and investment boom and to a lesser extent the 'large-scale distress borrowing' by firms in

Table 4.4   *UK banks, lending to UK residents, 1987/8–1992,*
annual % growth rates, Feb–Feb

Category	1987/8	1988/9	1989/90	1990/1	1991/2	1992 (end Nov.)
Lending to UK residents of which	22.0	28.0	21.0	10.0	3.4	3.5
to company sector	19.0	33.0	26.0	10.0	0.0	1.1
to non-bank financial sector	21.0	21.0	19.0	13.0	13.0	5.8

Source: *Bank of England Banking Act Reports* (various years).

the depths of the recession in 1981–2. In the 1980s bank lending to UK residents grew at an average annual rate of 19%.[18]

From Table 4.4 it can be observed that bank lending 'peaks' in 1988/9, just prior to the end of the economic boom. Lending appears to follow GDP and, perhaps, lags rather than leads aggregate economic activity. The behaviour of a prudent and profitable lender should lead rather than lag. Keynes (1931) wrote 'Banks and bankers are by nature blind. They have not seen what was coming'.[19] By reacting to events rather than anticipating them the cautious practice of banking owes more to hindsight than to foresight. For example there is much evidence of 'relationship banking', with banks generally more supportive of existing customers[20] and cautious behaviour with the emphasis upon historical information and 'rules of thumb' influencing bank lending decisions: 'banks also tend to keep in step with fellow banks'.[21] This supports but does not settle the argument that bank lending and the general availability of credit influences the business cycle in the way earlier recognised by Schumpeter. For example, when commenting on the deepening recession in 1990/1 the Bank of England stated:

It is hard to judge, from the statistics showing the economy and credit both slowing down, how far changes in the economy are reducing.the demand for credit and how far changes in the availability of credit are causing adjustment in the economy.[22]

The financial intermediaries most involved in personal sector lending are the banks and building societies. Two features of macroeconomic importance over the past two decades have been the competition between the two sets of institutions for the greater share of personal sector deposits and the impact of interest rate policy on both sides of their balance sheets. The greater reliance placed upon interest rates as the instrument of monetary policy in the 1980s underlines the importance of banks and building societies in the economy during this period when competition was most pronounced.

To examine the effect of macroeconomic policies including both the supply-side measure of market liberalisation and demand-side management via interest rates on the behaviour of financial intermediaries it would be helpful to set up a simple model relating revenue and costs where net interest income is taken as a measure of profit. As an initial simplification, the model ignores those revenues and costs associated with off-balance sheet activities and also administrative and capital costs. Taking revenues from assets less the interest costs of servicing deposit liabilities to equal profit, P, we have:

$$r_R . R + r_S . S + r_L . L - r_D . D = P \qquad (1)$$

r_R, r_S and r_L are the interest rates on reserve assets R, government securities S and loans L. Generally it would be expected that $r_L > r_S > r_R$, and therefore it would be the intermediaries' objective to maximise L, subject to prudent behaviour and/or any statutory or supervisory requirements regarding holdings of R and S. (Where cash is the only reserve asset, $r_R = 0$.)

r_D is the average interest rate on interest bearing deposits D. To increase loans L it would be necessary for our intermediary to increase D, provided of course that the intermediary had no scope for selling R or S, and substituting a private sector loan book. The latter strategy has been described as 'asset management', and was the way that the UK banking system financed loans in the non-price competitive post-1945 era. However, since CCC in 1971, banks have been increasingly engaged in liability management – i.e. competing for deposits (retail, wholesale and foreign) – thus raising D to finance a rising loan book.

The economic theory of market behaviour predicts the 'law of one price', with a common margin of profit for firms operating in a fully competitive environment. We shall tentatively examine this prediction in the UK domestic market for personal deposits held in banks and building societies.

Before 1971, banks engaged in an interest rate cartel, setting both r_L and r_D, and effectively their interest spreads, by reference to the Bank Rate. The increased competition since 1971 between banks and between banks and building societies for both loans and deposits has had some significant implications for net interest spreads and margins. Interest spread is the difference between the interest rate earned on average interest earning assets and the interest paid on average interest bearing liabilities. The interest margin is (net) interest income as a percentage of interest earning assets. In terms of the simple model, if A represented the total of all assets $(R + S + L)$ and r_A was the weighted average of r_R, r_S and r_L then

$$\text{interest spread } (\%) = r_A - r_D \qquad (2)$$

$$\text{interest margin } (\%) = \frac{r_A A - r_D D}{A} \qquad (3)$$

Table 4.5   UK banks' sterling deposits and interest rates, 1981–92, end-year data

Year	Interest bearing deposits (IBELS)		Base rate %	7-day deposit rate %
	(a) as % of sight deposits	(b) as % of total deposits		
1981 (end)	24.5	73.9	14.5	12.5
1982	31.6	77.4	10.0	7.0
1983	35.7	77.4	9.0	5.5
1984	38.7	77.1	9.5	6.5
1985	49.4	79.4	11.5	8.0
1986	55.1	80.6	11.0	7.0
1987	68.1	81.7	8.5	3.6
1988	58.9	83.0	13.0	6.0
1989	68.3	86.7	15.0	6.6
1990	71.9	88.6	14.0	5.1
1991	78.0	90.4	10.5	1.5
1992	79.3	90.8	7.0	1–2*

*From January 1992, the rates quoted are for the lowest tier of an instant access savings account.
Source: British Bankers' Association.

Clearly, if interest was paid on all deposits then since the total of assets must be equal to the total of deposit liabilities, the interest spread would equal the margin. A beneficial difference (known as the 'endowment effect') arises for the bank if a proportion of deposit liabilities is non-interest bearing, as for example with some current or chequing accounts (see Table 4.5).

Interest spreads and margins are regarded as broad indicators of the profitability and efficiency in financial intermediation. Spreads are quite easily seen as subject to competitive market forces. As financial intermediaries compete for deposits r_D is subject to upward pressure, while competition for loans keeps r_L rates lower than they might otherwise be, thus narrowing the interest spread. However the evidence from Table 4.5 suggests that interest differentials have become wider rather than narrower, but this may be misleading. Spreads are now calculated from average net interest earnings over a wide range of assets and liabilities. This more traditional indicator of interest spread has become increasingly less relevant over recent years as banks have introduced new and varied products, especially on the deposit side of the balance sheet.

Goodhart (1989) notes that the rapid growth of private sector deposits with both banks and building societies and the corresponding increase in the lending and asset creation of these institutions has reduced the effective spread or 'cost of intermediation'. Goodhart suggests that this cheapening of

Table 4.6   Domestic net interest spread and margins, 1980–92,
selected UK banks and building societies

Year	Bank spread %	Bank margin %	Building societies margin* %
1980	n/a	6.86	1.56
1981	2.9	6.52	1.81
1982	3.1	5.91	1.86
1983	3.4	5.43	1.81
1984	3.4	5.62	1.65
1985	3.0	5.67	1.83
1986	3.4	5.59	1.86
1987	3.3	5.42	1.87
1988	3.0	5.02	1.93
1989	2.4	4.70	1.96
1990	2.3	4.28	1.94
1991	n/a	4.00	1.96
1992	n/a	3.80	2.07

*Not strictly comparable with bank margins (interest earnings as a percentage of end-year total assets for all building societies reported in UK).
n/a Not available.
Sources: Bank of England, British Bankers' Association and Building Societies' Association (Tables 5.5 and 5.9, *Housing Finance Fact Book 1993*).

the spread has resulted in a structural increase in the use of these services; in other words, the demand for intermediation becomes a function of its cost – i.e. the spread.[23]

Table 4.6 provides some selective information on net interest spreads and margins for banks and building societies. Whilst not strictly comparable for the two kinds of institutions because of differing asset and liability structures, the figures should be helpful when analysing first, the supply-side effects of competition policy and, second, the interest rate effects of monetary policy. Although spreads and margins in commercial banking have been subject to a significant decline, in particular since 1985, the reverse has been the experience for the building societies. Bank margins are generally higher than those for building societies because of higher operational costs and risk premiums – e.g. branching, money transmission and unsecured lending. However, to the extent that deregulation and competition have brought about less diverse and more equivalent services, the spreads and margins are likely to be similar.[24] Figure 4.1 illustrates these recent trends and movement towards the 'law of one price'.

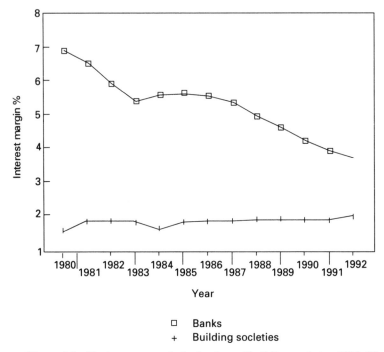

Figure 4.1   Net interest margin for banks and building societies, 1980–92

A distinguishing feature of significance in banking is the so-called 'endowment effect'. The existence of non-interest bearing deposit liabilities (NIBELS) is a potential source of profit through increased margins when interest rates are rising. This was certainly evident between 1972 and 1974 when the net margin almost doubled. However, it is also clear that the 'endowment effect' declined during the 1980s (see Table 4.6) as NIBELS fell from 26.1% of sterling deposits for the London Clearing Banks in 1981 to 9.16% for the major British retail banks – a slightly wider group – by the end of 1992. This in part explains the reduction in margins from 6.52% in 1981 to 3.8% in 1990. A further related causal effect has been the movement from low to higher interest bearing accounts.

Spreads and margins might be expected to move in tandem in the absence of structural changes. The 1980s, however, does not present a consistent pattern for both spreads and margins as the former increased in 1981–4 before declining in 1986–92. Spreads are susceptible to interest rates and market demand (see Figure 4.2).

Let $S(L)$ and $S(D)$ be the market supply curves for loans and deposits, respectively. $S(L)$ is higher than $S(D)$ to provide for non-interest costs such as the risk premium and administrative expenses. To the extent that there is an 'endowment effect', $S(D)$ is less interest elastic than $S(L)$ and cuts the horizontal axis at OE.

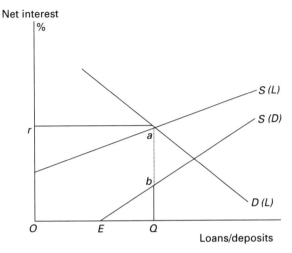

Figure 4.2   The net interest spread

If the demand for loans is given by *D(L)*, then the market clearing or equilibrium level of deposits is *OQ* at an interest rate of *Or*. The interest spread at this point is *ab*. With given supply conditions an increase in the demand for loans would narrow, the spread as rates tend to be increased more on deposits than for loans. As demand declines or becomes less competitive, so spreads should improve.

In general, the dynamic forces of competition and financial innovation would result in structural changes to both sides of the banks' balance sheet – assets (lending) and liabilities (deposits). For example, the period 1980–3 was characterised by deregulation and saw significant reintermediation into the banking system. This induced more competitive lending, such as the introduction by the banks of home mortgage loans. Such behaviour when interest rates were falling would on balance tend to raise net interest spreads, provided the lending continued to be profitable. However, loan default or loan loss provisioning reduces spreads. The declining spreads and margins observed in the 1980s, particularly the later years, may be explained in this way because bank assets have been at risk not only in home mortgages but also in loans to property developers and in 'sovereign' lending to middle income developing countries.

A similar analysis might also be applied to the banking crisis in the USA in 1929–32, when the banks were accused of over-investing or even 'reckless lending' to business and the stockmarket.[25]

The impact of interest rates and the stance of monetary policy should also be noted. With a given 'endowment' effect falling (rising) interest rates should perhaps be expected to lower (raise) both S_L and S_D equally, thus maintaining the net interest spread. This is evidently not the experience in UK banking. Short-term deposit rates are more sensitive than retail lending rates, thus 'interest rates charged to customers fall less rapidly than market rates generally'.[26] In 1992, banks reduced 'deposit rates on some savings earlier and by more than lending rates'.[27] Thus, *ceteris paribus*, spreads tend to rise when interest rates decline and, conversely, spreads will be expected to fall when monetary policy is tightened through higher short-term interest rates. Spreads have tended to move in this predictable fashion, whereas margins have been more influenced by structural changes in the balance sheets.

Recently there is some evidence that the rate of decline of spreads and margins has been reversed and that some interest spreads may have actually risen over the past two years. Since 1990 UK interest rates have been steadily reduced as inflation declined and the recession deepened. As may be observed from Figure 4.2, any fall in loan demand with the supply curves unchanged should result in some slight recovery in the interest spread. Because of the endowment effect with interest rates falling, a profit maximising bank would not wish to reduce loan rates as much as deposit rates and indeed, as explained earlier, market forces would not warrant this anyway. This may explain some of the recent criticism levelled at the UK High Street banks by small business customers, although a Bank of England Report into business lending margins refuted the allegation that banks had not passed on interest rate cuts. 'Although rising spreads placed upward pressure on the domestic interest margin this was more than offset by the impact of bad debts and the loss of 'endowment income'.[28]

The decline in net interest spreads and margins, together with the new capital adequacy requirement, only further emphasises the banking sector's desire and need for off-balance sheet activities and the increasing importance of non-interest income, as seen in Table 4.2 (p. 56). As noted by the Bank of England,

> Increased competition in traditional areas of business has prompted the large banks to seek other sources of operating income which require less capital as well as being less sensitive to recession.[29]

4. Conclusions

The twin forces of competition and technical change have led to widespread structural changes in the financial services sector, and in the economy as a whole. However, because financial markets respond much faster than do either goods or labour markets, we see these changes particularly evident in the product range of financial activities, operational systems and the pace of innovation, all of which combine to affect customer services, employment, productivity and profits, through spreads and margins. By themselves, these changes are interesting and rewarding areas of industrial investigation, but banks and other financial institutions are instrumental in providing money and capital to other sectors in the economy and overseas. We have seen that banking and finance are directly affected by the progress of the business cycle but as noted by Schumpter and illustrated in this chapter, banks in turn fuel both the booms and the slumps of the macroeconomy.

Notes

1. When attributing real causes, especially innovation and technical change, to an explanation of the business cycle, Joseph Schumpter writes
   We do not, of course, hold that the behaviour of banks has nothing to do with the cycle. There is no doubt that without credit creation amplitudes of cyclical fluctuations would be much smaller. (Schumpeter, 1939), p. 635.
2. Keynes (1936).
3. Beveridge (1944), para 159. In the prologue to the 1960 edn, Lord Beveridge notes
   I suggested a figure of 3 percent of the total labour force as likely to be idle at any time. Maynard Keynes, when he saw this figure, wrote to me that there was no harm in aiming at 3 percent, but that he would be surprised if we got so low in practice.
4. The theory and evidence at that time was reviewed by Friedman and Laidler (1975).
5. See, for example, Friedman (1968) and the Governor of the Bank of England (1978).
6. Fforde (1983).
7. Britton (199), p. 10.
8. House of Commons, HC328, p. 48 (HMSO, 1974).
9. There is a 'new classical' view, later but arguably described as 'The Ricardian Equivalence theorem', which suggests that the community is indifferent between taxes and bond finance as methods of financing the national debt. Endowed with foresight, altruism and rational behaviour individuals increase their savings to provide future generations with assets to offset the burden of increased taxes with which to service the increased debt. The expenditure increasing effect of a budget deficit is neutralised by the increased savings of households and fiscal policy is therefore regarded as neutral and having no real impact on the macroeconomy.
10. H.M. Treasury, *Economic Briefing*, 5 (August 1993).
11. See, for example, Vane (1992), pp. 31–3.
12. Goodhart (1992), p. 25.
13. *Barclays Economic Review* (First Quarter 1993).
14. See, for example, J.A. Frenkel, Research Director, IMF, reported in *IMF Survey* (26 November 1990), p. 352.
15. *Lloyds Bank Economic Bulletin*, 145 (1991).
16. See Chapter 5 in this volume; also Thornton and Stone (1992) and Davis and Lewis (1992).
17. Llewellyn and Holmes (1991).
18. *Bank of England Quarterly Bulletin*, 31 (4) (November 1991), p. 513.
19. Keynes (1931).
20. *Bank of England Banking Act Report* (1990–91), p. 5.
21. Dow and Saville (1990), pp. 20–1.
22. Bank of England, Memorandum, 'Is there a credit crunch?', submitted to the Treasury and Civil Service Committee (March 1991).
23. Goodhart (1989), pp. 377–8.
24. *Bank of England Quarterly Bulletin*, 30 (4) (November 1990), p. 509.
25. See, for example, Keynes (1931) and Schumpeter (1939).
26. *Bank of England Banking Report* (1991–92), p. 8.

27. *Bank of England Banking Report* (1992–93), p. 9.
28. *Bank of England Banking Report* (1992–93), p. 9.
29. *Bank of England Banking Report* (1992–93), p. 9.

Further reading

Bank of England Banking Reports, published annually each spring.

Beveridge, W.A., *Full Employment in a Free Society* (George Allen & Unwin, 1944).

Britton, A.J.C., *Macroeconomic Policy in Britain, 1947–87* (Cambridge University Press, 1991).

Britton, A.J.C., 'Monetary Policy in Britain 1974–87 – an empirical investigation', NIESR, *Discussion Paper*, 193 (1991).

Callen, T.S. and Lomax, J.W., 'The Development of the Building Societies Sector in the 1980s', *Bank of England Quarterly Bulletin*, 30 (4) (November 1990), pp. 503–10.

Chrystal, K.A., 'Don't Shoot the Messenger : Do Banks Deserve the Recent Adverse Publicity?', *National Westminster Bank Review* (May 1992).

Colwell, R., 'The Performance of Major British Banks 1970–90, *Bank of England Quarterly Bulletin*, 31 (4) November 1991), pp. 508–15.

Davis, T.K. and Lewis, M.K., 'Financial Innovation : Causes and Consequences', in K. Dowd and M.K. Lewis, *Current Issues in Financial and Monetary Economics* (Macmillan, 1992).

Dow, J.C.R. and Saville, I.D., *A Critique of Monetary Policy* (Oxford University Press, 1990).

Dowd, K. and Lewis, M.K., *Current Issues in Financial and Monetary Economics* (Macmillan, 1992).

Fforde, J.S., 'Setting Monetary Objectives', *Bank of England Quarterly Bulletin*, 23(2) (June 1983).

Friedman, M., 'The Role of Monetary Policy', *American Economic Review*, (March 1968).

Friedman, M. and Laidler, D., 'Unemployment versus Inflation – an Evaluation of the Phillips Curve', *Occasional Paper*, 44, Institute of Economic Affairs (1975).

Goodhart, C.A.E., 'Alternative Monetary Standards', Ch. 2 in K. Dowd and M.K. Lewis, *Current Issues in Financial and Monetary Economics* (Macmillan, 1992).

Goodhart, C.A.E., 'The conduct of Monetary Policy', *Economic Journal* (June 1989).

Governor of the Bank of England, 'Reflections on the Conduct of Monetary Policy', the Mais Lecture, *Bank of England Quarterly Bulletin* (March 1978).

Keynes, J.M., *The General Theory of Employment, Interest and Money* (Macmillan, 1936).

Keynes, J.M., 'The Consequences to the Banks of a Collapse in Money Values', in J.M. Keynes, *Essays in Persuasion* (Macmillan, 1931).

Llewellyn, D.T. and Holmes, M., 'Competition or Credit Controls?', Institute of Economic Affairs, *Hobart Paper*, 117 (October 1991).

Llewellyn, D.T., *Reflections on Money* (Macmillan, 1989).

Schumpeter, J.A., *Business Cycles, vol. 2* (McGraw-Hill, 1939).

Thornton, D.L. and Stone, C.C., 'Deregulation and Monetary Policy', in K. Dowd and M.K. Lewis, *Current Issues in Financial and Monetary Economics* (Macmillan, 1992).

CHAPTER 5

The Impact of Information Technology on the Financial Services Sector

Brian Anderton, John Davis, Guhlum Hussain and
Alan Staley

1. Introduction

The financial services sector has been at the forefront of the application of information technology in business. This is hardly surprising since, in most developed economies including the UK, the financial services industry has been one of the most dynamic and rapidly growing sectors of the economy. Such a rate of growth and change has created a fertile environment for the innovation of information technology.

As with any business, firms in the financial services sector have been most concerned with the impact on their 'bottom-lines'. Profitability has been influenced by the impact of information technology on both the cost and revenue sides of the business. However, the application of information technology has also had a qualitative impact, changing the mode of operation of the sector, modifying the range of services provided and linking together geographically isolated financial centres into a global financial community in which financial services are traded 24 hours a day. Some of the effects of information technology on the financial services sector are summarised below, followed by several more in-depth profiles.

2. The impact of information technology: an overview

In any business, information technology may be viewed as a strategic weapon which, if used effectively, may enable a business organisation to gain a competitive advantage. The financial services sector contains many examples, over the last 30 years, of the competitive use of information technology.

Cost minimisation

A financial services firm which is able to reduce its costs below those incurred by competitors providing a similar service, has the potential to enhance its profitability and/or gain a competitive advantage by passing on some of these cost savings to its customers. In the financial services sector, costs arise from two broad areas of operation: those connected with the management of information, and those connected with the execution of transactions. Information technology has made a contribution to the containment of both these areas of cost.

Financial services has always been a labour-intensive industry. The rising cost of labour, relative to the cost of other factors of production, has imposed a burden of rising costs as a proportion of total revenue earned in such organisations as retail banks. The application of information technology has been one very important way in which financial services firms have sought to contain their costs. For example, in commercial banking, the application of successive generations of computerisation since the early 1960s has dramatically reduced the size of 'back-office' staffing, while the growth of expensive paper-based systems for money transmission (cheque and credit clearing systems) has been curtailed by the development of paperless computerised payment systems such as BACS (Bankers Automated Clearing System) in the UK, and the development of EFTPoS (Electronic Funds Transfer at Point of Sale) systems.

Traditionally, the need to develop and maintain a significant network of branches has been a major barrier to entry for firms wishing to join the market in retail banking services. However, by the 1990s developments in information technology had greatly diminished these barriers to entry. New firms may now offer personal banking services without the need to offer a branch-banking network. This is well evidenced by the development of home banking services pioneered in the UK by the Nottingham Building Society/Bank of Scotland in the early 1980s, and brought to commercial success by First Direct in the 1990s. In addition, the reduced barriers to entry have allowed new firms, whose traditional business has not been in financial services, to enter the sector, for example Marks & Spencer.

Product development

Information technology might be thought of as impacting on the products supplied by the financial services sector in one of three ways.

- Enhancement of existing services
- Creation of new services
- Contribution to product differentiation, that is making the products of one firm appear different from, and superior to, those of its competitors.

In practice, the distinction between these impacts on product development is blurred. There are many examples of the way that financial services firms have sought to enhance their traditional services by the application of information technology. The development of alternative, cashless forms of payment is a good example. The innovation of debit cards and EFTPoS systems enables current account bank customers to make payments for goods and services without the need to carry a cheque book, and without the limitations on transaction size imposed by the cheque card guarantee of payment procedure. It remains the case that, numerically, the vast majority of transactions are still conducted using cash as the means of payment, and the provision of cash to customers and its receipt from traders paying into their accounts is both expensive and poses security hazards for banks. A very recent innovation currently being piloted by National Westminster Bank and British Telecom is the use of an electronic substitute for cash. Mondex is a plastic card with a microchip which stores 'electronic money' and which can be topped up over the phone. If successful, Mondex may be a significant step towards the cashless society, particularly as the card may also be used as a multi-currency product capable of holding up to five different currencies simultaneously. Development of new products has not been confined to the area of payments systems. The development of on-line and touch-screen share-dealing services have greatly simplified the procedures for buying and selling shares, and have gone hand in hand with the widening of share ownership through privatisation sales in the UK.

In one sense, it might be argued that these are not new services but simply new ways of offering traditional services to the clients of financial services firms. For example, the development of home banking mentioned earlier might be thought of as simply an alternative way of providing traditional account-based services to retail bank customers. However, the home banking service, with its reliance on telecommunications and information technology and its divorce from the conventional branch network, might be regarded as sufficiently novel as to represent a new product. Similarly, the provision of Automated Teller Machines (ATMs) and EFTPoS might be regarded as simply alternative ways of obtaining cash or making a payment. Yet the underpinning network of information technology links which allow bank customers to access these services on a national, if not an international, basis might be thought of as being sufficiently different to constitute a new product.

Many aspects of the financial services sector may be thought of as oligopolistic in organisation. In such markets, there is a tendency to avoid price competition and to compete instead on service quality. Product differentiation is an important part of such non-price competition and, in turn, information technology has contributed to product differentiation in the financial services sector. An interesting example of this has been the success of organisations such as Direct Line in the motor and household insurance sector. With its reliance on telecommunications and computerised processing, the company is able to offer insurance cover without the usual hassle of filling out proposal forms. Instead, information supplied by the client over the phone is used to generate a schedule which is sent to the client and which forms the basis of the contract of insurance.

Marketing tool

A successful business not only needs good products but also an effective marketing strategy to link potential customers to these products. In this respect, many financial services firms, most notably the banks, are in a unique position. As part of their business, they accumulate vast amounts of information about the financial and personal circumstances of their customers, and about their behaviour as consumers. The traditional problem has been to mobilise this data into information which could be used by the business in the marketing of its services to its customers.

The advent of database technology into financial institutions such as banks has revolutionised this process. It enables the bank to access data collected in connection with the provision of one of its services, and to utilise the information derived to identify potential customers for its other services. This is particularly fruitful in those sectors within financial services, such as banking and insurance, where firms provide a diverse range of services and need to find cross-selling opportunities. Very recently, financial services firms have been switching to the latest relational database technology, which is discussed in more detail later in the chapter.

Decision-making aid

Traditionally, most business-related decisions – for example, whether to lend, whether to sell or buy currencies, whether to invest in a particular way, etc. – have been based on the expertise and experience of individual managers. However, reliance on such 'expert managers' does pose problems to financial institutions.

1. Training managers so that they acquire the knowledge and experience to make good decisions is expensive for the financial services firm.
2. Good experienced managers may be difficult to retain, and their expertise may be lost to the organisation.
3. As a result of the 'human factor' experienced managers do not always behave in the same manner. In a large financial institution, this may lead to problems of consistency. For example, does the manager of bank branch *X* always appraise applications from business customers to borrow money in the same way as the manager of branch *Y*?
4. Processing of information leading to the making of decisions may be slow, even for experienced managers. Limitations imposed by the availability of experienced managers may, in turn, impose delays in the transaction of business. This may lead to customer dissatisfaction and a loss of potential business.

Many of the decision-making problems in financial services are repetitive yet complex. For example, the decision by a bank manager whether to lend money will tend to involve the assessment of a common set of factors which experience has shown to be important in distinguishing good and bad lending propositions. But each proposition will have unique features which make it subtly different. For this reason, the financial services sector has proved receptive to the development of decision-making aids based on an application of artificial intelligence systems such as Expert Systems and more recently Neural Networks.

Expert systems

Expert systems have been defined by Feigenbaum and McCorduck (1984) as:

> intelligent computer programs that use knowledge and inference procedures to solve problems that are difficult enough to require significant human expertise for their solution.

The principal components of an expert system are:

1. A *knowledge base*: The knowledge base is similar to a database, but it stores not only facts and figures but also keeps track of the series of rules and explanations associated with the facts. The knowledge base thus contains both factual knowledge and heuristic knowledge: a set of rules relating to the knowledge domain which allows the system to recommend a particular decision.
2. The *inference engine*: This may be thought of as the control structure for an expert system. Basically, it is a computer programme which provides a methodology for reasoning about information in the knowledge base using the rules (heuristic knowledge) which it contains.

Application of expert systems as an aid to decision-making has gained widespread acceptance in financial services. The following are good examples of the more important applications:

1. Customers applying for personal loans in most banks have their applications screened by a process known as credit-scoring. Data contained in the personal loan application form is fed into the bank's computer which, by using a rules-based expert system, makes a recommendation that the application for the loan be accepted or rejected. Similar systems are now being developed and applied in the more complex area of lending to business customers.
2. Some banks, notably Lloyds Bank, have computerised their 'Help Desks'. In the Lloyds Bank system, staff work with a computerised system containing around 2,000 rules, which is able to provide on-line advice and guidance in dealing with customer queries.
3. Credit card operations, such as Barclaycard, use an expert system to detect fraudulent transactions. The system monitors transactions on a daily basis, and detects those which are out of character with the normal operation of the credit card account. Early detection of potentially fraudulent transactions can subsequently reduce the cost of fraud to credit card companies. Insurance companies are also using similar systems to scan insurance claims, and to highlight potentially fraudulent claims.
4. Expert systems are also being used by the regulators of financial markets. For example, they have been used to scan some of the more recent UK privatisation issues, in order to detect illegal multiple share applications. This is a good example of the use of expert systems, since the tactics of people making multiple applications are well known and the knowledge base of the system can detect patterns which are consistent with multiple application.
5. Perhaps the most proactive use of artificial intelligence (expert systems and neural networks) to date is in the trading of financial markets. For example, Citibank's London currency dealing room commenced a trading operation at the beginning of 1993 using an artificial intelligence system. Currently, such models are based on a 'chartist' approach to forecasting movements in market prices. By 'training' the model on historical data relating to price movements, it should then be able to detect patterns which allow the future course of price movements to be projected, and hence for the financial institution to take a position in the market, whereby it will gain benefit when the price moves as the model predicts.

The advantages of using artificial intelligence systems as a decision-making aid in financial services are significant. Chief amongst these is the potential for cost saving. This may arise partially through 'deskilling' of jobs: facilitating less knowledgeable and less experienced staff, earning lower salaries, to make as good decisions as their more experienced but more expensive colleagues. Additionally, the efficiency of more experienced staff may be enhanced, since they spend less time sifting information in order to make decisions. However, there are other advantages than cost reduction. Since a standardised artificial intelligence system is scanning information and using a common set of decision rules, decision-making is likely to be more consistent across the organisation, while knowledge, once captured within the artificial intelligence system of the organisation, is permanently available.

However, it would be wrong to regard such decision-making aids as replacing human decision-makers. Artificial intelligence systems are currently applicable only within a narrow area of knowledge and do not purport to provide generalised problem-solving. Moreover, such systems are only as good as the knowledge base on which they are founded, while the current generation of systems (unlike human decision-makers) do not learn from experience. From this it follows that artificial intelligence systems can 'get it wrong'. They are, therefore, best thought of as systems which may supplement human managers and enhance the quality of their decisions, but not as replacements for human managers and the exercise of judgement.

3. Operational issues

The strategic issues regarding information technology are closely linked to operational issues, as the one (the strategic) should decide the other. The banking industry, because it was an enthusiastic early user of information technology in the 1960s (to reduce costs) now suffers from that early adoption. In information technology circles this is a universal difficulty known as the 'backlog problem', a carry-over effect from the early systems. Written in the COBOL language which has a difficult syntax, the banks now have systems which evolved nearly 30 years ago and which have been altered many times often with incomplete documentation and, when combined with 'de-bugging' and 'fixes', represent a major maintenance problem for all mature businesses. A further effect of the backlog problem is that since it was only in the 1980s that standardised system development methodologies became adopted, with some companies such as IBM developing their own and others using independently designed methodologies such as the Jackson methodology, it has been estimated that 75% of a computer systems department costs are spent in coping with backlog problems. Because banks are bigger than building societies, they have resultant bigger problems, as all new systems are constrained by this legacy of old code and the backlog problem occupies the time of the best staff who should be involved in developing new systems.

The first programmes written for banks were based on file processing which, although fast in operation and very efficient on memory (which was expensive in the early days of computing), suffers from the problem of inflexibility. The output from the computer was fixed in format and changing programmes to keep up with changes in the market place imposed great pressure on the computer and systems staff of the banks. The response to this approach in the 1970s and 1980s was to adopt a database approach. A database may be briefly described as an organised collection of data, and databases were adopted by banks for four main reasons:

1. As memory prices fell and processing speeds increased dramatically after the first file-based systems were introduced, the technological arguments against databases became redundant
2. The database approach overcame the problem of flexibility; reports can be written on an individual basis if necessary and so managers may look at data and information from many different perspectives – using a database reduces the problem of data duplication (data redundancy) and resultant inaccuracies (see below)
3. The database approach separates the data from the application (and the hardware); as new systems come along so the data can migrate to them much more easily than in the days of file processing – developing new applications and systems does not mean that previous data is obsolete
4. Finally, and most importantly, data stops being an overhead and becomes a resource to be used by the bank in a search for new markets and customers; banks in the UK can monitor spending patterns by customers by looking at credit and debit card spending patterns and by co-ordinating with other geographic and demographic data can plan effective delivery and marking programmes.

This use of technology as a creative as well as a bureaucratic tool supports the strategic thrust of the banks. For example, by monitoring spending patterns, banks have adopted a strategy of placing ATM machines away from the branch network in supermarkets, airports, railway stations, etc. ATM machines can do much more than deliver cash, they offer many other services as well such as statements, cash deposits and so forth. This means that long-term plans by the banks to reorganise, reduce or even eliminate the branch network may proceed without customers feeling negative effects. With the new information highways which blend telecommunications, computing and networks, the banks have the potential to respond by replacing the existing branch network with an electronic delivery system without losing their customer base.

The final operational issue regarding information technology is that of income and cost management. The adoption of the database approach to data management will enable banks to monitor pricing and costs more sensitively and carefully. Banks will have to price sensitively to maintain their market position, and the detail that is obtained from the new systems should enable banks to respond more rapidly to changes in market conditions, especially in the capital markets for corporate finance, and in the retail market in response to building society competition.

4. Relational databases

Banks and financial institutions have recognised that information is a *resource* of the business that can be harnessed strategically to provide competitive advantage. Information can now be used to identify new markets, to identify the need for new products and services, and to refine the targeting of customers. Customer databases allow the business to develop profiles on customers, and using 'geodemographic' techniques consumer groups can be identified by their lifestyles and postcodes. Rather than send mailshots to all customers which results in very low response rates, high costs incurred, and some irritated customers, the new systems focus on a small number of potentially interested customers. The move from account-based to customer-based approaches to business has largely been achieved by the development of *relational databases*.

File-based approaches to data storage

Traditional approaches to storing data were based upon having application-specific files where each part of the business had its own set of computer files. These files are illustrated in Figure 5.1.

Five points emerge from Figure 5.1:

- The same item of data may be repeated on many files. This is referred to as *data redundancy*. One of the consequences of this is that a number of

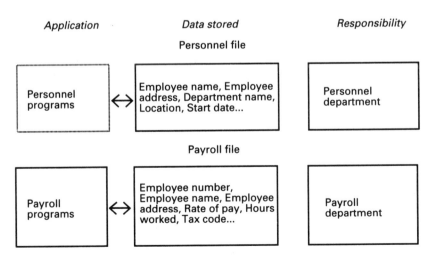

Figure 5.1   File-based approach to data storage

files need to be updated each time the duplicated data change – which is inefficient.
- If the duplicated data is changed on the one file but not others, then there is *data inconsistency*.
- Responsibility for the data is *dispersed*. Data is not seen as an organisational resource, but 'belonging' to individual departments. This can lead to a lack of standards and compatibility – e.g. 'employee name' in one file may be referred to as 'staff name' in another.
- There is *poor data integration*. It is difficult to relate information in one file with that of another, and therefore management information is also poor.
- If new applications are needed, *new files* will have to be created or existing files *re-designed*.

In addition, there is said to be *data dependence*. Each program will need to make reference to how the files are physically organised, for example the order of the records, and the length of each field. If the file organisation, or storage medium has to be changed, all the programs which use that file have to be modified. The programs are dependent on the data. Program maintenance therefore occupies a great deal of time. File-orientated applications are developed in a *piecemeal* fashion as individual needs arise. The approach therefore focuses on individual needs rather than the needs of the organisation as a whole.

Account-based data

The term 'account-based' (see Figure 5.2) was employed because data would be held on accounts rather than customers. If a customer had two accounts, there would be two separate records in the data file, one for each account. There would be no relationship between the two accounts and it would not be possible to develop a profile of a customer from the discrete accounts. To access each

ACCOUNTS

Account number	Name	Balance	Address
12345678	P Brown	10.00	2 Holland Park
25617811	J Day	427.64	82 Dunton Close
27421976	A Jones	148.00	4 Summer Lane
87112877	P Brown	5,000.00	2 Holland Park
91884213	L Smith	18.46	1 Milford Road

Figure 5.2   Account-based data

account to establish a balance, the user would need to know each individual account number.

5. The database approach

The database approach overcomes all the above problems by storing data in an integrated manner which is accessible to all applications. This shared data is highly structured to avoid redundancy and to allow the relationships between data types to be expressed. The approach is illustrated in Figure 5.3.

The term 'customer-based' is now employed because the use of relational databases have enabled the restructuring of data files into *relational tables* which can link all a customer's accounts together logically by creating a relationship between them (see Figure 5.4).

Notice how in Figure 5.4 information concerning P Brown (such as address) is only stored once in the customer table. The logical link between the two tables has been created by the common column 'Customer ID' in both tables.

The attraction of the relational database approach is its simplicity and flexibility. Users do not need to concern themselves with physical aspects of computer systems, and non-information technology specialists (such as marketing staff) can extract information from the database using simple English,

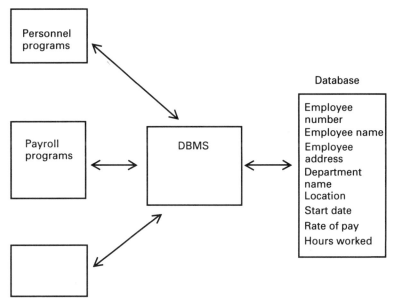

DBMS – Database Management System: software to control the data, programs, and user interfaces

Figure 5.3 Database approach to data storage

Customer table

Customer ID	Name	Address
376	P Brown	2 Holland Park
478	J Day	82 Dunton Close
621	A Jones	4 Summer Lane
782	L Smith	1 Milford Road

Account table

Account Number	Customer ID	Balance	Type
12345678	376	10.00	C/A
25617811	478	427.64	C/A
27421976	621	148.00	C/A
87112877	376	5000.00	D/A
91884213	782	18.46	C/A

Figure 5.4   Relational data tables

– as in *query languages*. SQL is an international standard for database query languages and an example of its use would be:

SELECT: Name, Address
FROM: Customer
WHERE: Age > 65

This would give the user a list of customers' names and addresses for only those customers over 65 years old.

Advances in technology and the use of graphical user interfaces has now resulted in users being able to construct such queries without the need to type the SQL command at the keyboard.

6.   Conclusions

In summary, the role of technology for banks and other financial services firms is central to their strategic and operational success. The original introduction of computing in the 1960s was for bookkeeping purposes, but the introduction and adoption of sophisticated networked databases has provided the banks with information which may be mined in the same way as any other resource. Information allows banks to identify new markets and products. It will allow banks to manage their balance sheets more efficiently and will enable them to reduce their cost ratios to meet the threat of new market entrants. New market entrants will arise because of the adoption of technology. If customers are indifferent to the delivery system of the product, and there is some evidence from the growth of First Direct that they are, then branch-less banking delivered to the home via information technology allows new banking businesses to start up without the disadvantage of the branch costs previously thought to be an insuperable barrier to new entrants.

Further reading

Chorafas, D.N. and Steinmann, H. *Expert Systems in Banking: a Guide for Senior Managers* (Macmillan, 1991).

Egner, F.E. *The Electronic Future of Banking* (McGraw-Hill, 1991).

Essinger, J. *Banking Technology as a Competitive Weapon* (Financial Times Business Information, 1991).

Feigenbaum, E., McCorduck, P., and Nii, H.P. *The Rise of the Expert Company* (Macmillan, 1988).

McFadden, F.R., and Hoffer, J.A., *Database Management* (The Benjamin/Cummings Publishing Company, 1991).

Violano, M. and Van Collie, S. *Retail Banking Technology, Strategies and Resources that Seize Competitive Advantage* (Wiley, 1992).

Welch, Ed. B. *Electronic Banking and Security: A Guide for Corporate and Financial Managers* (Blackwell, 1994).

The Tax Environment

Pandora Hancock

1. Introduction

Taxes are used by governments to raise funds for public expenditure. However, almost all taxes produce distortions in the economy of a country and affect the behaviour of its citizens. In fact governments often legislate in order to influence individuals' behaviour, for instance by offering tax incentives to home buyers to encourage home ownership.

In the UK there is thriving tax planning industry which devises packages of varying complexity in order to minimise its clients' tax bill. For example Tax Exempt Special Savings Accounts (TESSAs) were introduced on 1 January 1991 which paid interest free of tax provided that a number of conditions were met. Most building societies and banks 'jumped the gun' and offered deposit accounts which paid interest free of tax from the autumn of 1990, by the simple means of deferring interest payments until after 1 January 1991. On 1 January 1991 these deposit accounts were transferred to TESSAs prior to interest being paid. This scheme was successful because interest is taxed on a received rather than an earned basis, that is, a taxpayer pays tax when interest is received, regardless of the time period in which the interest was earned.

UK governments may try to prevent taxpayers from exploiting the existing legislation in unforeseen ways by implementing anti-avoidance legislation. For example the Taxes Act 1988 contains provisions intended to prevent the bond washing of fixed interest securities. 'Bond washing' involves the conversion of income into capital growth. A taxpayer holding fixed interest securities might prefer to make capital gains rather than earn income because capital gains on fixed interest securities are free of capital gains tax.

For most securities, interest will be paid on predetermined dates during the course of the security's life. Prior to these dates the securities will 'go ex int', that is the person who is registered as holding the stock on that date will receive the interest payment rather than the person who actually owns it on the date on which the interest is paid. The security's value falls, by approximately the amount of the interest due, on this date. Without the legislation, if a taxpayer bought a security when it is 'ex int' and sold it just prior to it next going 'ex int' no income would have been received but a capital gain approximately equal to the interest for the period of ownership would have been realised.

The accrued income scheme was designed to stop this happening. Rather than taxing interest on a received basis, this scheme enabled tax to be charged on accrued interest over the period of ownership. For example, if £100 worth of 10% debentures was held for 18 months the interest liable to income tax would be £15 (£10 for the first year and £5 for the remaining half year) regardless of the amount of interest actually received.

In this chapter we try to assess the impact that the UK fiscal law has had on the financial services sector. First we will consider the nature of taxation and take a quick look at some of the taxes which have been introduced in the UK in order to see what lessons can be learned from our past. We will then, briefly, discuss the general tax legislation that is currently in force before we examine the present tax legislation relating to saving and investing from both a political and an individual perspective. Finally, we will consider the current anti-avoidance tax legislation in the UK.

2.   An initial look at taxation in the UK

A tax is a compulsory levy, imposed by government, on income, expenditure or capital assets. The primary purpose of imposing a tax is to raise money for public purposes.

There are a number of ways of categorising taxes, but probably the most useful way is to think of them as being either direct or indirect. A direct tax is borne by the taxpayer, and is not passed on to another taxpayer. Examples include income tax, capital gains tax, inheritance tax and corporation tax. Indirect taxes, on the other hand, are passed on, so that the ultimate burden of their tax is borne by another taxpayer. Examples include VAT, and customs and excise duties.

A tax is *progressive* if in percentage terms, the levy on a taxpayer is greater, the wealthier is the taxpayer. For instance, income tax is progressive because the marginal rate of tax increases as the taxpayer's income increases. A taxpayer's marginal rate of tax is the rate of tax, s/he pays on his or her last pound of income. A tax is *regressive* if poorer taxpayers pay a higher proportion of their income in tax than wealthier taxpayers. VAT is a regressive tax, because poorer people spend a higher proportion of their income on standard rated items than better off taxpayers, who have large mortgages and save a significant part of their income.

3.   Taxation: the historical perspective

Whenever people have formed together into groups there has been a tendency for some form of taxation to develop. The purpose of this tax has usually been to raise money in order to finance the defence of the community. We can study the effectiveness of a number of different taxes which have been introduced in the UK in the past. In particular, we can assess the ease and cost of collecting taxes and the effect on the behaviour of individuals of the introduction of new taxes.

The earliest taxes were custom duties, levied on both exports and imports. In addition Kings of England claimed various feudal services from their subjects. When a poll tax was introduced in 1377 and 1380 the general populous rebelled and evaded the tax on a massive scale. It has been suggested that the uprising was not due to an inability to pay, but rather because the peasants were unaccustomed to paying tax. The hearth tax introduced in 1662 was readily avoided by the simple expedient of blocking up fire places. The window tax, introduced in 1747 was similarly avoided, and had to be abolished in 1851 on the grounds of public health.

There are a number of lessons to be learned from these early taxes. First, a tax may be introduced and have an unforeseen effect on people's behaviour, for instance the window tax encouraged householders to block up windows, leading to health problems. Secondly, new taxes should be introduced gradually and initially the rate of tax should be low. It is often argued that the community charge was not, in itself, unpopular: its downfall lay in the level of the charge. Thirdly, in general indirect taxes (VAT is the main example today) are regressive while direct taxes are progressive. Lastly, and somewhat surprisingly, major revolts against tax do not occur when people are over-taxed and impoverished, but when people are becoming more prosperous.

Income tax has it roots in the tax introduced by William Pitt in 1799 to fund the Napoleonic Wars. The excise duties which had been used by the medieval Kings to raise money had initially only fallen on the wealthy. By the end of the eighteenth century the scope of duties had been extended to include items such as food, so that they now fell heavily on the poorer people. Pitt introduced an income tax which was targeted on the rich middle and upper class, the people with the most to lose if the war was lost. The law did not allow for there to be any control over the correctness of the return, and in an attempt to reduce widespread evasion, withholding taxes were introduced. For example, the Bank of England paid dividends net of tax. Income tax was repealed in 1816, because it was seen as a wartime tax only. In 1842 income tax was reintroduced on a temporary basis, at a very low level. Income below £150 was exempted and income above this figure was taxed at 3%. The tax was supported because not only was it seen to be temporary and set at a low level but also because industrialists believed that for the government to raise all its revenue by means of indirect taxation was cutting consumer spending and increasing inflation. This is another important lesson to learn from history. Not only is indirect taxation regressive, but it may also have a recessionary effect by increasing prices and reducing consumer demand for goods.

4. Fiscal neutrality

A tax system can be said to be fiscally neutral if it does not discriminate between economic choices. That is, the introduction of the system does not change the economic choices made by taxpayers.

For example, VAT would be fiscally neutral if all goods and services were taxed at the same rate. If this was so, the marginal rate of substitution of one product for another would be the same including and excluding VAT. For instance if one unit of product A costs £1 and one unit of product B costs £2 before VAT, then after the cost of VAT is added on, a unit of product B will still be twice as expensive as a unit of product A. Of course, the total amount of either A or B which can be bought will be reduced because of the introduction of VAT. If VAT applies to product A only then product B is less than twice as expensive as product A and product B is relatively more attractive than before, creating the potential for economic inefficiencies.

Since VAT is charged only when money is spent, VAT makes saving relatively more attractive than spending money on consumer products. This is another example of the inefficiencies in our tax system, and explains why turnover taxes are considered to be recessionary, because they encourage saving at the expense of consumption. If investments are taxed neutrally the amount of tax paid will be related to the returns earned and will be independent of the particular investment vehicle used.

Hence, in a fiscally neutral environment, all forms of income and all types of savings would be subject to the same taxation. However, we do not live in a fiscally neutral world. It can be argued that it is the discrepancies in tax systems, and in particular the loopholes and anomalies, which cause people to behave in particular way. Certainly most, if not all, of the investments available today have been devised to exploit the lack of fiscal neutrality in the existing tax system.

5. Taxation today

As in the past, the primary purpose of taxation is to raise money for government expenditure. During the latter part of this century there has been an explosion in government expenditure, and this has been matched by the increase in taxes raised. However taxation is also used as an economic regulator and to modify individuals' behaviour. Taxation is levied by a series of Acts of Parliament, which form the legislative framework within which to operate, together with a substantial number of cases which have been used to both clarify the law and, in recent years, to extend it.

Some taxes raise very little money, but are seen to be equitable. The main example of this is capital gains tax which is often subject to rumour about abolition in a budget because so little revenue is raised, but remains in place because it is seen to be a 'fair' tax.

In order to set the scene for the interpretation of tax efficient investment vehicles in the 1990s, the main points of income tax, capital gains tax and inheritance tax are summarised below.

Income tax

All individuals are subject to income tax on the income, earned and unearned, which relates to a fiscal year. The fiscal year for income tax runs from 6 April to the following 5 April, for instance, the fiscal year 1994/95 covers the period from 6 April 1994 to 5 April 1995.

Unless income is specifically exempt, it is taxable under one of the Schedules and Cases of Income tax. For example, income from employment is taxable under Schedule E while the self-employed pay income tax under Schedule D Case I or II. Each Schedule and Case has its own rules. As we have already seen, interest is taxed on a received basis under Schedule D Case III. Until recently, interest was always paid after deduction of basic rate tax, but now certain interest payments are made gross. Dividends are also charged on a received basis under Schedule F and are paid together with a tax credit which is the equivalent of the basic rate tax. Income received by a child which is derived from capital transferred from his parents is assessed as if it were the parent's income.

The following is some of the income which is exempt from income tax.

- the first £70 interest on national savings bank ordinary accounts
- the increase in value of national savings certificates.

An individual is allowed a number of *deductions* from his total income in order to arrive at his taxable income, the amount on which s/he pays tax. All individuals are entitled to a personal allowance of £3445 in 1994/95. Married men and single parents are also given the married couple's allowance or the additional personal allowance for single parent. Both allowances are £1720 in 1994/95. Other allowances may also be available.

Deductions which may be allowed include interest on up to £30,000 borrowed to buy the taxpayer's only or main residence. Premiums paid under a personal pension policy are also allowable deductions.

The marginal rate of income tax increases as the taxpayer's income increases. Individuals on low incomes may not pay tax at all, while taxpayers with high incomes pay tax at a marginal rate of 40%. Most UK taxpayers have a marginal rate of tax of 25%. This rate is also termed the basic rate of tax.

Capital gains tax

Since 1988 only capital gains which relate to the period since 31 March 1982 are taxable. An individual has an annual exemption of £5800 and so can realise chargeable gains of up to this amount before incurring a tax liability. Capital growth becomes liable to tax only when the asset is disposed of. This provides many tax planning opportunities. Tax is paid at the taxpayer's marginal rate of tax.

In general, the computation of capital gain is relatively easy but the computation for shares is extremely complex because of the difficulty of matching purchases to disposals. If a taxpayer acquires shares of the same class in the same company on different dates and then makes a disposal, we need to find a way of matching the disposal to one or more acquisitions. This matching process is beyond the scope of this chapter.

Broadly, tax is payable on a chargeable gain which is equal to the sales proceeds *less* allowable costs and the indexation allowance. Proceeds are generally taken to be the net proceeds, that is the proceeds *less* any costs incurred in making the sale. These include commissions, fees and advertising costs. Allowable costs include all costs incurred to acquire the asset and to enhance its value. The indexation allowance is equal to the increase in the retail price index during the period of ownership multiplied by the costs of acquisition.

If an asset was acquired before March 1982, two computations are undertaken, one using the market value at March 1982 and the other using the original cost of the asset. In both cases, the indexation allowance is based on the higher of the market value at March 1982 and the original cost.

If the disposal was to a 'connected person', the market value will be substituted for the proceeds. An individual is connected with:

- his/her spouse and their relatives
- his/her relatives
- the spouses of all the above relatives
- business partners and their spouses
- trustees of any settlement where the individual is the settlor (any persons connected with the settlor are also connected with the trustees)

Inheritance tax

Inheritance tax is payable on some gifts and transfers to and from trust made during a taxpayer's lifetime as well as on his/her wealth at death.

Some lifetime transfers are exempt from tax and so are often useful for tax planning. These include:

- gifts of less than £250 per tax year per person;
- gifts of up to £5000 by a parent, £2500 by a grandparent or one of the betrothed and £1000 by anyone else, in consideration of a marriage
- normal expenditure out of income, this usually includes the payment of life assurance policy premiums paid for the benefit of another
- transfers between husband and wife.

Other lifetime transfers are potentially exempt, that is, if the taxpayer lives at least seven years after the date of the transfer, no charge to tax will arise and the transfer becomes exempt. Potentially exempt transfers include:

- gifts by an individual to another individual or into an accumulation and maintenance trust or trust for disabled persons and made on or after 18 March 1986
- transfers made on or after 17 March 1987 to either create or increase a trust fund in which an individual is entitled to receive the income for life.

If the donor dies within seven years of making a potentially exempt transfer it becomes a chargeable transfer. An individual receiving a gift has an insurable interest in the life of the donor for as long as there is possibility of a charge arising on the gift. Tailor-made insurance policies exist.

Other lifetime transfers are liable to tax, and are termed 'chargeable transfers'. A running total is kept of chargeable lifetime transfers and when this exceeds the nil rate threshold tax become payable. Tax is payable at 40% in 1994/95 and the rate has not changed since 1988. Lifetime transfers are taxed at half the normal rate of tax. Seven years after a transfer is made it is excluded from the running total and no tax liability can arise on that particular transfer. The nil rate threshold is £150,000 for 1994/95.

On death, an individual is deemed to make a final transfer of the whole of his estate. Any transfers made to an individual's spouse are exempt and so are excluded from the estate. Potentially exempt transfers made within three years of death are taxed at the full rate. The tax payable is reduced by 20% for transfers made more than three years but less than four years before the date of death. For each extra year between the date of the transfer and the date of death, the tax payable is reduced by a further 20%. Any tax due in this way is payable by the donee. If the tax already paid exceeds the tax due no repayment will be made.

Inheritance tax is clearly often totally avoidable if good use is made of lifetime transfers. However, the planning process may need to span decades. Life assurance policies offer scope for tax planning. If an individual takes out a policy and pays premiums then on death the maturity value will be included in the deceased person's estate. However, if the policy is transferred to the beneficiary during the policyholder's lifetime, the transfer value is the greater of the surrender value and the premiums paid. If the policy is transferred, then future premiums paid will be transfers of value. However, they are likely to be exempt as a gift out of income.

Trust

A trust is created when an individual, called the settlor, transfers assets to trustees who hold the assets for the benefit of one or more persons. The beneficiaries may receive income and/or capital from the trust. A trust can be created either during an individuals' lifetime or under the terms of his will. Lifetime transfers into a trust are potentially exempt, while in the case of transfers on death any inheritance tax due on the deceased's estate will be calculated before assets are transferred into a trust fund. A trust may be one of the following:

A trust with an interest in possession

An individual, called the life tenant, has a right to receive the income from the trust for a period of time. The trustees are charged basic rate tax on the income from the assets in the trust. No personal allowances are available and the trustee's expenses are not tax deductible. In addition, the beneficiaries are also liable to income tax on the income from the trust regardless of whether they draw it or not. However, the beneficiaries do receive a tax credit equal to the amount of tax paid by the trustees. If the beneficiaries' tax liability is lower than the tax credit, the difference is reclaimable. The trustees are also liable to capital gains tax at 25% on the chargeable gains on the trust. An annual exemption of £2900 for 1994/95 is available, but must be shared between all the trusts created by the same settlor. After the lift tenant's death, a beneficiary becomes absolutely enti-tled to the trust property. Although the trustees are regarded as having dis-posed of the property at its then market value, no capital gains tax liability arises, hence the gain is free of tax. If the trust terminates before the life tenant dies, for instance if a widow remarries, a capital gains tax liability may arise. A life tenant is deemed to own the underlying assets which provide their income for inheritance tax purposes. Hence, when the life tenant dies, the assets in the trust fund are included in their estate and the inheritance liability is calculated on the resulting value.

A discretionary trust

Nobody has an absolute right to the income from a discretionary trust. The trustees are liable to tax in the same way as for trusts with an interest in pos-session, but the rate is the basic rate of tax plus 10%. However, the trustees' expenses are an allowable deduction, though against the additional 10% of tax only. Beneficiaries must pay tax on the income they receive. They also receive a tax credit which is equivalent to the amount of tax which the trustees have paid. Hence, if a beneficiary receives £65 from the trust, he is deemed to have received £100 (£65 × 100/65) of income together with a tax credit of £35 (£100 × 35/100). This tax credit is reclaimable. Hence there is a tax incentive for trustees to pay out all of the trust's income to beneficiaries who are basic rate taxpayers. For capital gains tax purposes, the exemption limit is as for trusts with an interest in possession but tax is payable at 35% rather than 25%. Unless the trustee and beneficiary jointly elect to effectively defer the capital gains tax liability by transferring the asset at original cost, capital gains tax is payable when a beneficiary becomes absolutely entitled to trust assets. Inheritance tax is not payable on the trust funds. However, there is a charge of 15% of the inheritance scale rate on the value of the trust every 10 years. The same percentage is also charged when funds leave the trust. 15% of the inheritance scale rate gives a maximum rate of 6% on the current scale.

An accumulation and maintenance trust

Income is accumulated for minor children until they reach a specified age. Income which arose from capital provided by parents and used for the education or maintenance of unmarried children under 18 years old is treated as the income of the parents. Other income arising in the trust is taxed at 35% because the trust is discretionary. Once again the 35% can be used as a tax credit by the beneficiaries. When the beneficiaries reach the specified age the trust funds are transferred without any further income tax liability arising. However, capital gains tax is payable when a beneficiary becomes absolutely entitled to the trust's assets because the trust is a discretionary trust. Provided that the trust satisfied certain conditions, no inheritance tax liability will arise either 10 yearly or when the assets are transferred to the beneficiaries. To qualify for this preferential treatment the trust must terminate before the earlier of 25 years after its creation and 25 years from 15 April 1976. In addition, at least one of the beneficiaries must be 25 years old or younger when becoming either absolutely entitled to the property or gaining an interest in possession.

6. Recent developments in UK tax legislation

During the early part of the 1980s, with Geoffrey Howe as Chancellor, it seemed as if there was to be a move towards fiscal neutrality. Income tax rates were reduced, thus reducing the pressure for tax avoidance and evasion. The VAT standard rate increased from 8% to 15%, shifting the burden of tax away from direct towards indirect taxation. Tax reliefs were reduced or eliminated altogether, for instance the advantageous positions of friendly societies was restricted. Tax relief of life assurance premiums was removed. Some taxes, such as development land tax, were abolished.

However, these measures did not herald a new era of fiscal neutrality. The advantageous tax positions of pensions, always available for the self-employed and those in company pensions schemes, were extended to everybody who had earned income. The Business Expansion Scheme (BES) was introduced to provide tax relief for individuals who invested in certain unquoted companies. Personal Equity Plans (PEPs) provided tax relief for individuals investing in quoted securities. Finally TESSAs were introduced to provide a tax incentive for those prepared to save for five years (see p. 90). The many changes in tax legislation, together with the deregulation of the financial services sector, led to a myriad of new tax efficient investment vehicles being developed.

Interest bearing deposits are among the few types of investment which do not offer any tax advantages. We will start by considering these, and then discuss the new tax efficient investment vehicles introduced by the Conservative government.

Interest bearing deposit accounts

From 6 April 1991, interest on deposit accounts held with banks, building societies, local authorities and specified credit and finance companies is paid net of basic rate tax unless the depositor completes a certificate stating that s/he is a non-taxpayer when interest is paid gross. Depositors who receive interest net of basic rate tax who are non-taxpayers may claim back the tax deducted and higher rate taxpayers must account for extra tax.

Stocks, shares and Personal Equity Plans

Individuals invest in stocks and shares in order to gain an income and/or to achieve capital growth. Income is received in the form of dividends. UK companies pay dividends together with a tax credit which is equal to 20% of the gross dividend from 1994/95 onwards. For example, a dividend of £800 carries a tax credit of £800 × 20/80 = £1000. A non-taxpayer may reclaim the tax credit of £200. A basic rate taxpayer has not further liability to tax which means that his dividends are taxed at an effective rate of 20%. A higher rate taxpayer must pay an extra £200 (£1000 × 40% – £200) in tax.

Individuals may invest in the stock market via a personal equity plan (PEP). An individual may invest up to £6000 per annum in one ordinary PEP. Taxpayers may also invest up to £3000 a year in a single company PEP which only invests in the shares of one company. An investment in a PEP is totally exempt from capital gains tax and all dividends and interest payments are exempt from income tax. Clearly a PEP is more advantageous to higher rate taxpayers, but all taxpayers can use them to build up a significant holding of tax exempt funds.

Tax Exempt Special Savings Accounts (TESSAs)

TESSAs completed the government's portfolio of tax efficient investment vehicles. Many taxpayers are already retired and so cannot invest in a pension scheme and are perhaps unwilling to take the risks inherent in the stock market. Other taxpayers may also be risk adverse, or lack sufficient resources to invest in the stock market.

The legislation for TESSAs was enacted in the Finance Act 1990, and the schemes were formally available from 1 January 1991. In the UK, interest is taxed when it is received rather than when it is earned. Many financial institutions exploited this, by offering savings accounts in the autumn of 1990 which did not pay interest until 1991 when they were converted into TESSAs (see p. 80). Individuals may open one TESSA with either a building society or a bank. Interest earned is free of income tax provided that capital is not withdrawn from the account for a period of five years. Interest net of basic rate tax can be withdrawn without penalty. However, if an amount in excess of this is withdrawn all interest credited to date becomes liable to tax immediately at the rate then in force, this could be disadvantageous if the rate of tax has increased. In addition, the interest tax could be enough to put the taxpayer into a higher tax bracket, and so more tax could be due.

The individual may start with an initial deposit of up to £3000 and then may save a maximum of £1800 in each of the following three years. The maximum which can be deposited in the final year is £600 and the total amount which can be saved is limited to £9000. Each year an amount equivalent to the basic rate of tax on the interest earned is retained. For instance if £400 interest is credited to the account £100 (£400 × 25%) will be retained. At the end of five years the interest retained is credited to the account which ceases to have any special tax status. Hence, interest earned in the future is subject to tax in the normal way. The taxpayer is then free to start another TESSA s/he wishes.

It should be noted that the potential tax savings are not high: a basic rate taxpayer with £9000 invested in the final year at an interest rate of 10% will save £9000 × 10% × 25% = £225 in tax and savings in earlier years will be much less than this.

While TESSAs have proved to be very popular with many taxpayers opening an account, initial evidence suggests that most of the money invested in TESSAs has been transferred from other deposit accounts. This implies that the tax forgone by the treasury may have been wasted in that people's behaviour, in terms of the amount saved, has not been significantly affected.

Pensions

Probably the most important tax efficient investment vehicles are pensions. An individual may be a member of a company pension scheme or a personal pension scheme. A personal pension scheme is used by the self-employed and employees who are not members of a company pension scheme. Individuals who are members of company pension schemes can choose to make additional contributions to a pension through an AVC (additional voluntary contribution) which is linked to the company pension scheme of a free standing AVC which is independent of the company scheme. Contributions of up to 15% of income into approved pensions schemes are allowable deductions for income tax purposes up to a contributions limit of just over £10,000 a year. The investments made with the contributions are free of both income tax and capital gains tax. However, the pension finally received by the beneficiary is treated as earned income and is subject to income tax.

Hence, contributions to a pension fund are free of tax but the pension is taxable, whereas contributions to a PEP are not eligible for tax relief but funds withdrawn from a PEP are not subject to tax!

Housing

Finally, it its worth considering the privileged tax incentives available for home owners. The interest paid on the first £30,000 borrowed to buy the taxpayer's main or only residence attracts tax relief at the taxpayer's marginal rate of tax. The average mortgage in 1979 was £11,837 (excluding first-time buyers). In the 1980s the limit was increased to £30,000 but already many homebuyers were borrowing more than this and by 1991 the average mortgage had risen to £46,556. Then the relief was changed to be given only at the basic rate of tax rather than the taxpayer's marginal rate of tax and now relief is only available at a rate of 20%. But during much of the 1980s the real tax advantage of housing was that capital growth did not give rise to a capital gains tax liability. Imagine the attitude of home owners to increases in house prices if a quarter or more of the increase had to be paid in tax when moving!

Because of the privileged tax position of housing, people have often been persuaded to commit more of their wealth to their main residence than would otherwise be the case. (Remember product A and B in the section on fiscal neutrality. The distorting effects of taxing A and not B made buying units of B relatively more attractive. Hence the tax advantages of owning a house over other forms of investment create a propensity to hold wealth in property.)

The tax legislation may also encourage some individuals to move house or to borrow more when they move house. If a loan is raised, perhaps to buy a car, then no tax relief is available to individuals on the interest paid on the loan. But if an individual moves house and retains capital from the sale of the house to buy a car, thus increasing the amount of the mortgage needed to purchase the new house, the same total amount will have been borrowed but, provided it is less than £30,000, all of it will be eligible for tax relief.

The Conservative government of the late 1980s and early 1990s has interfered in the operation of the housing market on a number of occasions by amending the tax laws. In the budget of 1988 the Chancellor announced that there would be an end to tax relief whereby mortgage interest relief was calculated with respect to the individuals buying the property but it would, from the end of August be calculated by reference to the property. If two individuals, who were not married, bought a house prior to this change they were each eligible for relief on interest paid by them on a mortgage up to a maximum of £30,000. Hence two people who were not married could claim relief on a loan of up to £60,000 compared to a married couple who could get maximum relief of only £30,000. The Chancellor could have made the change in the law immediate, perhaps by allowing the higher relief only if the contract had been signed by the end of that day. There are a number of precedents for this, for instance life insurance premiums, were allowable for tax purposes only if they had been agreed by midnight on the budget date. By allowing the delay of nearly six months, the Chancellor fuelled an already buoyant housing market by providing an incentive for multiple purchasers to complete quickly, thus increasing demand. This delay has been blamed for some of the increase in house prices which was seen in 1988, thus making the subsequent slump worse.

In 1992 the government attempted to exploit this behaviour by abolishing stamp duty on house purchases under £250,000 for a limited period of eight months in an attempt to boost the failing housing market.

Anti-avoidance

As we have already seen, throughout history people have responded to tax legislation by seeking ways of avoiding paying tax. People are still seeking to reduce the tax they pay and today they have professionals who devise increasingly sophisticated vehicles to enable individuals and companies to minimise the tax they pay. The British government has traditionally used legislation to plug loopholes. This has led to extremely complex Finance Acts which have become longer each year. In addition, professionals try to find new loopholes. In the last half of the 1980s the courts, primarily the House of Lords, moved away from merely interpreting legislation toward a situation where they were actually creating new law. The first case involved an 'artificial scheme', that is, a scheme which was made up of a series of preordained steps which were to be carried out in rapid succession. The scheme required that all steps must be completed once the first one had been made. At the end of the series of steps the taxpayers would be in the same position as they had been at the beginning and any loss created would not be a real loss. In the case of *W. T. Ramsay* v. *IRC* (1981) the scheme was used to create a capital gains tax loss which could be offset against a capital gain which had been realised. In fact, the only losses which had been suffered were the professional fees which were paid for the scheme's operation. The House of Lords decided that, although each step in the scheme was a separate legal transaction, it was possible to view the scheme not as a series of separate legal transaction but as a whole, by comparing the position of the tax-payer in real terms at the start and finish of the scheme. When this was done no real loss was incurred and the scheme was self-cancelling.

The Ramsay principle was extended in *Furniss* v. *Dawson* (1984). This time the objective was to defer capital gains tax by using an intermediary company based in the Isle of Man. The scheme was not circular or self-cancelling. The House of Lords decided that the scheme should still be set aside for tax purposes because, once again, the scheme required a series of steps to be carried out in quick succession.

The case of *Craven* v. *White* (1989) was used by the House of Lords to limit the application of the *Ramsay* principle. Once again, an intermediary company in the Isle of Man was used to defer a capital gains tax liability. The key difference between *Craven* v. *White* and *Furniss* v. *Dawson* was that, when the shares were transferred to the Isle of Man company, the final disposal of the shares had not been agreed. Hence, no preordained series of steps existed at the time that the first transaction was undertaken. Consequently, the House of Lords refused to view the series of transactions as a whole and the scheme was successful. This case has great significance for anti-avoidance schemes generally. It makes planning well in advance critical. If transactions are undertaken before the final step is known with certainty, there is a greater likelihood of the scheme being successful.

7. Conclusions

There is an old saying 'you are what you eat', which has recently been superseded by 'you are what is eating you'. This describes the way in which an animal adapts itself to deal with its enemies, particularly parasites. The financial services sector can be considered in much the same way. It constantly adapts itself in response to new legislation. Through a number of examples, this chapter has sought to show that the tax environment has been a major formative factor in the evolution of the post-war financial services industry. In fact, it may not be going too far to suggest that the 'taxation tail is wagging the financial services dog'.

Further reading

Hancock, P. *An Introduction to Taxation and Tax Planning*, 2nd edn (Chapman Hall, 1994).

Homer, A. and Burrows, R. *Tolleys Tax Guide 1993/94* (Tolley Publishing Co. Ltd, 1993).

CHAPTER 7

Institutional Investment – Theory and Practice

Stephen Curry

1. Growth of institutional investment

One of the major changes in the UK capital market over the last quarter of a century and more has been the extent to which institutional investors have replaced individuals as the most important holders of ordinary shares. During the 1980s the Conservative government under Margaret Thatcher encouraged individual share ownership through the privatisation of nationalised industries. But although the number of adults owning ordinary shares increased from 3 million in 1979 to around 11 million in 1990, their relative importance in the stock market continued to decline. There was 'widening' rather than 'deepening' of share ownership – the number of personal shareholders rose, but their percentage of the total market continued to fall. In fact, a survey by London Stock Exchange in 1990 showed that 60% of personal shareholders held shares in only one company, and only 14% held shares in four or more companies. Between 1963 and 1992 the proportion of ordinary shares in UK listed companies held directly by individuals fell by two thirds – from almost 60% to under 20%. At the same time, the proportion held by the major institutional investors more than doubled – from 28% to 60% (see Table 7.1).

An institutional investor is a fund which takes savings from individuals and invests them in its own name as a principal. The individual investor thereby acquires a fractional stake in a 'pooled' fund, rather than having an individually managed portfolio. In the UK the four major institutional investors are the pension funds, life assurance companies, unit trusts and investment trusts, of which the fastest growing in recent years have been the pension funds.

*Table 7.1   Percentage of total market value of UK listed ordinary shares (equities),
held by different groups, 1963–92*

31 December	1963 %	1979 %	1992 %
Pension funds	7	23	31
Insurance companies	11	21	19
Investment trusts and financial companies	9	9	4
Unit trusts	1	3	6
Total institutions	28	55	60
Persons	59	30	19
Charities	3	3	2
Industrial and commercial companies	5	4	4
Government	2	4	1
Overseas	4	5	14
Total %*	101	101	100
			£589 billion

*Subject to rounding.
Source: Figures for 1963 are from the Diamond Commission; those for 1979 and
1992 are estimates by UBS Phillips and Drew.

The main types of asset held by institutional investors are shares, bonds,
property and cash. The differing weighting given to these four types of asset
varies over time and between different types of institutional investor. Shares
held by institutional investors are mainly ordinary shares (commonly known
as 'equities'), while bonds comprise largely UK government securities (generally known as 'gilt-edged' or simply 'gilts'). 'Cash' represents short-term
money market investments, such as money on short-term deposit within the
banking system, or short-term securities, such as Treasury bills.

Individuals with modest sums to invest can purchase both gilts and equities
(often referred to as 'stocks' and 'shares') through a stockbroker. Gilts can
also be bought and sold relatively cheaply through the Post Office via the
National Savings Stock Register. In recent years, with the de-regulation of
banks and building societies, there has been a proliferation in 'cash' accounts
paying competitive rates of interest to personal investors requiring instant
access, or access to funds after a short period of notice.

The one type of UK asset individuals have difficulty in acquiring directly is property. This is not to deny its importance in most households; after all, over two thirds of all homes are now owner-occupied. But individuals are largely restricted to residential property. The large sums required restrict commercial, industrial, and to some extent, agricultural property, to institutional investors, only they have the necessary funds to acquire major office blocks, or shops, in prime city centre locations.

Why have individuals, or households, preferred to invest via financial intermediaries, such as institutional investors, when it is perfectly feasible to construct similar portfolio for themselves? Table 7.2 illustrates this fact, showing that households have normally been net sellers of direct holdings in UK company securities (principally 'equities'), while at the same time investing increasing amounts in life assurance and pension funds.

Households were net sellers of UK equities every year from 1955 to 1991, but at the same time net investors in life assurance and pension funds. Individuals and households have in effect replaced direct holdings of equities with indirect holdings via their fund investments. The main reasons for this switch have been:

● tax efficiency
● diversification
● professional management
● marketing
● legislation.

Tax efficiency

Prior to the tax-cutting Budgets of the 1980s, tax on investment income was levied at rates as high as 98%! Investors, particularly higher rate taxpayers,

Table 7.2   Personal sector, acquisition and sale of financial assets, 1989–93

Year	UK company securities £ billion	Inflows to life assurance and pension funds £ billion
1989	−21.2	+28.5
1990	−10.1	+27.9
1991	−5.3	+29.4
1992	+2.8	+28.5
1993	−6.1	+30.7

Source: *Financial Statistics* (November, 1994 Table 8.1J).

sought investments which provided some form of tax shelter. Owner-occupation was one such investment, because of the exemption from capital gains tax of a principal private residence, and mortgage interest tax relief. Approved pension schemes have been the main indirect investment which enabled investors to reduce the incidence of tax. Contributions into an approved pension scheme, whether an occupational or personal pension, are an allowable charge against taxable income; the fund itself is tax-free, enabling income to accrue gross of tax; and on maturity any lump sum received is also tax-free.

The tax efficiency argument for indirect investment has weakened in recent years. Firstly, there has been the reduction in tax rates, lessening the advantages of tax reliefs. Secondly, in the Finance Act 1989 the Government 'capped' the absolute level of earnings for which pension contributions would provide tax relief. Nevertheless, the contribution limits still remain attractive. Contributors to occupational pension schemes can invest up to 15% of their earnings, and for personal pensions, the contribution limit ranges from 17.5% to a staggering 40% of income for persons aged 61 or over. The limiting of tax relief on pension contributions by the imposition of a 'cap' on eligible earnings was a government response to the increasing cost of such remission, and a reaction to the increasingly vocal criticism of the fiscal bias favouring institutional investors.

Prior to 1984 new life assurance policies attracted Life Assurance Premium Relief (LAPR). This was a subsidy on contributions, and it still applies to policies taken out before that date. For new policyholders, life assurance has little in the way of tax advantages – income can accrue within the fund net of basic rate tax; 'qualifying' policies, which are basically regular premium policies taken out for a minimum of 10 years, are tax free on maturity; and single premium policies provide a withdrawal facility with deferral of higher rate liability. But the life assurance fund itself pays tax on income and realised capital gains at a rate of 25%. This tax treatment would only be of advantage to higher rate taxpayers. Authorised unit trusts and approved investment trusts also have only modest tax efficiency. They can buy and sell investments without having a capital gains tax liability – this is deferred until the personal investor sells them – and they are tax free if held within a personal equity plan, but the latter also applies to direct holdings of equities.

Diversification

'Don't put all you eggs in one basket' is a central tenet of investment. Institutional investment provides the personal investor with access to a widely diversified portfolio for a relatively modest outlay. The extent of the diversification depends upon the type of fund chosen. The greater the spread of investments the less the risk of one poorly performing investment, or market, affecting the overall performance. Some indirect investments provide minimum guaranteed returns. Economies of scale enable investors to acquire a wide range of assets without having to pay prohibitive dealing charges. Diversification into overseas assets and into large-scale property assets would be difficult, if not impossible, on an individual basis.

Professional management

For most investors it is convenient to have someone else constantly monitoring their portfolio and dealing with its administration. Just as many people prefer to take their car to a garage rather than do their own servicing, or employ a decorator rather than undertaking DIY, exactly the same applies to investment. Specialist expertise can be acquired for the cost of a management charge. Fund managers are trained to understand specialist markets, to know whom to deal with, and how to deal. The personal investor is spared the chore of a lot of the necessary paperwork, such as calculating income and capital gains from numerous individual investments and resulting tax liabilities.

Marketing

Institutional investment products are actively marketed. Life assurance, in particular, is traditionally said to be sold, not bought! This partly reflects the inertia of buyers, but also the high commission often paid to life assurance salespersons. Marketing pressure has increased in recent years because of the deregulation of the banks and building societies (see chapters 2 and 3): increasing competition has led them to seek out additional profit opportunities. There was recognition that they held an under-exploited resource in the form of their depositors and borrowers; cross-selling of life assurance and other investment products to their existing customers was the natural development.

The Financial Services Act 1986 was intended to curb the wilder excesses of financial salespersons, often euphemistically known as financial or investment 'consultants'. The rule book of the Securities and Investments Board (SIB) and those of the relevant Self-Regulatory Organisations (SROs), require 'Know-Your-Customer' and 'Best Advice', and specify requirements for disclosure of charges and commission, advertisements, illustrations of benefits, 'cold-calling', and 'cooling-off' periods. Despite these controls indirect investments can be sold in banks, building societies, or by salespersons calling at or telephoning the home, methods which are not permitted for the sale of direct investments such as shares. There has recently been criticism of the high surrender rates for life assurance policies in the first few years of the policy, particularly for policies bought from 'tied' salespersons: the surrender values of such policies was almost always far below the contributions made. Endowment mortgages almost entirely replaced the traditional repayment mortgage, and many borrowers were led to believe it was the only type of mortgage available to them. It is perhaps ironic that life assurance has been marketed most aggressively at a time when its tax advantages have been at their most minimal.

Legislation

The most important recent legislation affecting the growth of institutional investment has been the Social Security Act 1986. Until relatively recently, many persons did not regard their pension entitlement as an investment, because they had very little control over it. The 1986 Act made personal pensions available to anyone with eligible earnings. The government was particularly concerned to encourage employees to opt out of the State Earnings Related Pension Scheme (SERPs) and into a Personal Pension Plan (PPP). SERPS is a 'Pay-As-You-Go Scheme'. It is 'unfunded' – not backed by an investment fund; each generation relies on the succeeding generation to pay their pension. The government became concerned about the financing implications for such a scheme, given the demographic trend towards an ageing population. A fiscal incentive was given for employees to switch out of SERPS into personal pensions which are fully funded. Consequently there was a boost to funds under institutional investment management.

2.   Institutional investment – the theory

Currently the orthodox academic approach to analysing fund investment management is known as 'Modern Portfolio Theory' (MPT). The methodology was developed in 1952 by Harry Markowitz.[1] The basis of this method of analysis is the assumption that investors are concerned with both risk and return. An investor is assumed to seek the highest rate of return for a given level of risk, and the lowest level of risk for a given rate of return. This is termed 'risk aversion', and is a consequence of investors' utility maximisation. An assumption is that of the diminishing utility of wealth: if utility increases with wealth, but at a decreasing rate, a certain sum of money provides greater utility than an uncertain sum with the same expected monetary outcome (see Figure 7.1).

For example, in Figure 7.1, assume that there are three investment possibilities *A*, *B* and *C*.

A	£50,000	–	100% certain
B	£75,000	–	50% probability
	£25,000	–	50% probability
C	£100,000	–	50% probability
	£0	–	50% probability

A, *B* and *C* each have expected returns of £50,000, i.e.

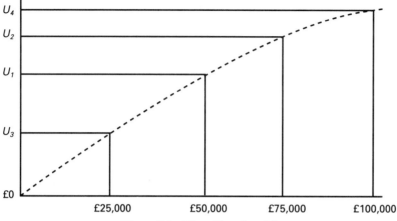

Figure 7.1   The utility of wealth

A	=	£50,000
B	=	£75,000 × 0.5 + £25,000 × 0.5
	=	£37,500 + £12,500
	=	*£50,000*
C	=	£100,000 × 0.5 + £0 × 0.5
	=	£50,000

If *A*, *B* and *C* were investment opportunities which could be repeated *ad infinitum*, they would provide identical returns. But for the personal investor there may be no opportunity to have a second chance! If investment *C* is accepted, and the outcome is £0, the whole of the investor's wealth is lost. The 'expected' utilities $(\bar{U})^2$ are as follows:

$$\bar{U}_A = U_1$$
$$\bar{U}_B = 0.5 \times U_2 + 0.5 \times U_3$$
$$\bar{U}_C = 0.5 \times U_4$$

It can be seen from Figure 7.1 that $\bar{U}_A > \bar{U}_B > \bar{U}_C$. Provided that utility increases less then proportionately to wealth, there will be some degree of risk aversion, and therefore less risk will be preferred to more risk for the same expected monetary outcome.

Markowitz's method of portfolio analysis is generally known as the 'mean–variance' approach, because portfolios are examined in terms of two dimensions – their expected return, and their risk, measured by the standard deviation [or its square, the variance] of possible returns. According to this approach, the standard deviation of the possible returns of a portfolio depends upon three factors – the weightings given to all of the assets; the correlation coefficients of the returns for all possible pairs of assets; and the standard deviations of all the underlying assets in the portfolio.

Using the Markowitz formulae for risk and return it is possible to generate an almost infinite number of portfolios by varying the weightings given to the individual investments. Some assets could be totally excluded by giving them a zero weighting. The feasible portfolios are illustrated in Figure 7.2. The efficient frontier illustrates the highest returns for given levels of risk, and the lowest levels of risk for given returns. If a risk free asset, with a return of r_f, such as a government short-term security, is added to the population of risky equities, a single optimum risky portfolio, m emerges. This will be the optimum portfolio irrespective of the investor's risk preferences. According to the model, investors should adjust the proportions of the risk free asset and risky portfolio m according to their risk preferences, rather than moving along the efficient frontier.

William F. Sharpe developed the work of Harry Markowitz, and in 1963 produced a simplified version of Markowitz's full covariance model, known as Sharpe's Single-index Model. Instead of calculating the correlation of the return of every asset with every other asset, Sharpe followed up Markowitz's suggestion of correlating the returns of each asset with the returns on some broad-based index, such as the FT-SE Actuaries All-Share Index in the UK. In a bull market most shares tend to rise, in a bear market almost all shares go down together – in the Wall Street aphorism 'when they raid the brothel they take all the girls!'. Basically what Sharpe did was to measure the slope of a line of best fit between the returns on an asset (e.g. a share) and the returns on an index. This regression line is called the 'characteristic' line, and its slope is known as the beta (ß) coefficient.

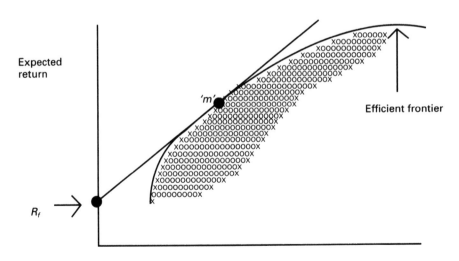

Figure 7.2   Efficient portfolios

The Single-index Model developed by Sharpe became the basis for an economic model, subsequently known as the Sharpe–Lintner Capital–Asset Pricing Model (CAPM)[3]. The CAPM (1964) used the concepts of portfolio theory, but postulated what would happen if investors operated in perfect capital markets, with perfect information. They argued that if everyone operated with the same information set there would be an efficient frontier and an optimal portfolio common to everyone. Since in equilibrium all assets must be willingly held by investors, the optimal portfolio had to be the overall market portfolio, for which the Index was a proxy (see Figure 7.3).

What are the implications of portfolio theory and the CAPM for investment management? The two models suggest different approaches to investment management. Portfolio theory does not necessarily imply an 'efficient' market for investments, whereas the CAPM depends on shares being fairly valued, as described by the efficient market hypothesis. Portfolio theory implies active management, to optimise risk and return, whereas the CAPM suggests that an efficient market automatically provides the optimal risk–return trade-off, even if with random selection. According to the CAPM, a passive investment policy, which minimises expenses, is likely to outperform an active 'buy and sell' policy, which fruitlessly seeks above-average returns.

The implications of portfolio theory have been summarised by Haugen[4]:

In the 1970s, after techniques for estimating the required inputs to the model were perfected, packaged and marketed as computer software, modern portfolio theory took off in terms of practical application in the

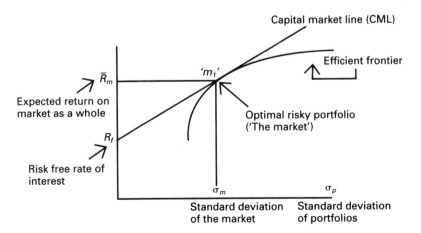

Figure 7.3   The capital market line

real world. Now the Single-index Model is widely employed to allocate investments in the portfolio between individual common stocks (i.e. equities), while the original, more general model of Markowitz is widely used to allocated investments between types of securities such as bonds, stock, venture capital, and real estate.

The role of the investment manager who believes in the CAPM and efficient markets was described by Lorie and Hamilton.[5]

Under this strategy, the portfolio manager has the following six tasks to perform:

(1) determination of the appropriate level of risk for the portfolio under management;
(2) achievement of the desired level of risk by constructing a portfolio of well diversified common stocks which is either dampened through the inclusion of riskless assets or levered by purchasing on margin;
(3) the periodic review of the appropriateness of the level of risk;
(4) the maintenance of the desired level of risk;
(5) management of additional investment or for the reduction in investment in order to make disbursements; and
(6) minimisation of transaction costs.

In other words, the role of the fund manager is to set the appropriate risk (or beta) for the fund and hence the likely expected return according the CAPM, and then simply deal with administrative matters.

A slightly different role for the fund manager is simply to provide a means for the small investor to acquire an adequately diversified portfolio at minimum expense. The growth of 'index' or 'tracker' funds is evidence of such passive investment, whereby the fund guarantees to 'match', rather than try to outperform, a specified share index. The fund manager is in effect setting the beta of the fund at 1 relative to that particular index. Personal investors can adjust their risk level by selection of other investments in their overall personal portfolio.

It is possible to adopt a 'half-way house' policy, which implicitly at least accepts the idea of a fairly efficient equity market, but does not accept that all types of asset are efficiently valued at all times. In other words, it is possible to reconcile an active portfolio management policy in terms of asset allocation between equities, gilts, property and cash, but at the same time adopt a fairly passive policy within the equity market itself. The evidence suggests that such policies are followed by the major UK institutional investors.

3. Problems in applying modern portfolio theory

To what extent has portfolio theory, and the capital–asset pricing model, been incorporated in fund management? To date, the evidence suggest only to a limited extent in the UK. Although portfolio optimising software is widely available, its application has been limited. Most funds still practice 'traditional' rather than 'modern' portfolio management. The reasons for this state of affairs include some or all of the following.

Asset allocation

For large insurance companies and pension funds, the primary determinant of performance is not the choice of individual shares, but the decision on how to weight the portfolio between equities, gilts, property, and cash. For large funds, this is likely to be a decision taken by an investment committee, and reviewed on a periodic basis. The decision on where to invest funds is likely to reflect the subjective judgements of the committee members. Often, the decisions relate more to the new money coming in, rather than to the existing portfolio, where the weightings will be heavily influenced by past performance. O'Barr and Conley (1992) investigated the investment decision-making behaviour of nine large US pension funds. Their most significant finding was the extent to which economic and financial analysis did *not* dominate decision-making:

> We heard instead about quirks of history, seemingly petty personal disputes and bruising political battles – the stuff of culture, not finance. We were struck repeatedly by fund executive's willingness to accept inherited structures and strategies without question. Again and again we heard that investment practices were 'instinctive' or 'part of the corporate culture'.[6]

Data requirements

Portfolio theory assumes that investment managers have the necessary information regarding expected returns, standard deviations, and correlation coefficients. In practice, reliance is usually placed on historical estimates, particularly for risk. Also assets such as individual properties, unlike quoted shares, have no regular market valuations making it difficult to calculate risk and return.

Size of portfolio

Most institutional funds contain far more different investments than would be deemed necessary by portfolio theory in order to diversity risk. This is partly historical, partly prudence, and partly reflects a recognition of problems in dealing in large-sized holdings, particularly in the case of equities other than the FT-SE 100 constituents.

Screening

One particular problem with portfolio theory is that it may involve 'contrary thinking'. Often the equities to which the model gives a high weighting will be those currently 'out of favour', or in sectors which have become unfashionable. The fund manager would be reluctant to go out on a limb and give the appropriate weighting to such investments, which might provoke detailed questioning from an investment committee, particularly if it resulted in short-term adverse performance. Such investments may therefore be effectively screened out.

Constraints

Fund managers may not have complete freedom to invest funds because of constraints imposed by the nature of the fund. These may be legal requirements, or imposed by relevant regulatory bodies. The nature of the liability of the fund may be an important constraint. For example, pension funds with final-salary-schemes' liabilities require assets whose returns correlate with real economic activity.

Brokers

Institutional investors undertaken a mixture of primary and secondary research. Secondary research involves reviewing investment recommendations received from stockbrokers. The choice of assets, equities in particular, may therefore not be based on a review of the portfolio as a whole, but rather the research and persuasive powers of brokers over a period of time.

Return versus risk

Portfolio theory gives equal weighting to return and risk in constructing an efficient frontier. But the general public, and popular investment journals such as *Money Management*, judge performance much more in terms of compounded return, irrespective of the risk involved. This may not be rational behaviour, but fund managers may feel that they have to acknowledge it. Performance tables in advertisements must include 'wealth warnings' – 'values can go down as well as up' – but the risks are rarely quantified. The contracting-out of fund management puts pressure on independent fund managers to continually demonstrate short-term performance in order to retain the funds.

The over-riding impression is that portfolio management in the UK is at present still mainly conducted on a subjective rather than a scientific basis. On the equity side, the ideas of passive management implied by the CAPM and efficient markets have received increasing recognition. 'Index' funds have been used by pension funds in the USA since the early 1970s. They received a boost from the Employment Retirement Investment Security Act (ERISA) 1974, which placed great emphasis for fund trustees, known in the USA as 'plan sponsors', to demonstrate that they had acted prudently. Around 15% of the assets of UK pension funds were managed in an index fund in 1992, compared with around 25% in the USA. In the UK index funds have been available to the general public since 1988, but to date form only a small proportion of unit trust and unitised life assurance and pension funds. They are available for single country indices, such as the FT-SE 100 Index in the UK or the Standard and Poor's 500 Index in the USA. There are also funds which track indices of a region, such as the James Capel Tiger Index fund, for the smaller Far East markets such as Hong Kong, Singapore, Thailand and South Korea.

Simply 'matching' an index is anathema to many fund managers because it explicitly recognises that they cannot pick shares on a regular basis which will outperform the market. Nevertheless, with large funds there is an element of 'closet indexing' whereby widespread diversification ensures that an equity fund's performance is roughly in line with the market, or markets, of the underlying shares. 'Closet indexing' may enable the fund to levy higher management charges than would be achievable with formal indexation! The conclusion is therefore that fund performance is generally determined far more by choice of asset type – equities, gilts, property, or cash – and choice of country, than by share selection within a particular market.

Asset allocation – empirical evidence

At the end of the Second World War in 1945, pension funds and insurance companies were principally invested in gilt-edged securities. Although interest rates were low, so was inflation. Interest rates on Treasury bills were 0.5%, 2.5% Consols yielded 2–3%, while equities had dividend yields of 4–5%, and earnings yields of 12–13%. Although there was a positive yield gap, in that equities had a higher immediate yield than gilts, the latter provided a guaranteed return, and the prospect of capital appreciation if interest rates were to fall even further.

3.5% War Loan reached 108 in October 1946. Many people feared a recession, as after the First World War. Equities were thought to be risky;

memories were fresh of the liquidations and dividend cuts experienced in the 1930s. The 'cheap money' policy was abandoned by the Conservative government in 1951: Bank Rate was increased to 2.5%, having been held at 2% for no less than 12 years.

The prosperity of the 1950s led to a belief that demand management of the economy might reduce the threat of a 1930s-style depression, but lead to an alternative problem, endemic inflation. In the early 1950s, following the lead set by the Imperial Tobacco pension fund headed by George Ross Goobey, there was an increasing recognition that equities, unlike conventional fixed-interest gilts, could provide a hedge against inflation. Thus the 'cult of the equity' was born. Pension funds and insurance companies during the 1950s began to orientate their portfolios more towards equities, and to a lesser extent property, and away from fixed-interest investments. By October 1959 the persistent rise in share prices had driven the average dividend yield on equities below the yield on 2.5% Consols for the first time since records had been kept – this was the beginning of the so called 'reverse yield gap'.

The increasing equity orientation of institutional portfolios undoubtedly proved to be a correct move. To what extent it proved to be self-justifying is a matter of debate. The 'weight of money' theory is a belief that the level of share prices is determined to a large extent by the amount of new money invested by the institutions. But, world-wide, equities proved to be the star performers of the 1970s and 1980s as a whole. The UK Stock Market collapsed between 1972 and 1974, but then rose almost continuously from early 1975 until 'Black Monday', 19 October 1987. After the crash Share prices subsequently recovered to new highs.

According to Combined Actuarial Performance Services (CAPS),[7] the cumulative annual return on UK equities over the 10 years to the end of 1991 was 19.6%, as compared with 16.9% for overseas equities, 14.7% for gilts, 11.9% for sterling cash, and 9% for UK property. The best period for equities was that preceding 'Black Monday'. According to County NatWest WoodMac,[8] in the five years to mid. 1987 the annualised returns on UK equities, gilts, and cash were 34.9%, 15.6%, and 10.1% respectively. But in the subsequent five-year period to mid-1992 cash was the best performer, with respective figures of 6.1%, 9.4% and 12.5%. Over the same period the property market crashed across the board – industrial, commercial, agricultural and residential were all adversely affected.

The superior performance of equities has been evident over very long periods of time. The BZW Equity–Gilt Study[9] shows that UK equities consistently outperformed gilts and cash over the period 1918–92. The nominal annual geometric mean return on equities was 11.9% (7.3% in 'real' terms) compared with 5.7% (1.2%) for gilts and 5.4% (1.0%) for cash. Equities thus recorded a risk premium in excess of 6% over both gilts and cash.

The riskiness of equities, measured by the standard deviation of returns, was almost twice that of gilts, and therefore equities would be expected to provide an overall return greater than that of gilts. But the size of the premium is perhaps excessive. Using the data of returns from 1918–92 BZW found that gilts did not feature in portfolios on the efficient frontier except at the minimum level of risk. Low risk, average risk and high risk portfolios consisted of combinations of cash and equities, the low correlation between the real returns on cash and equities (0.30) making them an attractive combination, except for maximum return portfolios, which were entirely equities. Gilts did well during the late 1920s and early 1930s when retail prices were falling, but they subsequently suffered badly because of the largely unanticipated inflation from the late 1960s to early 1980s. Long dated fixed-interest securities are much more vulnerable to an upsurge in inflation than 'cash' investments, for which the interest rate will adjust to some extent for inflation.

Mehra and Prescott[10] found similar results in the USA to those reported in the BZW Study. They referred to the 'equity premium puzzle', the phenomenon that in the USA over the period 1889–1978 equities appeared to offer excessive returns relative to bonds, even after allowing for differences in risk. Siegel[11] extended the work in the USA back to 1802. He found that the equity risk premium had increased over the period of nearly 200 years. The real geometric mean return on equity in the USA was remarkably constant – 1802–70 5.7%; 1871–1925 6.6%; 1926–90 6.4%; and over the entire period 1802–1990 6.2%. The increasing equity risk premium was due a decline in the real return on bonds. Over the same three periods, the real geometric mean returns on short-term US bonds were 5.1%, 3.1% and 0.5% respectively, averaging 2.9% over the whole period 1802–1990. Similarly long-dated US bonds real geometric mean returns were 4.9%, 3.8%, and 1.4% respectively, averaging 3.4% over the entire period. In the USA, the equity risk premium over short-term bonds/cash was thus 1802–70 0.6%, 1871–1925 3.5%, 1926–90 5.9%. The equity risk premium over long-term government bonds was similarly 0.8%, 2.8% and 5.0% for the same periods respectively. Siegel also found a remarkable similarity in the trends of UK and US bond returns; the sharp decline in real yields on fixed-interest securities in the USA, particularly in the nineteenth century, was closely mirrored in the UK.

Siegel's results suggest that the long-term real return on cash and bonds in the USA has been 3–3.5%, and the equity risk premium has averaged around 3%, roughly half the mean figure in the USA and UK for most of this century. Siegel highlighted the fact that the 1980s in the USA provided the highest average annual real returns (10.5%) on long-term government bonds for any consecutive 10-year period since 1884, and the highest real returns (3.7%) on cash since the nineteenth century except for the period of the Depression. Similar results were found in the UK. Siegel concludes:

It is not unreasonable to assume that the current higher real rates will turn out to be more characteristic of future returns than the unusually low real rates of the earlier part of this century. If they do, then the advantage of holding equities over bonds will shrink from the levels reached over the past several generations. The holders of fixed income investments should enjoy enhanced real returns in the future.

In the UK index-linked gilts provide guaranteed real returns until well into the twenty-first century. In early 1995 these guaranteed real returns were nearly 4% p.a. This suggests an equity risk premium over index-linked gilts of 3–3.5% in the future in the UK.

In an efficient market, conventional fixed-interest gilts should offer similar real returns to index-linked ones. The expected equity risk premium over conventional gilts would also fall to around 3–3.5%. Before September 1992 a strong case was made for increasing the proportion of fixed-interest bonds in institutional portfolios because of UK membership of the Exchange Rate Mechanism (ERM). The basis of the argument was that UK involvement in the ERM meant that inflation could no longer be accommodated by a depreciating currency. A fixed exchange rate would be good for fixed interest securities because of the downward pressure on inflation, but less favourable for equities, since it might involve adverse effects on profit margins and growth. But this strategy was quickly undermined by the UK's decision to suspend membership of the ERM in September 1992 and to float the pound. The immediate consequence was an upsurge in share prices. As Siegel concluded, 'Equities still appear to be the best route to long-term wealth accumulation.'

4.   Asset allocation by type of fund

Pension funds

Pension funds are probably the best indicators of asset allocation policies, since many of them have complete discretion on investment, and being gross funds, their decisions are not distorted by tax bias. Funded occupational schemes in the public and private sectors provide pensions either based on final salary (defined benefit) or on the performance of the fund (contracted-out money purchase schemes – COMPS). In either case, the fund manager is expected to earn a real rate of return of around 4% on investments in order to provide pensions of the required level. In this respect, UK fund managers have much greater freedom of manoeuvre than their counterparts in many other countries. The Trustee Investments Act 1961 allowed funds to invest up to 50% in equities, but many funds now have 'beneficial owner' clauses in the trust deed. This permits them to override the 1961 Act, and invest as if they were managing unrestricted funds. Table 7.3 shows the major changes in pension funds between 1978 and 1993. It relates to all self administered schemes in the private and public sectors, but excludes those run by insurance

Table 7.3   Selected asset holdings of self-administered pension funds,
1978 and 1990

	Year-end	
	1978 %	*1993* %
Short-term assets (net)	4.7	3.4
Gilts	20.9	6.8
UK Company securities	47.2	55.0
Overseas company securities	4.7	17.2
UK land, property and ground rents (including property unit trusts)	17.2	4.4
Other	5.3	13.2
Total assets	100 £31.3 billion	100 £464.1 billion

Sources: Wilson Report, Appendix 3, Table 3.51; (12) *Financial Statistics* (November 1994, Table 5.1B).

companies. Personal pensions are managed by life assurance and unit trust groups, and included in their figures (see below).

The most notable changes in pension fund portfolios during the 1980s and early 1990's were the increased investment in overseas securities – overwhelmingly equities – and the reduced weightings given to gilts and property. Changes in weightings partly reflect changing market values, and also net purchases and sales. During the 1980s overseas equities effectively displaced gilts in UK pension fund portfolios. Overseas securities provide greater diversification of the equity element of the portfolio. But, on the other hand, this means that more than two thirds of portfolios are on average invested in company securities, nearly all of them equities. The dramatic collapse of the Japanese Stock Market in the early 1990s (a fall of 60% by August 1992) indicates the volatility of equity returns, particularly in overseas markets. Index-linked gilts comprised nearly a half of the gilts holdings but only 3.3% of total portfolios. At the end of 1957, in contrast, total holdings of company securities (29%) were less than gilt holdings (34%).

Combined Actuarial Performance Services (CAPS), which measures the performance of around 2800 portfolios, generally the smaller funds but worth around half the total value of pension funds, noted an even more dramatic trend. They found that the 'typical' British pension fund had a total of 83% of its overall investment in UK and Overseas equities – the highest figure they had ever recorded! On their measure, property had fallen to a mere 2%, and gilts were only 5%. In contrast, according to the Bank of England[13] in 1988 pension funds in Japan held 55% of assets in bonds, in Canada 47%, in USA 38% and in Germany 28%. UK pension fund managers were clearly prepared largely to ignore risk in order to achieve the highest possible returns. They are assisted in this policy by the Accounting Standard for Pensions SSAP24, which effectively insulates them from short-term price fluctuations. In the UK, defined benefit pension schemes are valued not on the basis of market prices but on an actuarial valuation basis, which focuses upon the present value of expected future investment income. In contrast, in the USA the equivalent accounting standard FAS87 is based on market values, and deficiencies in meeting future liabilities resulting from a fall in market values have to be met from the parent company's profit and loss account. Naturally US companies would be reluctant to allow the pension fund to invest too heavily in volatile equities.

Another factor relevant to the UK is the increasing maturity of pension funds. When a fund is new, outgoings in the form of pension payments are low and income from contributors is high. But the ageing of the population in the UK means that many pension funds are reaching maturity – outgoings relative to inflows are increasing – and this may cause a shift towards investments producing a high immediate yield, such as gilts.

Insurance companies

Insurance companies are active in both life assurance and non-life (general) insurance, and they also manage the pension schemes for many employers. Long-term business – mainly life assurance – has an emphasis on the spreading of risks over time, whereas general business is mainly concerned with the spreading of risks between persons and organisations at the current time. Consequently, long-term business has greater investment funds to manage.

The overall portfolio mix of long-term funds is governed by the Insurance Companies Regulations 1981, and the Insurance Companies Act 1982. Insurance companies in the UK generally have much greater freedom to invest than is the case in many other countries. Where the controls do have an effect is in the solvency valuation conditions. Some types of asset, for example, are totally or partially inadmissible for solvency purposes. A company's freedom to invest depends upon the extent to which its admissible assets exceed its liabilities together with the required solvency margin.

Taxation is not a dominant consideration in investment policy since life funds are taxed at 25% on both income and chargeable gain (1994–95). The investment policy of managers of long-term insurance funds is constrained to some degree by the nature of the policies sold. Traditional endowment and whole life policies – 'with' or 'without' profits – and 'managed' bonds leave investment policy entirely to the fund managers. 'With-profits' policies pay reversionary bonuses and a terminal bonus. The relative size of these two forms of bonus is at the discretion of the company. Terminal bonuses provide more flexibility because they are determined solely in the year when the policy matures, whereas reversionary bonuses accumulate, usually on an annual basis, and once declared cannot be withdrawn, despite any downturn in investment markets.

Unit-linked policies, specific to a particular type of asset, such as equity, gilt or property bonds obviously predetermine the type of asset which can be held – that decision has been made by the investor, not the fund manager. The same range of policies, endowment or unit-linked, are available in the form of personal pensions, which have the advantage of a tax-free fund.

Long-term life funds have followed the trend of self-administered pension funds in increasing the emphasis on equities, although not to quite the same extent. This has been brought about by the growth of unit-linked equity funds; increased pension business, both corporate and personal; and increased emphasis on performance statistics in the marketing of life and pension business.

100 years ago, the major type of asset held by life offices was mortgages on property within the UK – 43% of total assets in 1890 (J. Dodds[14]). But by 1952 mortgages were only around 11% of life office's assets, with 25% of funds invested in gilts. After the Second World War, equity holdings increased from negligible proportions to around 20% of total assets. By 1978, equities at 32%, including unit trust units, were the most popular type of asset held, with gilt holdings at 25%. Property assets increased from 10% of total funds in 1961 to 22% on 1978.

As with pension funds, there has been increased emphasis since 1978 on equities, particularly overseas, at the expense of gilts and property. At the end of 1993, UK equities alone comprised 39% of total assets, and overseas equities were an additional 10%. These figures do not take account of unit trust holdings, which are almost exclusively equity-based. Changes in the tax

Table 7.4   Selected asset holdings of long-term insurance funds, 1978 and 1990

| | Year-end | |
	1978 %	1993 %
Short-term assets (net)	4.3	3.5
Gilts	25.4	16.5
UK company securities	32.0	46.7
Overseas company securities	3.0	10.3
Unit trust units	2.7	8.8
UK land, property and ground rents	22.3	7.5
UK loans and mortgages	7.9	2.0
Other	2.4	4.7
Total assets	100	100
	£37.8 billion	£412.9 billion

Sources: Wilson Report, Appendix 3, Table 3.46; *Financial Statistics* (November 1994, Table 5.1A).

treatment of life assurance holdings of unit trusts in 1991 means that their holdings of unit trusts are likely to decline rapidly, to be replaced by direct holdings of the underlying shares.

Table 7.4 includes life offices' pension funds.

It should be recognised that it is very difficult for a large life office to drastically restructure its portfolio in the short term. For funds like the Prudential, with over £70 billion under management, changing the portfolio's asset allocation weighting is akin to a large oil tanker turning at sea.

Unit trusts

A unit trust is constituted by a trust deed, drawn up by the managers and the trustee, two parties who must be independent of each other. The purchaser of units, the unitholder, becomes the beneficiary of the trust fund, and his or her interests must be protected by the trustee. The managers of a unit trust are its promoters. They are responsible for the day-to-day management of the fund. The trustee – invariably a bank or insurance company – retains custody of the trust assets, controls the issue of units, maintains a register of holders, and generally watches over the management of the trust. The trustee does not interfere in the purchase or sale of investments unless the actions of the managers conflict with the interests of the unitholders. If, for example, the trust is to invest exclusively in Far East securities, the trustee should ensure that only such securities are held.

Authorisation by the SIB (see Chapters 2 and 3) means that units can be advertised and marketed directly to the public, and the funds themselves are

Table 7.5   Selected asset holdings of UK authorised unit trusts, 1978 and 1993

	Year-end	
	1978 %	1993 %
Net short-term assets	10.3	3.1
Gilts	0.8	1.0
UK company securities	73.1	56.9
Overseas company securities	15.6	36.6
Other	0.2	2.4
Total assets	100 £3.9 billion	100 £92.3 billion

Sources: Wilson Report, Appendix 3, Table 3.36; *Financial Statistics* (November 1994, Table 5.2D).

exempted from capital gains tax (instead, the liability, if any, rests with the ultimate investor).

The investment powers of UK authorised unit trusts have until recently been restricted to shares and fixed-interest securities, as shown in Table 7.5. Company securities are mainly equities. In fact, at the end of 1993 equities alone constituted 90% of the total assets of unit trusts – 54% of total assets being UK equities, and 36% overseas equities. Gilts at 1.0% had barely changed in importance from 15 years previously. The most notable movement has been in the increasing importance of overseas diversification, particularly with 'emerging market' funds.

Shares and bonds are nearly always quoted on 'approved markets'. These are the 'Official Lists' of the countries of the European Union; plus the principal markets of the remainder of Europe, North America and the Far East; plus the Unlisted Securities Market (USM) in the UK. Up to 10% of an authorised fund can be invested in transferable securities which are not quoted on an approved market. The rules have been relaxed somewhat since the Financial Services Act 1986 extended the investment powers of authorised unit trusts to invest in money market securities, property, commodities, and options and futures contracts. By holding a combination of interest bearing investments, futures and options, it is possible for funds to offer investors the combination of security of capital together with participation in stock market appreciation.

In the case of UK authorised unit trusts investing in equities, there are restrictions on the amount which can be invested in individual holdings. Generally no more than 5% of the fund can be invested in any one company, and no more than 10% of the issued equity capital of a company can be held.

The choice of authorised unit trusts available to the investor is bewilderingly wide. In 1993 there were in excess of 1500 such trusts available from over 150 management companies. The Association of Unit Trusts and Investment Funds allocates each trust to one of the 20 or more categories, e.g. UK General, UK Equity Income, UK Growth, UK Balanced, plus a whole range of International Funds. The unit trust fund is constrained by these objective specified in the trust deed and the advertising material. A UK Balanced Fund, for example, according to the AUTIF criteria, should have no more than 80% of portfolio invested in either equities, or gilts and other fixed interest securities. On the other hand, a Japanese, Far East or Australasia fund should be, at least, 80% invested in the specified location. 'Ethical' funds also specify criteria used to select or de-select particular securities. Income or Growth funds, by their nature, limit the range of securities which can be held. The guidelines specify that a UK Equity Income fund should have at least 80% of its assets in equities, and have a yield in excess of 110% of the yield of the FT-Actuaries All-Share Index. In some cases, such as 'index' or 'tracker' funds discretion is almost entirely removed from the fund managers because they simply replicate a specified index.

Because unit trusts are 'open-ended' they must have sufficient liquid assets to meet any net redemptions from the fund.

Investment trusts

Unlike unit trusts, investment trusts are not truly 'trusts' – they are in fact limited companies, subject to the provisions of the Companies Acts like other companies. The Companies Act 1980 created an entirely new class of public company – the investment company – although investment trusts had been in existence since the middle of the nineteenth century, well before unit trusts were devised. However, they have not been as actively promoted or aggressively sold as unit trusts. There are around 260 different 'approved' investment trusts, far fewer than the number of 'authorised' UK unit trusts. At the end of 1993 the total funds under the management of investment trusts was £39.5 billions, around half the £92.3 billions managed by unit trusts. However, in recent years, the number of investment trusts has increased, after many years contraction, principally because their inclusion along with unit trusts in Personal Equity Plans (PEPs) enabled investors to hold them as tax-free investments. In addition, a number of them launched imaginative capital structures, with securities including loan stock, warrants, 'stepped' preference shares, zero-coupon preference shares, income shares, and capital shares. They thus created securities to meet all needs for combinations of income or capital growth, with high, average, or minimal risk.

Like unit trusts, investment trusts offer a wide range of funds, which are categorised by the Association of Investment Trust Companies. Traditionally, investment trusts have had a greater overseas orientation than unit trusts, and 'International General' and 'International Capital Growth' are the largest types of fund. The general trusts aim to produce balanced income and growth. Assets are primarily equities spread throughout the world. According to the AITC definitions, international general funds can have up to 80% of assets in one geographical area. Most of them hold the majority of assets in the UK, and the rest in USA, Japan, the Far East and Europe.

The type of fund must be specified in the investment trust's articles of association, and in its Stock Exchange 'Continuing Obligations'. In order to exempt the fund itself from capital gains tax, an investment trust must be 'approved' by the Inland Revenue as conforming with the definition contained in the Income and Corporation Taxes Act 1988. The chief requirements of the Act are:

- the company's income is derived wholly or mainly (i.e. 70%) from securities
- no single holding must represent more than 15% of the overall fund (reduced to 10% for new applicants)

- its own shares are quoted on the London Stock Exchange
- the company must not distribute realised capital profits as dividends;
- it does not retain more than 15% of the income it receives from investments in shares and securities.

New applicants for a Stock Exchange listing are also required to state an investment policy by which no more than 25% of the fund is invested in securities not listed on a recognised Stock Exchange. Investment trusts have greater freedom to invest in unquoted shares because they are 'close-ended' funds. This means that their shares can be traded without affecting the capital within the fund. There is no fear of having to realise illiquid assets to meet redemptions. Because the shares of the trust trade independently of the fund itself, they can deviate in price from the net asset value of the fund; usually they trade at a discount to their underlying asset value.

There is very little fiscal bias for unit or investment trusts. The ultimate investor is taxed in almost exactly the same way as if he or she held the underlying assets directly. A funds freedom from capital gains tax does, however, mean that shares can be bought and sold within the fund without incurring capital gains tax, which means that it is cheaper for a fund to restructure its portfolio than would be the case for an individual. Investment trusts are treated unfavourably for unfranked income – e.g. gilt interest – on which they pay the full rate of corporation tax, whereas unit trusts pay only the equivalent to basic rate tax, which is reclaimable by non-taxpayers. This distinction matters very little as investment trusts, like unit trusts, are overwhelmingly invested in equities (see Table 7.6).

Table 7.6   Selected asset holdings of UK approved investment trusts, 1978 and 1993

	Year-end	
	1978 %	*1993* %
Net short-term assets	4.7	4.0
Gilts	3.5	2.7
UK company securities	58.5	41.7
Overseas company securities	32.3	48.7
Other	1.0	2.9
Total assets	100	100
	£6.7 billion	£39.5 billion

Source: Wilson Report, Appendix 3, Table 3.41; *Financial Statistics* (November 1994, Table 5.2C).

At the end of 1993 equities were still the dominant asset held by the investment trusts, accounting for 87% of assets in total – UK (40%) and overseas (47%). Despite the wide investment powers traditionally held by investment trusts, unlisted company securities were only 2.0% of total assets in 1993, and property holdings were a derisory 0.1%. Investment trusts still have a greater overseas orientation than unit trusts although, as mentioned earlier, unit trusts have also increased their overseas diversification. In addition to the overseas company securities, investment trusts held 1.2% of their funds in overseas government bonds (this is included in the total 'Other' figure, 2.9%).

The gearing of investment trusts is modest, at around 8% of total assets, when including all forms of medium-and long-term debt, plus preference shares. The servicing cost is not likely to have a significant influence on the types of asset held.

5. Summary and conclusions

The common feature of all four major institutional investors is that since 1980 they have increased their investment in overseas equities. Pension funds and life funds have also increased their weightings in equities overall, at the expense of gilts and property.

The decline in the proportion of property assets among pension and life funds is surprising in terms of 'efficient' portfolios. Smith, Proffitt and Stephens,[15] report the results of four studies in the USA comparing the risk and returns of property and equities. They state that in the USA

> On the whole, real estate returns have compared favourably with common stock (i.e. equity) returns in the post World War 2 era. Real estate investments performed especially well during the highly inflationary 1970s. Generally, the returns on real estate have also been less volatile than common stock returns.

They add that

> Since real estate returns seem to be quite independent of the returns on stocks and bonds (as indicated by small, often negative correlations) adding real estate to a portfolio containing stocks and bonds may produce significant benefits.

Fogler[16] demonstrated that the presence of a significant amount of real estate in the portfolio made the expected return higher at a given level of risk, or the risk lower at a given level of expected return than would have been attained by a portfolio composed only of equities, bonds, and cash.

The BZW Equity–Gilt Study also reviews the performance of house prices. In the UK, residential property prices have performed in line with equities over long periods of time. Real assets such as houses tend to outperform equities when inflation is in excess of 6%, but do worse at rates below 6%. But over the period 1918–88 the ratio of equity prices to house prices in the UK remained unchanged. Between 1918 and 1936 equities did much better, and the ratio rose from 1 to 4, but from that date onwards house prices recovered lost ground. Between 1962 and 1992, the average house doubled in value in real terms, compared with a 22% real increase in the market value of equities.

In the short term, changes in the proportions of portfolios held in different types of asset may simply reflect the relative performance of those assets. Take self-administered pension funds as an example. In 1993 they disinvested £2.0 billions from UK equities and invested £3 billions into overseas equities, but between the year ends of 1992 and 1993 the market value of their total holdings increased by £46 billions and £15 billions respectively. If fund managers were attempting to maintain optimal weightings by market value, the portfolios would have to be continually readjusted in order to maintain those desired weightings. Ironically, it would mean reducing investment in those assets which had been the best performers.

The 1980s was a time of deregulation across the whole range of financial services (see Chapters 2 and 3). There was much greater competition and a corresponding need to demonstrate performance. Unit-linked life funds became increasingly popular relative to traditional with-profits policies, and unit-linked policies also became widely available in the form of personal pensions. Many of these unit-linked funds are entirely equity-based. Many new unit and investment trusts were also introduced, often based on specialist sectors or geographical regions. Such funds inadequately diversify risk. In terms of modern investment theory it is irrational for investors to hold such funds in isolation; they should be held only as part of the investor's more widely diversified portfolio. This tendency has been accentuated by the intensified competition between fund managers. The steady smoothing of performance provided by 'with-profits' policies, backed by wide diversification, has been replaced by emphasis on shorter-term performance. In the short term highly specialist funds tend to do either much better or much worse than the more general, diversified funds. Not unnaturally advertising tends to emphasise the winners, not the losers. Return has been stressed, but risk largely ignored. Fund managers of traditional life funds and self-administered pension funds have also shifted their stance more towards equities. The high returns earned on equities have justified this policy, but investors have been exposed to greater risk.

There is a view that a diversified portfolio of equities is less risky for a long-term investor, such as a pension fund or life fund, than for a short-term investor. According to Smith, Proffitt and Stephens[17]

Long term investors receive the benefit of 'time diversification', which means that if a diversified portfolio of common stocks is held for many years, the investor can be quite sure the good performance in the up years will more than offset the bad performance of the down years.

According to the BZW Equity–Gilt Study, an investor who was a non-taxpayer would not have lost money in real terms in any 25-year period from 1918–1992. In the very long run, according to this argument, mean return is all important. Portfolio theory and the CAPM are both based on the assumption that investors are concerned with short-term variability in returns because they wish to maximise utility at the end of a single time period, say three months, or one year. In a multi-period model, maximisation of the utility of terminal wealth many periods hence may produce optimal portfolios different from those identified by the Markowitz mean–variance approach.

Many investors, however, do not invest for a lifetime, even in pension schemes and life policies. To deal with this problem, fund managers have been assisted by the growth of financial derivatives, such as futures and options contracts. Through 'financial engineering' the fund can combine derivatives based on equity indices with cash or gilts to enable investors to participate in the upside of an equity market, but be protected against the downside. A typical formula would be a 70:30 fund. The 70% invested in gilts or cash would be expected to grow sufficiently to return the original sum invested after, say, five years. The remaining 30% is invested in futures and options to give the investor the full gain on the equities. The drawback of such schemes are the loss of income, the minimum holding period, and the management charges. At present, these are largely restricted to life funds and personal equity plans. It has yet to be proved that such 'guaranteed' or 'stabilised' funds provide a better risk–return trade-off for most investors than traditional diversification.

Notes

1. Markowitz (1952).
2. $\bar{U}$ indicates the mean expected utility derived by multiplying each possible level of utility by its probability of occurrence.
3. Sharpe (1964).
4. Haugen (1993), p. 2.
5. Lorie and Hamilton (1973), p. 109.
6. O'Barr and Conley (1992).
7. *Financial Times* (7 May 1992).
8. *Financial Times* (28 June 1992).
9. The BZW Equity – Gilt Study (1993).
10. Mehra and Prescott (1985), pp. 145–61.
11. Siegel (1992).
12. Wilson Committee (1980), Appendices.

13. Bank of England, *Quarterly Bulletin,* Aug 1991 vol. 31 (3) pp. 380–390.
14. Dodds (1979).
15. Smith, Proffitt and Stephens (1992), pp. 629–30.
16. Fogler (1984).
17. Smith, Proffitt and Stephens (1992), p. 612.

Further reading

Dodds, J.C., *The Investment Behaviour of British Life Assurance Companies* (Croom-Helm, 1979).
Fogler, R.H., '20% in Real Estate: Can Theory Justify It'?, *Journal of Portfolio Management* (Winter 1984).
Frost, A.J. and Hager, D.P., *A General Introduction to Institutional Investment* (Heinemann, 1986).
Haugen, R.A., *Modern Investment Theory*, 3rd edn (Prentice-Hall, 1993).
HMSO, Report of the *Committee to Review the Functioning of Financial Institutions* (Wilson Report), CMND 7937 (HMSO, 1980).
Lorie, J.H. and Hamilton, M.T., *The Stock Market: Theories and Evidence* (Irwin, 1973).
Markowitz, H.M., 'Portfolio Selection', *Journal of Finance* (December 1952).
Mehra, R. and Prescott, E., 'The Equity Premium: A Puzzle', *Journal of Monetary Economics*, 15 (1985).
O'Barr, W.M. and Conley, J.M., 'Managing Relationships: The Culture of Institutional Investing', *Financial Analysts Journal* (September–October 1992).
Pawley, M., Winstone, D. and Bentley, P., *UK Financial Institutions and Markets* (Macmillan, 1991).
Sharpe, W.F., 'Capital Asset Prices: A Theory of Market Equilibrium under Conditions of Risk', *Journal of Finance* (September 1964).
Siegel, J.J., 'The Equity Premium: Stock and Bond Returns', *Financial Analysts Journal* (January–February 1992). [Reprinted in Lofthouse, S. (ed) 'Readings in Investments' (Wiley 1994) Chapter 17]
Smith, R.K., Proffitt, D.L. and Stephens, A.A., *Investments* (West Publishing, 1992).
The BZW Equity–Gilt Study, 38th edn (Barclays de Zoete Wedd Research, 1993).
Winfield, R.G. and Curry, S.J., *Success in Investment*, 5th edn (John Murray, 1994).

CHAPTER 8

Corporate Credit Analysis

Tony Sawyer and Ken Andrews

1. Introduction

Providing finance (lending) means risk-taking by the banks. There are a multitude of things which might happen to cause both businesses and private customers to be unable to repay their debts, and so bankers will often wish to take collateral (security) to cover themselves. However this latter action is well recognised to be only for control purposes. Thus, the borrowing proposition and subsequent repayment must be considered in isolation from the security: money should not be lent unless the bank is satisfied there is good probability of the money being repaid, without recourse to security.

To reach the above stage, every bank carries out a series of investigations, often called credit appraisal, discussion of which is the purpose of this chapter. The first half of the chapter focuses on traditional techniques, which have been developed over many years of lending by working bankers. The second half of the chapter reviews current progress in the development of more objective approaches to credit–risk analysis. These involve the application of quantitative analysis to financial data, in order to make predictions about the likelihood of financial success or failure of companies.

2. Bank lending – a traditional approach

The 'mnemonics' of lending

The word 'mnemonic' comes from the Greek language, and by definition means 'the art of improving memory'. All banks have for many years followed this idea – that is, to give their lenders an alphabetic-based guide to follow.

The rationale is to ensure a consistency of approach to credit appraisal across the many different managers who make lending decisions in branch banks.

The first of these mnemonics was:

C – Capital
C – Character
C – Capability

The belief was, at that time, that if lending bankers could satisfy themselves on these three issues then a positive decision to lend could follow. The weakness of this mnemonic was that it tended to look backwards, only considering those issues from the customer's *past*, on which the decision to lend *future money* would be agreed.

It is vitally important to realise that lending needs to consider both *past history* and *future intentions*, so this led to the development of alternative mnemonics.

For example, Lloyds Bank and TSB Bank make use of the following lending mnemonic

Capital	Purpose
Character	Amount
Capability	Repayment
	Terms
	Security

Addition of the word 'PARTS' has opened up new areas of investigation, making it easier to identify sections of analysis.

The mnemonic is quite a good one as lenders can quite easily relate to the meaning of each key letter. A possible improvement would be to place the word *CAPABILITY* after the word *TERMS*, so that bankers would construct future budgets to test the recovery of their lending. But this of course destroys the mnemonic! Mnemonics used in some of the other large UK clearing banks are shown below.

Barclays	*Nat West*	*Midland*
Character	*C*	Personality
Ability	*A*	Amount
Means	*M*	Repayment
Purpose	*P*	Security
Amount	*A*	Expediency
Repayment	*R*	Remuneration
Insurance	*I*	Services
	and	
	*I*nterest	
	Charges	
	Extras	

These mnemonics are very similar to *CCCPARTS* in the issues they highlight; note that words like 'Character' and 'Personality' come early on. These are an investigation into the owners of the business as to their track record/ability/experience. 'Security' (or 'Insurance') tends to come towards the end, to be considered only after the borrowing proposition has met the other criteria.

Rationale for the traditional approach to credit–risk appraisal

From the mnemonics of lending mentioned in the previous section, it is possible to see that decisions are made on two types of information:

● knowledge of the past
● prediction of the future (see Figure 8.1).

If we then ask which is the most important of the two, we come up with the answer that the future is more important, as it can give repayment from surplus cash generated (i.e. Income *less* Expenditure if a private customer or Revenue *less* Expenses if a business). Whereas if we lend on knowledge of the past only, with little heed to the future, we are implicitly relying on security to ensure repayment (see Figure 8.2).

Attempting to integrate the above with the areas of investigation in each of the mnemonics, the following emerges.

LEND

THE PAST ----------------- **or** ----------------- **THE FUTURE**

DECLINE

Figure 8.1   The traditional approach to risk–credit appraisal

LEND

THE PAST ----------------- **or** ----------------- **THE FUTURE**

DECLINE

Implicitly relies on
security to underwrite
repayment

Can give us
repayment
from surplus
cash generated

Figure 8.2   Lending with knowledge of the past and the future

The *past* requires us to:

- report on the *people* in the organisation which picks up character, integrity, etc.
- report on the business's *past financial record*, where strengths and weaknesses must be identified, and above all *trends* which will help us plan the future.

The *future* requires us to:-

- Critically consider the *proposition* before us, initially as to its *purpose* and *amount*. Both of these help us to identify the *risk* we are taking if we go ahead.
  The proportion of a bank's lending in relation to what their customer is contributing from his own resources (known as gearing) will also be of concern to the bank in assessing risk. We now naturally turn to the possible need for *security*, where both its quality and value will have to be determined in relation to the level of risk.
- Calculate the bank interest charges, and annual capital repayment; we will need to see the future *projections* of our customer (whether a private or business account), as we attempt to test our margins of cover for repayment.

To summarise, the traditional lending model, as it has been developed by the banks, may be regarded as appraising credit risk against four headings (see Figure 8.3).

1. The people
2. The past financial record
3. The proposition
4. The projections.

The decision to lend, or to decline to lend, derives from a collection and assessment of information under each of these headings. The next section seeks to amplify this approach by use of a case study in which the principles are applied to a lending proposition.

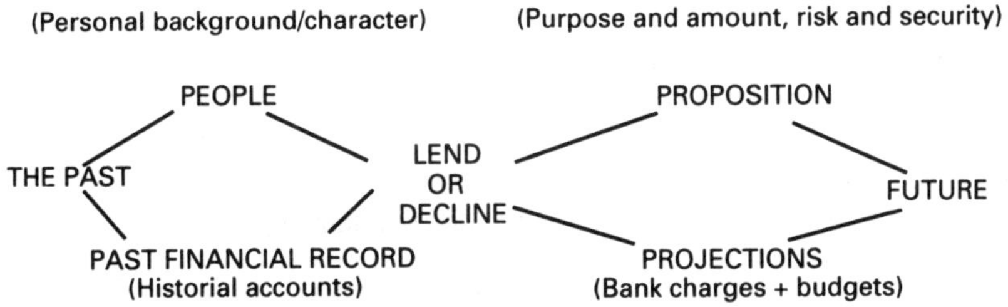

Figure 8.3   Traditional lending model

3.   Case study: John James Precision Engineering

The proposition – would you lend?

John James Precision Engineering Ltd has maintained a bank account with your branch since the company was incorporated 10 years ago. The account has worked in credit throughout its history, and you have little information on file regarding the company other than that the directors are John James and Mary James.

Mr James calls to see you today by appointment. He explains that he lives with his wife in a house owned by the local government authority. He has just started negotiations with the local government authority to purchase the house for £15,000, a price that represents a 40% discount on the market value. He had intended to approach you shortly to discuss the transaction but a problem has now occurred with his company. Apparently, Mr James' largest customers have indicated to him that if he wishes to retain their work he must upgrade his machinery; their orders could then increase from £3,000 to £10,000 per month.

The machinery and the associated equipment is available but would cost £25,000. Mr James is uncertain what to do and has approached you today for the first time for your advice. He produces accounts for the past two years to 31 March 1992 and 31 March 1993.

You have been given the information in Figures 8.4 and 8.5 regarding the company's account covering the past 12 months:

Analysis

A   Personal background

1. Turnover suggests a 'small' company: Mr James is probably a good engineer but low on financial ability.

2. Two good opportunities:
    (a) buy his council house,
    (b) invest in new machinery with a definite sales boost.

B   Past financial record

	1992	1993
1. *Capital base*	27,800	29,300

This shows a slight increase only, but due to retained profit.

Gearing	NIL	NIL
	27,800	29,300

This suggests that it would seem appropriate to contact the loan givers should a good opportunity arise.

2. *Fixed asset investment*

	1993
Net Value at start	13,200
Less Depreciation for year	(2,600)
	10,600
Net Value at year end	11,300
Therefore Net Purchase	700
% Investment	5

This shows a lack of investment which could be of concern. Will he remain competitive?

3. *Working capital*	1992	1993
Current Ratio	33,900	33,700
	19,300	15,700

In this case 1.8:1, and 2.1:1, which is quite adequate for most manufacturers.

4. *Revenue accounts/profitability*

	1992	1993
Sales	109.4	111.6
Gross Profit	40.5	39.0
GP%	37	35
Less overheads:		
Directors' Remuneration	(10.1)	(8.8)
Depreciation	(3.1)	(2.6)
Others (administration and selling)	(24.9)	(25.1)
% of Sales	22.7	22.5
Net Profit before Tax	2.4	2.5

The above shows:
(a) Sales – no progress, really a backward trend.
(b) Gross Profit – falling margins on 'falling' Sales give great concern.
(c) Overheads – show control, but only by a reduced living standard, and falling depreciation (a bad sign).
(d) Net Profit – provides insufficient retentions to invest in better fixed assets.

	£
Present balance	4,100 credit
Debit turnover (value of cheques, etc. drawn on the account)	126,000
Range	8,700 credit to £1,200 credit
Average balance	4,300 credit

Figure 8.4   John James Precision Engineering Ltd: company data

Figure 8.5   John James Precision Engineering Ltd

		Balance Sheets as at 31 March		
		1992		**1993**
	£	£	£	£
Fixed Assets				
Plant and Machinery		9,100		8,200
Motor Vehicles		4,100		3,100
		13,200		11,300
Current Assets				
Cash/Bank	6,400		5,600	
Debtors	22,900		24,000	
Stock/Work-in-Progress	4,600		4,100	
	33,900		33,700	
Current Liabilities				
Trade Creditors	9,900		8,300	
Other Creditors	9,400		7,400	
Directors' Loans	16,000		15,600	
	35,900		31,300	
Net Current Assets (liabilities)		(2,000)	2,400	
Net Tangible Assets		£11,200		£13,700
Financed by:				
Share Capital		100		100
Profit and Loss		11,100		13,600
		£11,200		£13,700
Sales		109,400	111,600	
Gross Profit		40,500	39,000	
Net Profit		2,400	2,500	
After directors' remuneration		10,100	8,800	
Depreciation		3,100	2,600	

C   Proposition (and Risk to the Bank)

How much:	What for:	How long:
£25,000	New Machine	On loan over 5 years

Acceptable, but is it enough? (Will more Working Capital, or better motor vehicles be needed?)

The future gearing

$$\frac{25,000 + \text{any Working Capital}}{13,700 + 15,600}$$

In this case probably low geared and acceptable for this good quality customer.

Security to support the gearing

Unlimited Debenture
a   which picks up: Plant and

	Machinery	$(8,200 + 25,000) \times 20\%$	say =	6,640
	Motor Vehicles	$3,100 \times 20\%$	say =	600
	Debtors	$24,000 \times 50\%$	say =	12,000
				19,240
			=	

Joint and Several
b   Guarantee with 1st
mortgage support
(house subject to a 3   = unlimited
year Council clawback)

Key man insurance on
c   the directors

Note: Security is only taken for control.

D   Projections (repayment of the bank)

(a) *The charges* (Year 1)	£
Capital Repayment	5,000
Interest @ say 15%	3,750 max.
Arrangement Fee 1%	250
To find	9,000

(b) *The budgets*

Sales Existing Business	110.0
New Contracts, 12 × £7,000	84.0
Gross Profit	68.3
GP%	35

Less Directors' Remuneration	(12.0)	say
Depreciation	(7.6)	say
Others, Administration and Selling (see notes)	(34.0)	say
Bank Charges (Interest + Arrangement fee)	(4.0)	
	10.7	

Interest cover = $\dfrac{10.7 + 4.0}{4.0}$ = 3 times cover which is considered adequate.

Capital repayment (see Figure 8.6)

Figure 8.6   John James Precision Engineering Ltd: budgeted cash flow statement for year ended 19..

		£000
(1)	Operating Profit	14.7
	Add Depreciation	7.6 say
	Stock Increase	(3.1)
	Debtor Increase	(18.3)
	Creditor Increase	12.0
(2)	Interest Paid	(4.0)
(3)	Corporation Tax paid	Nil say
(4)	Fixed Assets Bought	(25.0)
(5)	Loans taken	25.0
	Loans repaid	(5.0)
	Improvement in Bank Balances	3.9

Capital Repayment = $\dfrac{3.9 + 5.0}{5.0}$

= 1.78 : 1   which may seem a little lower than the 2.0 : 1 which banks normally expect

E   Decision

From our tests:

(a) Background low on financial skills – bank in credit but business failing!
(b) Past financial record static at best, and will plummet if the £3000 turnover monthly is lost.
(c) Risk to the bank gearing low, and just enough security.
(d) Repayment of the bank can easily be met on the projected sales (is the extra £ 7000 certain and who is the debtor?)

We lend subject to debtor knowledge, and would prefer Mr James' accountants' budgets, showing all overheads (fixed, semi-variable and variable). It is a wonderful chance to get this business going again (new machinery and a higher turnover).

Notes on the case

(1) The 'size' of the Company is indicated by the turnover, £100,000 or £2,000 a week which is very small – one or two workers only, where Mr James must cover all aspects *buying, selling, overhead control, finance* and all *management duties*. The 'stay in credit at the Bank and use old machinery' approach does not impress.
(2) The accounts show that the business is going nowhere. If the large customer pulls out £36,000 of the turnover (12 × £3000), he'll surely be under the breakeven point. *He must modernise his machinery.*
(3) The proposition is about the business *not the house*, as correction of profit levels in the former, will lead to ease of purchase of the latter.
(4) Security can then include the house. Any council tenant buying his rented house usually receives an excellent discount due to years of paying rent. *(One stipulation is that if it is sold within 3 years then a proportionate clawback of the discount will be made,* more in the 1st year less in the 3rd year.) This clause effects the bank's security value for 3 years.
(5) The debit turnover of £126,000 with a nominal range of account balance is supposed to give you an estimate of the *credit turnover*, i.e. Sales, so as to construct the budget:
(a) Assume debit turnover = credit turnover – due to low range of movement on the account.
(c) *Takings will include VAT.*
(d) Takings × $\frac{40}{47}$ = Sales ex VAT (sales in the Trading Account are always without VAT)

$£126,000 \times \dfrac{40}{47} = £107,234$, (rounded to) £110,000

(6) The historical 'other' overheads are about 22.5%. Applying this to £194,000 of projected sales gives £43,650 But this presupposes that all these overheads are *fully variable*, which cannot be the case for Administration and Selling expenses (unlike the bulk of Manufacturing expenses). Neither could we insert £25,100, last year's figure, which would assume they were all fixed overheads. The real answer is somewhere between the two figures and to be determined so we have assumed £34,000, a mid-point.

(7) Excellent margins appear to exist, which should put this business right. Mr James will now be able to buy his own home.

Monitoring lending

Using the four lending criteria can enable a bank to distinguish between good and bad lending propositions. However, subsequent to the decision to lend, both internal and external factors may lead to a change in the borrower's ability to repay. Consequently, it is essential for the bank to take an active interest in the borrower, and to monitor his/her continuing ability to repay the debt.

Enquiries will centre around two things:

(a) What are (in the case of businesses) the *actual* sales each month? These will be compared with monthly *budgets* and reasons sought for any *variances*, whether positive or negative.

(b) Management figures. These are the monthly (or quarterly) submission to the bank by the business customer of its itemised working capital (see Figure 8.7):

1. If the total Working Capital is rising on a monthly basis, then this suggests that a profit is being made. Continual falls suggest losses.
2. The level of debtors and stocks indicate the amount the bank can rely on as security where the business is a limited company and where the company has executed a debenture as security for the bank.

	£
	Stocks
	Debtors
less	Creditor
less	*Cash Book* overdraft
=	Working Capital

Figures 8.7   *John James Precision Engineering Ltd: itemised working capital calculations*

3. Whether the 'formula' is being adhered to. This is a form of security, or rather more a safety requirement, as under the terms of the loan the banker may stipulate, for example... 'that at all times the business shall keep its debtors 1.5 times greater than its overdraft, or, keep its stocks and debtors 2.5 times its overdraft'.

To summarise, keeping in touch with its borrower on a regular basis will enable the lenders to receive early warning of any problems, so that it can take action to avert or reduce loss to itself.

4. Corporate credit analysis – a modern approach

Introduction

Lending institutions, until very recently, have based their lending decisions on a subjective assessment of their clients. Banks, for example, who have dealt with their customers over a period of time, and who have lent them the money to buy some of their fixed assets, feel uniquely qualified in this respect. More recently, however, a more systematic analysis of company financial statements has led to a modified approach, in an attempt to enhance the traditional subjective approach.

This modified approach can be characterised in the following four ways:

1. The choice of financial variables for the assessment of company performance.
2. The various issues involved in using financial ratios, which provide the bulk of the financial variables used.
3. Taking care to avoid the duplication of financial information.
4. The evaluation of risk indices using multivariate models.

Of these, 1 and 3 are interlinked, as we shall see.

Choice of financial variables for the assessment of company performance

With very few exceptions, the variables used are *financial ratios*. Trend measures have been used in a few instances, and so have combined variables incorporating several pieces of financial information. The problem is how to select them.

The choice is dictated by the need to represent important aspects of company performance. Traditionally this led to the placing of ratios into groupings incorporating profitability, leverage, liquidity, and activity. This approach was intuitively attractive, as it seemed to help in avoiding the duplication of financial information. Courtis (1978) used this grouping 'approach' to produce his categoric framework, incorporating Profitability, Managerial Performance and Solvency. Several of the subsequent empirical studies in the area have used Courtis' framework as the starting point in their choice of variables.

Courtis used his framework to group 79 financial ratios, having taken a fair amount of trouble to identify them in the first instance. 28 of these ratios were identified 'as possessing some utility in predicting various forms of corporate difficulty'. Interest in predicting corporate difficulty had been stimulated by the work of Beaver (1966) and Altman (1968) in the USA and by Taffler (1982) in the UK. Of the remaining ratios, 34 came from a study of contemporary literature, and 17 were either used in a specific study or sponsored by organisations like investment houses.

During his work, Courtis identified the problem of the duplication of financial information, and appreciated the fact that 'only a small number of financial ratios are needed to capture most of the information'. An outline of his framework is shown in Figure 8.8.

Issues involved in using financial ratios

Ratios have been traditionally used in two ways. One way is to compare a ratio value with some standard or benchmark, to say whether it is high or

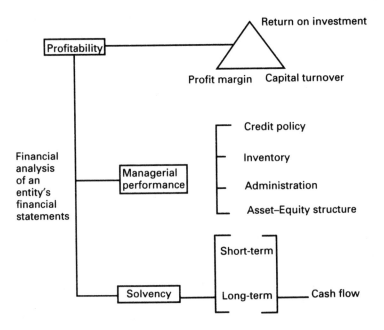

Figure 8.8   Financial ratios categoric framework
Source: Adapted from Courtis (1978).

low. The question then arises of a suitable standard to use. The second way has been to compare ratio values between firms, as a measure of comparative performance.

Returning to this issue of a suitable standard for a particular financial ratio, it is important to examine the statistical distribution in the first instance. Using MINITAB, for example, it is an easy matter to examine the relevant histogram. This is important, because there is a tendency to use the industry or sector average value as a benchmark. If the distribution is reasonably symmetrical, this may be all right. If, on the other hand, the distribution is characterised by the presence of one or more extreme values, which would distort the calculation of the average, then the median may be a more appropriate benchmark or standard to use. It goes without saying that the particular ratios, and their benchmarks, which are being used, need to remain confidential. Once knowledge of a particular benchmark becomes widespread, then firms wishing to present their results in a favourable light will take steps to adjust their results accordingly. There is plenty of evidence to support this.

In considering the way in which ratios are used to compare the performance of firms, one has to appreciate that what one really wishes to do is to compare numerator values, the effect of size having been taken into account. In other words, for a ratio y/x, x represents some measure of size, e.g. total assets. To ensure that the comparison is a fair one, one needs to examine the relationship between y and x values for a random sample of firms, from the industry or sector. The easiest way to do this is to regress y values against x values, assuming a linear relationship. The result when plotted will look similar to that in Figure 8.9.

A problem arises if the intercept α is significant. Dividing $y = \alpha + \beta x$ by x, one obtains the relationship $y/x = \alpha/x + \beta$. Then the term α/x will tend to distort comparative performances. Specifically, if the size of the firm, represented by x, is comparatively small, then the term α/x will be comparatively large, and vice versa. If this is the case, then a firm whose ratio values lies above the line $y = \alpha + \beta x$ can be said to be performing better than the average, and leave it at that.

Avoiding the duplication of financial information

There are two issues to consider here. One wishes to represent all the major independent sources of financial information, whilst avoiding possible duplication.

There are many instances where it is important to recognise the possible duplication of information. The presence of multicollinearity in regression analysis is one instance. Accountants quickly appreciate that ratios like

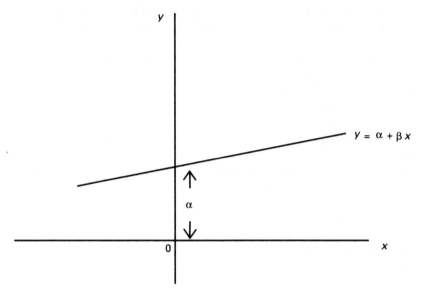

Figure 8.9   Comparing the performance of firm

'return on equity' and 'return on capital employed' are measuring similar aspects. If they need convincing, a correlation analysis, measuring the correlation between two similar ratios, will soon provide the evidence.

Correlation, in fact, provides the background to the best technique to employ. Principal component analysis both identifies the independent aspects of financial information, but also evaluates the contribution which these independent aspects make to the overall scene. The independent aspects are known as components or factors.

The studies of Laurent (1979), Pinches *et al.* (1973), and Taffler (1982) are well worth examining. Of these Laurent (1979) is easiest for a non-expert to follow. He set out to identify a small independent set of 45 financial ratios which would account for most of the financial information required. He identified 14 components or factors, of which the leading 10 were found to account for almost 90% of the informational content. He, however, made no attempt to deal with the outliers or extreme ratio values.

Pinches *et al.* (1973) and Taffler (1982) very deliberately set out to take account of outliers, using ad hoc methods. Pinches and his colleagues were working in the USA, whereas Taffler was using UK data. Both identified seven major components. In Taffler's case, the leading five components accounted for about 86% of the informational content.

The conclusion seems to be that provided 'reasonable' steps are taken to alleviate the effect of outliers, principal component analysis will provide an empirical justification, at a point in time, for the choice of a small independent set of ratios to represent most of the informational content. It will also enable one to identify the dimensionality of a possible multivariate model, and a suitable data set for its construction.

Evaluation of risk indices using multivariate models

Currently three different techniques are being used; discriminant analysis, logistic regression and neural networks.

Altman (1968), in talking about the use of Multiple Discriminant Analysis for corporate failure prediction, made the case for the use of multivariate models when he said that

> the primary advantage ... is the potential of analysing the entire variable profile of the objects simultaneously rather than sequentially examining its individual characteristics.

Because the application of neural networks in the area is in its early stages, it seems reasonable, to begin with, to consider the applications of discriminant analysis and logistic regression. The approach adopted will be to consider how the outputs from the two models complement one another, in seeking to establish the creditworthiness of a potential borrower. The real problem, from the lender's point of view, is how to identify potential failure in good time. Current legislation suggests that a warning period of at least three years would be a reasonable benchmark.

Again, from the lender's point of view, there are two types of error; s/he may classify a firm as a good risk, lend, and then the firm fails. Alternatively s/he may decide not to lend where the firm is a good risk. The lender would really like to avoid the first of these errors, and it is to this end that most of the effort is directed.

The discriminant approach

Altman's (1968) model is typical of the z-score models which have been constructed. His model

$$z = 1.2X_1 + 1.4X_2 + 3.3X_3 + 0.6X_4 + 1.0X_5$$

utilised data from company accounts to evaluate ratios X_1 to X_5. Of course X_3, Earnings before Interest and Taxes/Total Assets, and X_5, Sales/Total Assets, seemed to contribute most to the discriminating process. Identifying the relative importance of individual model variables has been one of the problems in using discriminant analysis.

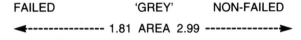

Figure 8.10   Z-score for discriminant analysis

When the z-score model was applied to the firms forming the database for the model, the z-scores fell into the ranges shown in Figures 8.10

Firms whose scores fell in the 'grey' area were a mixture of failed and continuing firms, and those with scores below 1.81 all failed subsequently. Clearly, if one wishes to avoid lending to a firm which is likely to fail, a 'cut-off' value for z would be nearer 2.99 than 1.81.

Up to this point in time, no theory of corporate failure has emerged. Without such a theory, successive researchers have developed their methodologies on the basis of accumulated wisdom. Two of the methodological issues are of interest:

1. the selection of failed and non-failed firms, and
2. the variables employed.

The selection of failed and non-failed firms   Having assembled data on a sample of failed firms – a major task – two alternative approaches may be used. One is to pair failed and non-failed firms, using a set of criteria. The other is to use a sample of non-failed firms which is larger.

If one pairs firms, one may do so on the basis of industry, size and accounting year. The advantage in pairing is that inter-firm differences in, for example, industry and size should not affect the magnitude of the independent discriminating variables. The disadvantage is that it eliminates any predictive power these factors may have had. Using a larger sample of non-failed firms ensures that the sample is more representative of the whole population, and is statistically more attractive. The non-failed firms may be selected by a stratified sampling procedure, to include loss-making firms as well as healthy or sound ones.

The variables employed   There are three issues to be considered, namely the choice of financial variables, the possible duplication of financial information, and the statistical distributions of the variables. These have been considered in a general manner already, but in the context of the discriminant approach a little more detail is required.

The choice of variables, usually financial ratios, has developed pragmatically. Effectiveness in previous studies, and popularity in the literature are often cited as reasons for the choice. The categorical framework of financial ratios developed by Courtis (1978), as we have already seen, provides another useful starting point.

Because data for the construction of corporate failure models needs to be gathered over several years, and also because one wishes to use the models for a reasonable period, it is necessary to consider the use of principal component analyses over several years. In other words, one wishes to examine the stability of the financial patterns over a relevant period. The empirical work of Pinches *et al.* (1973) sets the scene. Pinches *et al.* set out to

(1)   develop empirically-based classifications of financial ratios and (2) measure the long-term stability/change in these classifications over the 1951–1969 time period.

They concluded that

meaningful empirically-based classifications can be determined and that the composition of these groups are reasonably stable over time. It is this stability that can justify the continued use of multivariate models, apart from the very obvious justification of model performance.

The statistical distributions of the variables are important because of the requirements of multiple discriminant analysis (MDA). A particular requirement of MDA is that the variable should be multivariate normal in distribution. In practice, approximate marginal normality of the individual variables is all that can be reasonably achieved. There are various ad hoc approaches which may be used, for example, taking logarithms, some of which are reasonably systematic. Taffler (1982) includes a description of the winsorisation approach in dealing with outliers. Tests based on assessments of skewness and kurtosis are principally used to check for normality.

The logit approach

Deciding between discriminant and logit models to assess corporate viability, depends largely on the intended use. If only a dichotomous classification is required, then discriminant analysis should be adequate. On the other hand, for a banker making a commercial loan decision, or an investor where the assessment of commercial risk is important, then logit models may better 'fit the bill'. There is empirical evidence (Martin, 1977) to show that logit models provide better probability estimates, for example of failure, from the same data than discriminant models.

Zavgren (1985) and Keasey and McGuinness (1990) both referred to the work of Pinches *et al.* (1973) to justify the choice of variables used in their analyses. Keasey and McGuinness (1990), working in the UK, extended their dataset to make it more suitable for use in the UK.

Apart from identifying potential corporate failures, Keasey and McGuinness (1990) set out 'to determine which financial variables were significant in explaining the financial failure of UK industrials'. To help them, they were able to use the ability of logit models to assess the relative importance of individual model variables. This approach is reasonable as long as the variable set is a representative one. The only problem is that the classification results were rather disappointing. This can only mean that the original variable data set did not contain a sufficient number of good discriminators.

Subsequent empirical research – as yet unpublished – used a much more comprehensive data set to build a series of models, which helped to identify, what seems to be, a rather better set of discriminating variables.

5. Conclusions

In practice, one suspects that the traditional approach may continue to be used for 'small' loans. In addition, as knowledge of the modern approach becomes more widespread, and with the benefit of the very extensive databases available to lending institutions, some comparison between the traditional and the modern approach may help to provide the best answers. The approaches are really complementary, and should be viewed in this way.

Further reading

Altman, E.I., 'Financial Ratios, Discriminant Analysis and the Prediction of Corporate Bankruptcy', *Journal of Finance,* 23(4) (September 1968), pp. 589–609.

Beaver, W.H., 'Financial Ratios as Predictors of Failure', Empirical Research in Accounting, *Selected Studies,* Supplement to the *Journal of Accounting Research,* 5, pp. 71–111.

Courtis, J.K., 'Modelling a Financial Ratios Categoric Framework', *Journal of Business, Finance and Accounting,* 5(4) (1978), pp. 371–95.

Hutchinson, H.H. and Dyer, L.S., *Interpretation of Balance Sheets* (Chartered Institute of Bankers/Bankers Books, 1990).

Keasey, K. and McGuiness, P., 'The Failure of UK Industrial Firms for the Period 1976–1984, Logistic Analysis and Eutropy Measures', *Journal of Business, Finance and Accounting,* 17(1) (1990), pp. 119–35.

Laurent, C.R., 'Improving the Efficiency and Effectiveness of Financial Ratio Analysis', *Journal of Business, Finance and Accounting,* 6(3) (1979), pp. 401–13.

Martin, D., 'Early Warnings of Bank Failure', *Journal of Banking and Finance* (1977), pp. 249–67.

Pinches, G.E., Mingo, K.A. and Caruthers, J.K., 'The Stability of Financial Patterns in Industrial Organisations', *Journal of Finance* (June 1973), pp. 389–96.

Rouse, C.N., *Applied Lending Techniques* (Chartered Institute of Bankers/Bankers Books, 1991).

Rouse, C.N., *Bankers' Lending Techniques* (Chartered Institute of Bankers/Bankers Books, 1991).

Sawyer, A., Lending: *Q & A Workbook* (Department of Financial Services, University of Central England, 1994).

Taffler, R.J., 'Forecasting Company Failure in the UK using Discriminant Analysis and Financial Ratio Data', *Journal of the Royal Statistical Society,* A, 145, Part 3, pp. 342–58.

Zavgren, C.V., 'Assessing the Vulnerability to Failure of American Industrial Firms: A Logistic Analysis', *Journal of Business, Finance and Accounting,* 12(1) (1985), pp. 19–45.

CHAPTER 9

The Problem of Costs and Cost Identification

John Davis

1. Introduction

This chapter uses the banking sector to illustrate the problems of low profits and problems of strategic and operational profitability, together with the response made by banks towards improving their profitability relative to the new competitive environment in which they operate. The financial services industry in the UK has moved since the 1980s from a traditional domestic retailing service centred around the main High Street banks to a competitive industry where the retail credit market is dominated by a number of leading players with new entrants to the market jostling for position. This increased competition has been partly the result of the growth of the market for retail credit, but is closely connected to a complex mixture of other factors arising from political, commercial and cultural changes in the 1980s. These changes are detailed in more detail below, but in essence they arise from the increase in consumer credit, the diversity of the banking industry, a generally low industry profitability, an expensive product delivery system and a general problem of cost identification in an industry where many costs are fixed and the products sold are intangible.

2. The significant rise in consumer credit

A major social change in the 1980s was in the growth of consumer credit. The following statistics indicate the growth of this business, and reflect the changes which took place in British High Streets during those years. This can be clearly seen in Table 9.1.

This rapid expansion of consumer credit was a reflection of the high profile given to the retailing sector, and the decade of the 1980s could be seen in

Table 9.1   The rise in UK consumer credit, 1982–92

Year	New credit advances £ million	Credit card turnover £ million
1982	15,791	2,384
1983	18,891	3,153
1984	22,307	3,955
1985	26,112	5,032
1986	30,212	6,287
1987	36,370	8,156
1988	42,707	9,418
1989	48,709	10,816
1990	52,878	11,970
1991	53,765	12,686
1992	52,927	13,064

Sources: *Financial Statistics* (London: CSO); British Bankers' Association, *Annual Abstract of Statistics* (1993).

retrospect as the decade of retailing. Gardner and Sheppard (1989) admirably summarises how in the (mid) 1980s a customer passing from a retail shop such as Next and entering the High Street bank next door would in effect be stepping back a decade or more in attitudes to customer services, decor, atmosphere and so forth; it was only at the end of the decade and early 1990s that this attitude began to change. The major visible changes from the customers' point of view were less 'back room' staff on view, and the general opening up of the premises to give a much greater proportion of the floor space back to the customers with more automated teller machines (ATMs) available for use. This change in the role of banking is examined in the next section.

3.   The complicated business of retail banking and the diverse financial services industry

Banks are different in a way that is not readily apparent to the lay observer; they actually own the whole process of delivering credit. Credit is created by banks through the concept of lending multiples. Banks invent their products (for example, an account aimed at the young saver), market it, sell it, and withdraw it from the market at a time that they control. This complete vertical integration has implications for the management of profitability. If we were to observe a traditional manufacturing firm, the firm developing a new product would generally have some interaction with outside organisations – for instance, a manufacturer would deal with its suppliers – and the process of adding value would be identified in terms of labour inputs, added materials and services. This process of adding value is not directly observable in retail financial services, although some costs are subcontracted, credit scoring as part of card processing being a good example.

The other major changes that have taken place in the financial services industry to create increased diversity have arisen because of the impact of deregulation and the creation of an open market in financial services. Legislation such as the Building Societies Act 1986 and the Financial Services Act 1986 have had the effect of opening up the industry to create a level playing field. The business of banking is much more than that of taking deposits. Banks enjoy (or suffer) a much greater range of products or services than building societies. The common factor behind all financial products is that they are *derived products*. (The term 'derived product' is used to describe a service or product which is a stepping-stone to some other form of customer satisfaction.) By encouraging the customer to enter the bank the opportunity is provided to offer to the customer a range of financial products which, being money-based, should be cheap to deliver if not to service.

The problem for the banks is that they do not have monopoly of these services. They operate in probably the most competitive market it is possible to imagine and this competitive market exists because entry to certain sections of it is relatively easy and in some cases cheap. For example, Marks and Spencer have both the stores and the technology (the delivery channel), the customers and, when combined with a good credit rating to obtain low cost funds, can set up selling pension schemes and loans in their stores. Another example of the ease of entry to new financial products is the way banks and building societies have allied themselves with insurance companies to sell products in this area. Lloyds Bank in the first half of 1993 (a recession year when bank profits would be expected to be low) reported UK retail banking profits of £17 million, and profits of Lloyds Abbey Life (the insurance and unit trust arm) £153 million.

Banks are also difficult businesses to define. The concept of banks as they have been known in the past is changing – it is possible to save with an insurance company, open a current account with a building society, purchase insurance at the local high street bank and buy investments (gilt-edged securities) at the post office. Furthermore, you can obtain a loan from your local branch of Marks & Spencer and it is possible to obtain a credit card from Ford and General Motors. Banks, then, may be viewed as operating in an area which is extremely broad, has many competitors and is very fast moving. The business of banking is also closely tied to the prevailing economic climate and, as an industry, suffers when its customers suffer. A good example of this is the property slump of the late 1980s when many banks suffered heavy losses because of their high exposure to property risk.

4. Low bank profitability and the problem of the financial services industry's cost structure

The first problem to be addressed is, what makes banks special? In a deregulated financial services industry anyone can take part in providing credit and money transmission services and, in fact, many non-bank firms who sell frequently provide credit to their customers, albeit at zero interest. However, the usual rationale for this credit provision is for operational efficiency and marketing reasons rather than from the desire to emulate banks. The banks have developed economies of scale in money transmission and in dealing and other activities, and it is information costs that give them a competitive edge as financial intermediaries. This is evidenced from the changing role of building societies arising from the Building Societies Act 1986, as a result of which building societies in the High Street now provide many of the same services as banks and are themselves becoming participators in the London money markets. Building societies face problems in joining the major High Street banks because of problems of scale and their need to accumulate information. This can be evidenced from Abbey National, who now enjoy plc status but still only operate in the traditional arena of personal finance, the corporate sector being as yet avoided even though, with an asset base of £36 billion, Abbey National is comparable in size to Lloyds Bank with assets of £55 billion.

Building societies and banks share many attributes. First, as previously noted, their products are merely a stepping stone to another consumer preference. People generally do not aspire to own a loan or have a mortgage, but rather wish to purchase a new boat or a house suitable to their personal needs and, from the viewpoint of the customer, banks and building societies provide services which are functionally the same. This perspective of banking products as derived products creates major problems for bank marketing which, in the 1980s and 1990s, was aimed at 'lifestyle marketing'.

Secondly, banks are financial intermediaries. This means that a major part of their revenues is based on a differential between their costs in the money markets and their selling prices in the High Street, known as 'spread'. Unfortunately for banks, this key area of their activities has seen a steady erosion of margins as international competition has narrowed bank spreads (Table 9.2). The link between deteriorating spreads and margins and the economic policy environment is discussed in more detail in Chapter 4.

Despite their large size (all the main High Street banks are in the FTSE 100 index), bank profitability in terms of return on assets remains stubbornly low. If the four major High Street retail banks are taken individually, it can be seen that the post-tax return on average assets remains very small. Table 9.3 shows the average return for the four High Street banks since 1986.

In broad terms, all the High Street banks are less profitable in 1992 than they were in 1986. They do not control the market, which is becoming more

Table 9.2   Domestic bank spreads, 1986 and 1990

	1986 %	1990 %	% change
Barclays	2.9	2.0	−31
Lloyds	3.9	2.9	−26
Midland	3.3	2.0	−39
Nat West	3.1	2.1	−32

Source: *Bank of England Quarterly Bulletin* and *Annual Reports* of the relevant banks.

Table 9.3   Post-tax percentage return on average total assets, 1986–92

Year	Lloyds %	Midland %	Nat West %	Barclays %
1986	1.10	0.46	0.80	0.90
1987	(0.48)	(0.94)	0.50	0.30
1988	1.27	0.74	1.00	0.90
1989	(0.87)	(0.35)	0.20	0.40
1990	0.67	(0.34)	0.20	0.30
1991	0.79	(0.07)	0.00	0.20
1992	0.97	0.17	0.20	(0.20)

Losses are shown in brackets.
Source: *Annual Report* of the relevant banks.

sophisticated, with customers having access to up-to-the-minute financial information, and the banks are finding that the greater amount of market information is altering the pattern of their profitability; this may be simply summarised as the erosion of the interest income on which banks have traditionally relied. For example, Midland, except for 1988, had a run of losses until 1992. In any other industry, this would be regarded as the most abject failure.

Banks, until the mid-1980s, were viewed by governments as vehicles for the extension of government macroeconomic policy, and so to some extent were protected from the cold wind of competition; but these losses, in a deregulated market for financial services, have meant that banks will have to change dramatically to survive. Up until deregulation, such changes would not have been considered necessary as banks have been in the business of banking for 200 years and have made a very successful business doing it. This then is the new scenario of retail banking: spreads are being reduced and there is greater competition resulting from deregulation. How should banks react to these changes?

5. Retail branch banking is very expensive

The business of banking in the 1990s encompasses much more than the traditional activities such as the taking of deposits and making of loans with which banks have been traditionally associated. This diversity of operations, to maximise their market share in financial services, has had significant effects on bank profitability. One major effect of this multiplicity of products and services has been that, since the 1980s, bank cost ratios have remained stubbornly high. The high cost of delivering traditional retail banking in the UK may be attributed in general terms to the following main reasons.

Branch networks are too large and expensive

That the banks have recognised the long-term nature of these costs may be seen from the changes in the branch network over the decade to 1992. There was an overall fall in the number of branches of one-fifth over the decade and, except for small niche market banks, all the main high street retail banks have closed marginal branches and concentrated the business into larger branches. Midland Bank have been most active in this field possibly as a result of the move by the group in setting up First Direct, a completely telephonic and postal bank. Midland, strategically, should be the first of the major retail banks to reduce its cost base. Table 9.4 shows how banks have started to adjust to the changing competitive environment by reducing the size of the branch network.

Banks may be perceived as only having two kinds of cost: information costs and transaction costs. The traditional information gathering costs were based on account and ledger records, and because of the labour-intensive nature of both of these activities, gathering information and dealing in investments, the regional/branch network developed. In an age of technology such systems are partly redundant. Whilst there is a need for local intelligence, the accumulated records of the main High Street banks are now computerised and creditworthiness of all current customers and even of potential customers is easily assessed, either from existing databanks or from credit scoring activities. The bank branch network is becoming a liability for the large High Street retail banks; these banks are tied into computer systems up to 20 years old, and the introduction of new computer systems is inherently more difficult in a large branch network than in a smaller organisation, not least because there is more institutional inertia than in smaller companies (see Chapter 5).

Table 9.4   *British banks* and building society branch size, 1982 and 1992*

| | Number of branches | | % change |
	1982	1992	
Abbey National	664	680	+2.4
Bank of Scotland	567	409	−27.9
Barclays	2,959	2,281	−22.9
Lloyds	2,284	1,884	−17.5
Midland	2,441	1,716	−29.7
Nat West	3,253	2,541	−21.9
Royal Bank of Scotland	901	663	−29.7
TSB	1,602	1,369	−14.5
Co-operative	73	106	+45.2
Yorkshire Bank	207	266	+28.5
Total Retail Banks	14,951	11,885	−20.5

*Excludes building society agencies and Standard Chartered Bank, which does not service the retail bank market.
Source: British Bankers' Association, *Annual Abstract of Statistics* (1993).

Competition from other financial institutions, both bank and non-bank

More important than size in the growth of the market shown in Table 9.1 is that of the constituent components. Table 9.5 illustrates how the market share of differing institutions has changed over the decade from 1982 to 1992.

It can be seen that in this decade the banks managed to hold on to their market share (by aggressive marketing of credit cards); the main losers were retailers, who saw their market share halved.

The range of products on offer and the associated staffing costs

Building societies have a far more restricted product range than banks, mainly due to their absence from the corporate sector. Whilst the societies participate in taking deposits, the granting of loans, money transmission and payment services, that is effectively the limit of their product range. Banks offer a whole further raft of products ranging from executorship, share dealing, tax planning, private banking, corporate finance and many more. The result is a staffing structure which is large compared to building societies and with a resultant cost. Table 9.6, is simplistic, but illustrates the gulf between banks and building societies.

There is a managerial difference: building societies generally have fewer staff but one manager may control up to four branches. This is in stark

Table 9.5   UK consumer credit,* new advances, 1982 and 1992

Institution	1982 £ million	1982 %	1992 £ million	1992 %	Change %
Banks	12,602	80	42,974	81	+1
Building societies	NIL		743	2	–
Non-bank credit	1,278	8	5,024	9	+1
Insurance companies	317	2	1,581	3	+1
Retailers	1,594	10	2,605	5	–5
Total credit	15,791	100	52,927	100	

*'Consumer credit' is broadly defined as all non-commercial lending other than to finance the purchase of land or buildings.
Source: *Financial Statistics* (London: CSO).

Table 9.6   Comparative staff costs, 1992

	Woolwich Building Society 1992	Lloyds Bank 1992
Employees	6,812	45,427
Number of branches	523	1,884
Employees per branch	13	24

Source: *Annual Accounts.*

contrast to the traditional bank branch manager, and the banks' response to this has been to move more of the back office staff to the regional office, move to banking clusters to obtain economies of scale, and close branches where business is not seen to be economic. In this way, banks continue to reduce their staffing costs in order to compete with the societies. The wide product portfolio of banks, however, and especially operations in the corporate sector, will continue to need more staff than building societies. There is a further problem for banks – their size itself is a problem when compared to other institutions. Building societies, because of their smaller branch network, can develop new information systems more quickly and most importantly can change them more quickly. Banks suffer the inertia that large systems bring; in a similar way to turning a super tanker around, it takes longer, and more care is needed to avoid hazards. Building societies have always been committed to new technology and generally writing in pass books has been obsolete for five years or more. This greater competition, especially with interest bearing current accounts, has had the effect of decreasing the traditional bank reliance on interest as a source of profit. This would not matter if every other financial institution suffered costs to the same proportion, but they do not. Strategically, banks have an insurmountable problem with the current method of product and service delivery, because building societies deliver their products much more cheaply. Table 9.7 illustrates the high cost of the banking system compared to building societies.

This is not a new problem. To take Midland Bank as an example, the cost–income ratio for 1984–92 never fell below 70%, and it was this persistently high cost ratio, when compared to the building societies, that contributed to Midland's decision to set up the First Direct telephone bank, to avoid the cost of the branch network and to bring cost ratios down. Branches of the main banks have graced prime city and town centre sites, often with prestigious architectural designs, so that customers can see and be reassured by their solidity and permanence. These branches represented the current technology at the time of their construction which was based around paper and the associated high labour intensity of record keeping. Large numbers of staff required a management structure of commensurate size and, because probity was important, staff were needed for policing the bank systems. Modern banking systems do not need the quantity of staff or even the same staff with the same traditional skills and there is no reason at all to house them in the same building that was used 100 years ago. The cost ratios, which remain stubbornly high for banks, are the legacy of the branch network with the associated high premises and staffing costs. To reduce these costs implies that banks will adopt new delivery systems for their products. Such systems could be telephonic such as First Direct, but given new interactive services on satellite television and the integration of technologies within computing, telecommunications and information

Table 9.7   Operating costs as a percentage of operating income, 1992

	1992 Woolwich Building Society £ million	1992 Lloyds Bank £ million
Interest income	462	2,226
Other income	157	1,767
Total income	619	3,993
Operating expenses	314	2,458
Operating expenses as % of total income	50.7	61.6

Source: *Annual Accounts.*

technology, all banks will be forced by strategic cost pressures to radically alter the method of service delivery to customers.

6. The problem of costing intangible products

Banks basically incur two kinds of costs, transactions costs and information costs. Transaction costs include money transmission through the clearing systems, risk management in the money markets and dealing costs. Information costs include credit scoring, record keeping, market research and so forth. The problem for banks is that many of these costs are not readily identifiable, as many costs are jointly incurred and cannot be (and possibly may never be) separately identifiable. A ready example of this is the cost of central computing facilities. Many functions benefit from this activity yet it is difficult to attribute the cost of this service to specific tasks. Many such information costs incurred by banks are similar to this and are fixed in nature and are near-impossible to allocate to products or service activities. Information processing is notoriously expensive and continuing to rise in importance and cost, yet accountants cannot devise any methodology for cost allocation which satisfies all users. Staff costs in banks account for up to 56% of operating expense (Lloyds Bank, 1992) yet without accurate measurement of staff time in servicing products and customers, the £1.4 billion Lloyds spent in 1992 may possibly be allocated to divisions of service, but there will always be some arbitrary allocations to specific services and products.

This is not a new accounting problem and accountants have usually solved the fixed overhead problem by ignoring it and adopting an economic marginal cost approach, or using market cost comparisons to gauge whether costs attributed to products meet known industry norms. Most recently, the banking community has borrowed from the manufacturing sector in adopting a costing technique known as activity-based costing.

Accounting textbooks and most management accounting literature are based firmly in a tradition of manufacturing, and the service sector has tended to be ignored. There are many reasons for this, mainly historical. General Motors had sophisticated product costing systems in place in the 1920s because of the complexity of their products, together with an awareness of the importance of product profitability, but also because there was a recognition that shareholder needs could only be satisfied with rigorous financial planning. These costing systems identified automobile costs to the nearest cent and the costs were continuously monitored. Competition forced many companies to behave in a similar manner, and a generally accepted methodology of product costing using a standardised terminology (such as direct cost, indirect cost, allocation cost, cost and work centres, etc.) developed. These ideas were formalised through accounting literature and specialist accounting organisations such as the National Accounting Association in the United States and the Institute of Cost and Works

Accountants (now the Chartered Institute of Management Accountants) in the UK, who came into being to formalise professional standards.

However, the bias towards manufacturing remains. The financial services industry, although it is not the same as motor manufacturing, has perceived similarities. These are high fixed costs, standardised products, a high service element, problems of labour categorisation, etc., and it is easy to see how the product costing techniques from manufacturing could be applied to the financial services industry. An important development for banks was the development of segmental marketing in the 1980s. Because of the vertical integration of the industry it can develop new products quickly and, depending on market conditions, withdraw or expand their scope as market conditions change. An example of this is the Midland Bank which in 1991, following poor financial results, withdrew certain bespoke accounts such as 'Orchard' to concentrate on more core business. Whether there were other costs of withdrawal not measured, such as loss of customers to other banks, is not known.

The low profitability of retail banking being based on low margins and high turnover creates problems for the banks, and a good example is how to identify on the one hand product profitability and on the other customer profitability. The problem is further compounded by the fact that, for retail banking, disaggregation of costs is very difficult. Some banks, for instance Barclays, have rearranged the front office into specialised staff so that staff dealing with financial products such as mortgages can be distinguished from staff who deal with payment services (fewer and fewer, with ATM machines). In this way, branch costs can (perhaps) be more clearly identified with activities, but many costs remain central, for example, head office costs, computing costs, building costs, etc. This problem of cost identification is further compounded by the falling spreads of commercial retail banks. If this source of profitability cannot be relied on to deliver shareholder wealth, then banks will have to charge for services on the principle that everything has a price, even if the cost of the service cannot be ascertained with any degree of certainty. Table 9.8 illustrates this trend, for example, in the Midland Bank.

Table 9.8   Midland Bank, service delivery costs, 1989 and 1992

	1989		1992	
	£ million	%	£ million	%
Interest income	1,850	58	1,712	52
Other income	1,332	42	1,567	48
Operating income	3,182	100	3,279	100

Source: *Annual Accounts.*

Banks have responded to the problem of overall costs of service delivery and the problem of product cost identification, by strategically investing in new technology, with an associated plan to reduce staff numbers and branches in the long term. Whilst this can only be achieved by automating the cheque clearing system, or replacing it over a number of years, either through a massive expansion of debit cards or automated cheque reading, in the long term competitive profitability has to be maintained. Whilst the strategic thrust is to more automation, banks will have to ensure that all services are financially viable. All banks are reappraising their product and service profitability.

A common approach is to use *activity-based costing* to determine this product viability. Activity-based costing is a modification of absorption costing which has been introduced in manufacturing industry to adjust to the rapidly changing environment that manufactures face, namely, a reduction of the actual 'direct' labour input into the creation of a product and the complementary increase in technology and service labour costs. These changes in manufacturing are the result of changes in production technology, for example assembly robotics, numerical control machining, automated quality control procedures and so on. In these circumstances the old-fashioned cost accounting analyses of 'productive' and 'non-productive' labour becomes meaningless and therefore irrelevant. Furthermore, as automation reduces the overall numbers employed, compared to older technologies, the nature of the work performed also changes. People involved in manufacturing may well be a combination of production workers, inspectors, material controllers and so forth.

Activity-based costing, (and this is not the place to explain the methodology in full) focuses on the activities that *cause costs to happen*. Activity-based costing is based on the view that managers do not control costs, they control activities. Activities must thus be measured to make costs meaningful. This is a view proposed by Porter (1985). The thrust of his argument is that in traditional accounting measurement, accounting information flows do not match management information flows, partly because the things accountants class as 'overhead' are in fact important profit generators, for instance, service or quality costs. In the terminology of activity-based costing, these activities are called 'cost drivers'. Costs are allocated to cost pools (a service, for instance, which may not necessarily correspond to cost centres or work centres) and activity cost driver-based rates are calculated by comparing the level of activity and applying the rates to determine product costs.

The essential difference between the older averaging method of cost determination and activity-based costing is the identification of cost drivers. To provide an illustration, the role of material handling, an example borrowed from manufacturing, will suffice. Activity-based costing studies undertaken so far have revealed the high cost of material handling which can take place in manufacturing, moving stock from one machine to another, in and out of stores, to and from inspection, into packing, rectification and so on. Under conventional costing, this high cost of material handling remains hidden, being included in several departmental overhead rates. Under activity-based costing, the true high cost of handling is revealed and apportioned to products on a more "realistic" basis. Focusing on what causes costs to happen, proponents of activity-based costing suggest that a fairer product cost may be determined. A major factor behind activity-based costing is the rise of high powered low cost computing. Accounting analysis is now easier to perform using automated spreadsheets and databases, whereby information can be downloaded directly from the mainframe computer on demand.

These developments have not passed unnoticed by the financial services industry. Many of the conditions in modern manufacturing which have led to the exploration of activity-based costing have been prevalent for years within the banking industry, for instance, a very high fixed cost, a flexible labour force, automated production, a wide product range, intense domestic and international competition, and most importantly the high level of support costs needed to support the branch and product network. As yet, there is little evidence of whether the adoption of the activity-based costing approach will deliver higher shareholder value through identification of high cost areas or better pricing structures, because the methodology is new and little has been published. Sephton and Ward (1990) suggest three reasons for the adoption of activity-based costing:

1. A better understanding of cost drivers, as changes in the level of business can be assessed both for direct product-related activities and the link between products and customers.
2. Product costs would be more meaningful because high cost activities would be identified. For example, high cost activities with a high staff cost content may be suitable for investment with information technology, and an activity-based approach may identify the real cost of complexity in providing financial services instead of aggregating them as overhead burden.
3. Meaningful profitability analysis could be produced building up from product, product group, branch and division.

This activity-based approach may also provide better budgeting, forecasting and performance measurement. Such an approach also lends itself to measuring the profitability of customer relationships by measuring the activity levels created by each customer, the 'real' cost of each client (especially corporate clients, the heavy users of services). This change to relationship banking took a further step forwards towards market segment analysis when the Midland Bank in 1987 formed a UK Corporate Division and set up a chain of 600 corporate banking centres. There is no reason why this approach could not be applied in other areas, the analysis merely being a computer coding problem. Stuart White, Midland's enterprise manager, was quoted in October 1990 as saying:

Segmentation means that customers can go to a local centre where they can see bankers who specialise in the needs of the small or corporate market. The services available through these centres are carefully designed to be appropriate to the particular market. For example, the small trader may want a loan to buy a single delivery van, whereas a larger customer may need finance for a whole fleet of cars.

The problem with such a statement is that this view of segmentations is valid only with appropriate and meaningful analysis of product costs and product profits.

A more radical alternative view is proposed by Porter (1985), who suggests that conventional accounting can lead to incorrect strategies. His alternative view is that firms who wish to achieve or maintain competitive leadership should undertake *value chain analysis*. A 'value chain' is a way of looking at the business holistically, because the accounting information flows often do not match the business information flows within the organisation. Competitive edge, he proposes, is achieved through combinations of favourable industry structure, cost leadership or differentiation. In discussing activity-based costing previously, the importance of measuring activities was emphasised because management manage present and future activities. Porter's proposed value chain analysis views the firm as a series of inter-linked strategically relevant activities, so that the behaviour of the cost relationship of related activities may be understood. Porter's approach is particularly relevant for understanding bank costs because of the emphasis that he places on the supporting activities of a firm, the special services that make for product or service differentiation. Porter, though, is not without critics and, whilst there is a general recognition that support activities (viewed by the accountant as an overhead and therefore somewhat undesirable) are vital to business success, activity-based costing and value chain analysis only describes a company's existing business; nothing can be learned from the accounting system in any form about competitors or about the industry in general.

7. Conclusions

Banks have a major strategic problem, unique to their industry, of having their market share for their services undercut by outsiders to the banking industry who can deliver identical services at lower cost. They have, at the corporate level, to adapt to the new competitive environment to survive. At the same time, traditional services which may have benefited from cross-subsidies are being attacked by specialist firms (such as share shops). Finally, a major source of profit, interest income, has been falling, and continues to fall. From this three-pronged attack the banks are faced with many options. Whichever strategic choice is adopted, there remains the costing problem. Product costing is not an exact science and the allocation problem remains insoluble. From what evidence has been made public, all banks are adopting the activity-based approach and reorganising their internal organisation into business units, so that costs from main business activity types may be identified and better decisions made. Whatever the accounting changes that are made, the long-term decision will be hard. Technology will have a continual effect on employment levels in the industry. Even if they retain a rump branch network, banks will be delivering their products in different ways, possibly using the telephone or cable television systems. The lower costs of entry into banking services may mean new forms of banks, such as using a privatised post office, to provide cash transmission services. Whatever the future, banks will have to change radically from their existing cost structures to survive.

Notes

1. Gardner and Sheppard (1989).
2. Porter (1985).

Further reading

Clarke, T. and Vincent, W., *Banking Under Pressure, Breaking the Chains* (Butterworths, 1989). (A good overview of the changes in banking since the 1980s.)

Chorafas, D.N., *Bank Profitability, From Cost Control to Pricing Financial Products and Services* (Butterworths, 1989). (Good industry view of product costing in banking.)

Drury, C., *Management and Cost Accounting* (Chapman & Hall, 1991). (Good student text on activity-based costing.)

Gardner, C. and Sheppard, J., *Consuming Passions* (Unwin Hyman, 1989). (A good overview of the changes in banking since the 1980s.)

Innes, J. and Mitchell, F., *Activity Based Costing: A Review With Case Studies* (CIMA, 1990). (Good student text on activity-based costing.)

Management Accounting, 'Banks Segment Their Business Services', *Management Accounting (UK)* (October 1990). (Good industry view of product costing in banking.)

Porter, M.E., *Competitive Advantage* (Free Press, 1985). (Rationale and underlying thinking behind activity-based costing.)

Royal, D., 'Are You Sure of Your Costs?', *ABA Banking Journal* (April 1988). (Good industry view of product costing in banking.)

Scapens, R.W., *Management Accounting: A Review of Recent Developments* (Macmillan, 1991). (A broad overview of the changes in management accounting.)

Sephton, T. and Ward, T., 'ABC in Retail Financial Services', *Management Accounting (UK)* (April 1990). (Good student article on activity-based costing.)

CHAPTER 10

Marketing and Corporate Strategies for Financial Institutions

David Deakins and Stephen MacKay

1. Introduction

This chapter will draw together some of the threads that influence corporate strategy that have been dealt with elsewhere in this book, for example the impact of deregulation, financial innovation and new legislation. Any organisation, to be successful, has to respond to the competitive environment in which it operates. This has been particularly important to the formulation of business strategy for financial institutions due to the rapid pace of change in this environment during the last decade. To discuss the formulation of corporate strategy, it is necessary to discuss these external factors, the rapid pace of change and internal influences on policy such as the aims and the aspirations of managers and the response of financial institutions to these factors. The processes that have led to change will be identified, and their consequent impact on marketing and strategy analysed, to determine strategic policy areas and the response of the financial institutions in terms of marketing strategy and techniques employed. Undoubtedly the major influence on strategy has been the rapid pace of developments in the competitive environment.

This chapter will maintain the inter-disciplinary approach, which is one of the themes of the book, by introducing economic theory to analyse the competitive position of the financial institutions. It is possible to identify the reaction of the major institutions within a classical oligopolistic framework, and some recent developments in economic theory will be applied to discuss these reactions.

2.   Corporate strategy

Corporate strategy can be described as the strategic planning of responses to competitive and other pressures from the competitive and legal environment in which the institution operates. Since the planning of strategy is determined by senior management, corporate strategy may be described as 'managerial strategy' or simply, 'business strategy'. Following Porter's seminal work (1980), there are now a number of texts that follow in Porter's footsteps that give detailed analysis of the determination of corporate strategy: (Rothberg, 1981; Grieve-Smith, 1985, Luck, 1989; Johnson and Scholes, 1989). However, the reader may also like to note that Porter was preceded by writers such as Schelling (1960) and Ansoff (1965).

Strategy is formulated from a complex series of factors arising from the external competitive and legal environment and also, internally, through the aspirations and objectives of senior management. Although the aspirations and characteristics of management are important, it is difficult to obtain any hard objective evidence on the importance of different objectives.[1] Managerial objectives will be discussed, but we will concentrate, in the first part of this chapter, on the factors that influence the competitive environment. These shape the competitive strategy of the major institutions. The emphasis is on competition between the banks, building societies and other institutions for retail deposits.

The strategy adopted in response to competitive forces may fall into one of Porter's (1980) three 'generic' competitive strategies: (a) cost leadership, (b) differentiation and (c) focus. Cost leadership is the pursuit of cost reduction in all departments to gain a competitive cost edge over rivals. For financial institutions, differentiation is the diversification into different services. Focus is the concentration of resources on improving one aspect of the organisation, for example meeting the demand from a particular market segment. We shall see later that all three of these strategic responses can be observed when we examine the competitive strategy of the major financial institutions.

3.   Market structure

Competition for financial services fits an oligopolistic framework for analysis, with six major banks and 15 large building societies. However, the key feature of oligopolistic competition is not the number or 'fewness' of firms, but the extent to which each firm has to consider the actions of its rival when formulating strategic decisions. An oligopolistic market structure means that the providers of financial services cannot make decisions in isolation. For example, if a bank makes a strategic decision to alter interest rates or launch a new type of current account or open for longer hours, it must consider its rivals' actions and reactions to this decision. Each operator is interdependent:

Each firm recognises that its best choice depends upon the choices its rivals make. The firms are interdependent, and they are acutely conscious of it. (Scherer, 1980, p. 151)

4. Some applications of theory

In oligopoly, firms' expectations of how rivals will react to strategic decisions becomes crucial. The term used by economic theorists to describe expectations is conjectural variations (*CV*). If providers expect no reaction by rivals to a strategic decision then $CV = 0$, if they expect decisions to be matched, then $CV = 1$. Note that *CVs* refer to expectations only, the actual decisions of rivals may well be different from what is expected. For oligopoly to be modelled there has to be some assumption made on *CVs*. It is the fact that decisions can be different from expectations that makes this form of competition difficult to model. Space limitations restrict us to examining two models that could be applied to the provision of financial services; the kinked demand model and the Cournot duopoly model. There are, however, several other theoretical models of oligopolistic competition and the interested reader should consult a standard text in this area such as Laidler and Estrin (1989) or Koutsoyiannis (1985).

The kinked demand model

This model was developed simultaneously by Hall and Hitch (in the UK) and Sweezy (in the USA) at the end of the 1930s to explain price rigidity in some markets. The model can be used to explain why prices, once set at a particular level, p^*, remain stable. Above p^*, $CV = 0$ and below p^*, $CV = 1$. The model is illustrated in Figure 10.1.

Firms will not increase price above p^* because they believe other firms will not follow a price increase. The relevant (elastic) demand curve is $D1D1$. However, price cuts, below p^* are believed to provoke reactions and firms hold the expectation that price cuts will be matched. The relevant (inelastic) demand curve is $D2D2$. It is possible for one firm to attempt a price reduction to, say, p_1 in the hope of capturing an increased market share represented by q_1. In practice, other firms will follow price cuts and the gain to the individual firm is relatively small (say, in new deposits attracted).

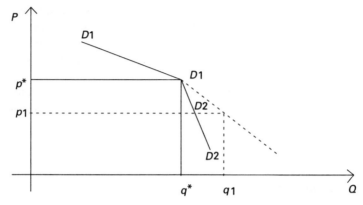

Figure 10.1   The kinked demand model

We could use the model to explain why interest rates (once set by govern-ment intervention) remain stable with little competition between institutions on rates. Indeed the industry is characterised by non-price competition. Institutions prefer to compete in the range of services and facilities offered to customers, and it is noticeable that marketing is geared around non-price forms of competition.

The Cournot duopoly model

There has been a resurgence of interest by Business Economists in the Cournot Duopoly model. It has been described as:

the benchmark model of oligopoly (Shapiro, 1989, p. 330).

The value of the model lies in the prediction of firm behaviour and the provi-sion of a unique equilibrium result, whatever the number of firms. One repre-sentation of the model is shown in Figure 10.2. To simplify the representation of the model we have the financial services industry represented as a duopoly with banks grouped together as one operator and the building societies grouped together as the rival operator. The model can be adapted to deal with an n firm oligopoly.

In the Cournot model, the strategic decision variable is the quantity of service provided. This is only one of a number of simplifying assumptions in the model.[2] $R1$ is the reaction curve of banks to building society decisions on services (for example if building societies provide q_2 then the banks will provide q_1). In the model, both providers operate with $CV = 0$. $R2$ is the building societies' reaction curve to service level provision of the banks.

The model predicts that a stable equilibrium will result at q_1^*, q_2^*. There is no benefit to either provider to deviate from this (it can be shown that profits

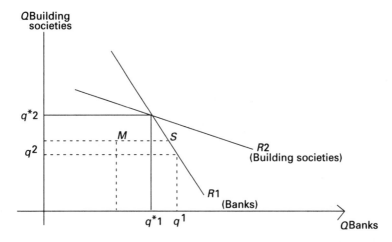

Figure 10.2   The Cournot duopoly model

are lower). Assume *M* represents a joint-profit maximisation level which has been obtained by collusion between banks and building societies, but if *M* is achieved through agreement between the two operators there is an incentive for both providers to renege on the agreement since *individual* profits can be increased if the rival does not respond to a service level increase. For example, at *M* it would pay the banks to increase provision to *S*, so long as there is no reaction from the building societies (i.e. realised $CV = 0$).

5.   The competitive environment

This section will outline some of the more important factors that have created the dynamic competitive environment and account for the rapid pace of change referred to in the Introduction. The oligopolistic structure of the market, mentioned above, belies the relatively competitive behaviour of the main providers. Banks have been forced to react to the increased competition for deposits provided by the increased importance of building societies, who have taken on some traditional banking functions such as money transmission services.

The providers

Following our analysis of the previous section, we can notice distinct periods when the nature of competition was altered between the dominant providers, reflecting their assumptions of their interdependence and how their rivals would react to strategic decisions.

In the 1970s the building societies operated a cartel on interest rates but they could rely on retail deposits for their funds. The banks, although operating relatively expensive money transmission services could rely on raising funds in the wholesale money markets. Also, both institutions traditionally saw different customers as their main profit source. The banks relied on corporate customers and building societies on the mortgage market.

In the 1980s this relative lack of competition for customers was to gradually break down as the banks realised that they could no longer rely on wholesale funds, that they needed to diversify their profit base and entered the mortgage market; and with the eventual break-up of the building societies' cartel. The 1980s also saw a period of merger activity in building societies, with the disappearance of many small, local or regional concerns. There were 95 members of the Building Societies' Association (BSA) in 1992 compared with 471 in 1970. This period of intense merger activity has left the big building societies in a strong position to exploit their large customer base and move into direct competition with banks in areas that the banks have traditionally seen as their own domain. The general effect was to intensify competition. Drake (1989) has commented that the result of these changes were that building societies are 'much more overtly profit orientated than previously'.

The changes that enabled the building societies to move more into direct competition include the deregulation of financial markets and institutions and changes in monetary policy. These two factors are considered below. It might be expected that one of the reasons for the mergers would be economies of scale, these are also considered later. The growth in the importance of building societies and their success in attracting new customers during the 1980s is also reflected in the growth of their deposits, illustrated in Table 10.1.

Table 10.1   The growth in shares and deposits with building societies, 1979–90, £ million

Year	Amount
1979	5,833
1980	7,175
1981	7,082
1982	10,294
1983	10,250
1984	13,249
1985	13,314
1986	11,847
1987	13,564
1988	20,146
1989	17,456
1990	17,855

Source: CSO database, Bath University.

The regulatory framework

We merely note here that changes in the regulatory framework including particularly the Building Societies Act 1986, the Banking Act 1987, and the Financial Services Act 1986, provided the necessary changes and removed restrictive practices that allowed the banks and building societies to compete directly with each other, and freed competition between banks and building societies. The regulatory framework is discussed in more detail in Chapters 2 and 3.

Monetary policy

The election of a Conservative administration in 1979 provided a period of emphasis on monetary policy for the achievement of government objectives of which, of course, the priority has been to control inflation. Three different periods of monetary policy have been identified by Goodhart (1989). From 1979 to 1982 there was a period of tight monetary policy and monetary targeting, from 1982 to 1985 a period of monetary 'pragmatism' and in the period since 1985 a concern with exchange rate mechanisms. The tight monetary policies of the early 1980s were gradually relaxed, and this provided the policy background which saw a remarkable period of growth in the demand for advances in the mid-1980s. Table 10.2 compares the growth in advances provided by banks and building societies in the 1980s. Since 1990, a fourth period of monetary policy

Table 10.2   Banks' and building societies' advances compared, 1980–90 £ million

Year	Building societies	Banks
1980	9,614	8,734[a]
1981	11,991	11,707
1982	15,339	13,983
1983	19,263	18,965[b]
1984	24,034	20,539
1985	26,491	23,640
1986	36,937	33,655
1987	35,529	49,754
1988	49,605	60,494
1989	45,160	71,463
1990	44,592	51,287

[a]Estimated.
[b]Total advances by banks.
Source: Adapted from the CSO database, Bath University.

has emerged, involving the withdrawal of sterling from the European Exchange Rate Mechanism (EMS) and reliance on short-term interest rates.

The relaxing of regulation combined with the easing of monetary policy saw a period of intense competition to meet the demand for advances and pressure to innovate to attract new customers. In terms of Porter's generic strategies it could be described as a period of differentiation. Goodhart comments

> The last decade has seen a wave of financial innovations – in part in response to the various pressures within the financial system brought about by the earlier policy regime switch towards monetary targeting and practical monetarism. (Goodhart, 1989, p. 298).

Of course, other aspects of government macro economic policy also encouraged the growth in advances, for example the policy of council house sales. The impact of government economic policy on the financial services sector is discussed in more detail in Chapter 4.

6. Strategy decisions

This section examines examples of strategic decisions that can be described as strategic responses to the changes in the environment which have been described above. Space limitations preclude more than a brief discussion of strategic decisions and no more than a cursory discussion and analysis of the reasons and motivations for these decisions can be given. Financial institutions have concentrated on non-price competition which we would expect for the marketing of a relatively homogeneous service, although pricing strategy is discussed below.

Innovation

Banks and building societies have sought to innovate both in terms of products and delivery of services. Examples include the introduction of ATMs, cash/credit cards, different accounts designed to attract a range of customers. Midland Bank, for example have introduced their 'lifestyle' accounts, each one designed to attract a different 'style' of customer. The three accounts that were initially marketed were, Vector, Meridian, and Orchard. Midland were also first in developing the high interest cheque account, an example of a strategic decision that forced the other retail banks to react with the introduction of their own, similar accounts. These strategies have been overtaken by events since the merger with HSBC (see below).

Product differentiation and diversification

Apart from the development of different brands, financial institutions have taken the opportunity to market different services often operating subsidiary companies to develop and market these services. Given uncertainty and imperfect knowledge, this diversification represents one way of reducing risk for the providers. The development of these products is now well known and includes financial planning services, hire purchase and more recently and less successfully, estate agency. These, of course, can all be cross-sold with other services. This lateral integration means that banks and other financial institutions can be called financial conglomerates (Maycock, 1986).

The insurance companies have also attempted to diversify their operations, most notably by buying into chains of estate agents. The slump in the housing market has forced them to re-think their expansion strategy and the Prudential, for example, decided to sell its estate agency chain in 1990.

Cross-selling

Financial institutions have been able to exploit a degree of customer inertia due to the inconvenience and personal costs of transferring accounts or operating multiple accounts. Banks, particularly, in the past have been criticised for their relatively poor attention to customer care. Increased competition has led partly to more emphasis on customer care and a move away from a passive selling role. Obviously, opportunities to cross-sell services have been developed as a natural extension of this changed emphasis, even if it has not met with the approval of staff as noted by one commentator, 'Selling appears to many bankers as a departure from the profession they originally selected' (Richardson, 1981).

The development of services associated with advances has been particularly attractive to banks. Mortgage lending, although not a traditional area of operation for the banks, has been attractive to them for cross-selling life assurance. The current account, however, remains the main vehicle for cross-selling services such as credit cards, loans, insurance and travel services. The current account also provides a good marketing channel through direct marketing of some services.

Takeovers and mergers

The extent of takeover and merger activitiy by the banks has been limited by the likelihood of mergers being rejected by the Monopolies and Mergers Commission (MMC). With the exception of the TSB takeover of Hill Samuel and the merger between the Midland and HSBC, merger activity has been predominantly between building societies (see above). One of the motives for the merger activity might be the desire to obtain economies of scale, but econometric work has found that inefficiencies (or diseconomies) outweighed any increased benefit from operating on a larger scale (Hardwick, 1989). There are, of course, many motives for mergers. It is more likely that motives deriving from the aspirations of executive management, such as increased security, greater market share, prestige and growth, are the main reasons for the high level of merger activity among building societies.

A major structural change occurred in 1992 with the merger of the Midland with the Hong Kong & Shanghai Banking Corporation (HSBC). A protracted battle for the Midland had emerged in 1992 between Lloyds and HSBC. Lloyds wished to merge to rationalise the UK branch network of both banks, they would have closed down one branch where both Lloyds and Midland operated branches, and consequently reduced operating costs. Despite a strong economic case for the takeover by Lloyds, since it would have provided an opportunity to rationalise the branch banking system, and a better share price offer, the threat of referral to the Monopolies and Mergers Commission meant that the rival offer from HSBC was favoured by the Midland board and Lloyds eventually withdrew. The motives for the HSBC of the merger were to acquire a strong branch network in the UK and the merger provided a convenient entry into Europe. The merger has affected the competitive strategy of the Midland and HSBC. They have sought to improve their market share. For example, in the small business market the Midland have been quite active in promoting the Small Firms' Loan Guarantee Scheme as one way of attracting new small business clients.

Pricing policy

It is possible to recognise a pricing strategy for institutions in some limited way, for example, price discrimination between customers (Channon, 1986). However, financial institutions have generally avoided price competition. There is effectively little difference in prices of services for the same *class* of consumer. Competition has, however, forced the paring of margins so that the spread between lending and deposit rates has narrowed and banks have been forced to reduce charges on current accounts to maintain customers in the face of competition from building societies. Building societies entered direct competition with the banks with the introduction of interest bearing current accounts. The first in the field, Nationwide Anglia, introduced its interest paying FlexAccount in 1987; similar accounts have appeared from Abbey National, Halifax and the Woolwich. They have been very successful in attracting customers away from the banks; the Nationwide, for example, has found it difficult to cope with demand. Building societies have also undercut the banks with their interest charges on credit cards which, although not likely to be profitable, are probably seen as a loss leader for those societies keen to get into retail banking.

Capacity

The traditional use of capacity by banks has been to devote the vast majority of capacity to administration, with a relatively small percentage of floor space devoted to sales and enquiries. Innovation has meant that the traditional banking functions can be carried out in far less space and banks (and building societies) are beginning to examine their use of space. Indeed it could be argued that there is no longer the need for the traditional High Street branch and there is no doubt that the banks, in particular, with their large number of branches have a large degree of over-capacity. Logically, it seems inevitable that the banks will rationalise capacity in the future, both to reduce costs and to better utilise assets, which are often in prime sites. This is discussed further in Chapter 9.

Joint ventures

There are examples of joint ventures both between banks and between societies and banks which are designed to reduce the launch and development costs of product differentiation and innovation. Examples include joint credit cards, collaboration over ATMs, a Visa card operation between the Halifax and the Bank of Scotland, and links between banks and building societies on the one hand and banks and life assurance companies on the other.

New entry

The market for financial services has also been subject to the entry of new organisations. For example, banks are facing increased competition not just from the willingness of building societies to enter retail banking but also from entrants such as First Direct, a Midland Bank subsidiary, who have decided to take on the banks in direct competition with few retail outlets, made possible, of course, by innovations in banking services. It is no longer necessary for customers to have the convenience of their local branch. It remains to be seen how successful these new entrants will be and whether they will attract new customers that do not have bank accounts or attract existing customers from retail banks. One of the reasons for the large branch network of the main retail banks has been the belief that customers valued convenience; that belief is being challenged by new entrants. Chapter 5 looks, in some detail, at the way developments in information technology have facilitated the growth of new competitors.

Preparing for Europe

Financial institutions had to prepare their strategy for the impact of the Single European Market after 1992. Given the over-capacity and restricted growth likely in the UK market, future expansion may only be achieved in Europe, a fact recognised by Norrington of Barclays – 'The UK market for financial services is mature and growth will become increasingly constrained' (IBI, 1990).

Insurance companies have also begun to prepare for Europe through acquisitions and joint ventures in Europe. The attraction of the size of the market (320 million people), and the freedom from restrictions, means that it is a targeted growth area for providers. However, as Chapter 11 makes clear, progress towards a unified European Market for financial services has been far from smooth, and poses significant challenges to UK financial institutions.

Business ethics and banking

In the 1990s the concept of the 'ethical firm' has become prominent (RSA, 1994). By 'ethical firm', we mean a firm that is concerned about how it trades and who it trades with, for example favouring suppliers that are concerned about the environment and have carried out environmental audits. In terms of competitive strategy, a firm may be able to achieve a competitive edge through association with good ethical practice by its customers.

This has been the strategy, pursued with some degree of success, by the Co-operative bank. In the 1990s the Co-op Bank concentrated on dealing with firms that are concerned with business ethics and the environment. It proved successful in gaining customers from professional occupations and social categories A/B. These were customers that had a high balance on current account and customers that could be targeted for the cross-selling of other services. In 1992 alone, the Co-op increased its number of customers by 13%. In terms of Porter's generic competitive strategies this is a remarkable example of a successful focus and niching strategy.

7. The marketing environment

Interfacing with the market place and its competitors is of immediate concern to a firm. However, it is also critical that a firm understands the environmental trends affecting the industry and the market place in the longer term. Environmental pressures, such as intensified global competition, improvements in information technology, and deregulation have had, and will continue to have, an impact on the structure of financial services in the UK.

Not only do the dynamics of the environment make it difficult to understand, but also the fact that it is boundless and that it is for the most part uncontrollable means that a special expertise is required to understand it. An organisation can never have full control of any environmental factors, but it can respond in ways designed to take advantage of an opportunity or dampen the effects of threat. For example, a company could try to identify market trends likely to affect the current product market entries and then adjust the marketing mix to take advantage (or reduce the negative impact) of those changes.

Earlier chapters of this text have considered the impact of deregulation, information technology and taxation. The following section, therefore, does not recover familiar ground, but considers other important environmental factors.

Personal assets and liabilities

The 1980s and early 1990s witnessed a shift in the composition of personal sector assets and liabilities. Financial assets in the UK personal sector rose, on a current price basis, over fourfold from 1981 to 1993 (see Table 10.3). Financial liabilities, such as loans and consumer credit, rose fourfold from 1981 to mid-1991 (see Table 10.4).

As far as assets are concerned, there has been a shift towards investment in equities, either directly or indirectly via unitised funds (discussed in more detail in Chapter 7). This trend peaked at 65% of assets immediately before the stock market crash of October 1987. Turning to liabilities, it can be seen that building societies have remained as the main source of housing finance, but banks and the so called 'central lenders', such as the Household Mortgage Corporation, have significantly increased their market share.

Home ownership

The 1980s witnessed a dramatic increase in the number of homeowners in the UK. By the end of the decade the proportion of housing stock occupied by owners was estimated to be over 60%. Running alongside this increase in home ownership the decade saw a concomitant rise in house prices. According to the Building Societies' Association the average house price at the start of the decade was £23,500. By 1990 this figure had reached £64,700.

As would be expected with this increase in house prices, the proportion of disposable income accounted for by mortgage payments has grown significantly for many families. Indeed, it is possible to argue that mortgage provision has taken a pre-eminent role in family financial decision-making. Financial services providers have obviously benefited from the increased significance of home ownership and mortgage finance. Few people can proceed to purchase a property without some form of mortgage and/or investment advice; indeed, the centrality of this process to family decision-making was a key motive in the diversification into estate agencies by banks, building societies and insurers.

Table 10.3   Financial assets of the UK personal sector, %, 1981, 1989 and 1993

	1981	1989	1993
Notes and coin	2.6	1.1	0.9
Bank deposits	12.3	12.7	11.0
Building society deposits	16.7	12.4	12.4
UK shares	10.9	13.5	11.4
Unit trusts	0.9	2.0	2.0
Equity in insurance and pension funds	36.3	45.0	51.5
Other	20.3	13.3	10.8
Total (%)	100	100	100
total (£million)	339,218	1,128,809	1,557,100

Source: *Financial Statistics* (London: CS0).

Table 10.4   Financial liabilities of the UK personal sector, %, 1981 and 1990

	1981	1990
Bank loans	17.6	20.0
Loans by credit companies and retailers	4.4	1.9
Housing: banks	4.8	19.9
Housing: building societies and insurance companies	48.8	48.0
Other	24.4	10.2
Total %	100	100
total (£million)	105,319	418,698

Source: *Financial Statistics* (London: CS0).

The late 1980s and early 1990s saw a downturn in the housing market, rising interest rates and falling house prices, especially in the South of England. An unfortunate by-product of these trends has been a rise in mortgage arrears and repossessions. Figures published by the Council of Mortgage Lenders revealed that repossessions peaked in 1991 at 75,500, though this had fallen to 31,800 by 1993. This compares to 13,470 for the whole of 1989.

Share ownership

The 1980s witnessed a rapid increase in private share ownership. In 1979 only 7% of the population owned shares. By 1985, this proportion had risen to 12.5% and by 1987 it stood at 21%. The reason for this upsurge in share ownership is most definitely due to the privatisation of state controlled industries. The introduction of tax exempt Personal Equity Plans in 1987 (see Chapter 6) also contributed to this trend. An interesting more recent development is the innovation of High Street share shops.

Demographic changes

An understanding of demographic trends is very important to financial services providers and the financial needs of individuals change quite substantially throughout their lifespan. The UK is undergoing some quite significant demographic changes. Perhaps the most important of these is an increasing proportion of older people. For example, in 1977 3% of men and 6% of women were aged over 75. Only a decade later, these figures stood at 5% and 8% respectively. Currently, about 15% of the UK population is aged over 65, with women outnumbering men in the ratio of approximately 3:2. By 2031 it is estimated that the proportion will have risen to about 25% of the population. This gradual ageing of the population profile of the UK will lead to an increased incidence of bequeathed wealth; this has obvious implications for financial service providers.

An interesting point worth making here is that this anticipated ageing of the population was a strong contributory factor in the decision of the government to weaken the earnings-related element of state pension provision and introduce personal pensions in the Social Security Act 1986. As state provision is less able to deal with an increasingly ageing population, this will create further opportunities not only in pension provision, but also in areas such as making financial provision for future health and residential care.

Household changes

In the 1980s there were many changes to the traditional household structure. In 1991, the average household size was 2.50 persons compared to 2.67 in 1979 and 2.91 in 1971. This reduction in the average household size can be attributed mainly to an increase in the proportion of one person households and a decrease in the proportion of large households. In fact, between 1971 and 1991, the proportion of households containing only one person rose from 17% to 27% while the proportion of households with five or more persons fell from 14% to 7%.

In 1961 approximately 40% of households had dependent children. By 1988 this proportion had fallen to 26%, reflecting falling birth rates throughout the period. The proportion of all families with dependent children which are lone parent families increased from 8% in 1971 to 14% in 1988, largely reflecting the rise in divorce rates, the increasing incidence of births outside marriage and the decline of the traditional nuclear family structure. These trends have continued into the 1990s.

The financial services implications of these changes include a growing role for females in household decision-making, and responses have included flexible life insurance products where the proportions of the premium apportioned to investment or protection cover can be varied as personal circumstances change.

Growth in self-employment

Self-employed persons are defined as those who, in their main employment, work on their own account, whether or not they have any employees. One of the most noticeable trends in the composition of the labour force during the 1980s has been the growth in the number of self-employed. During the 1970s there was little change in the number of self-employed but from 1979 to 1988 the total rose from 1.7 million to 3.1 million. This rather dramatic rise can be at least partly attributed to the prevalence of an 'enterprise culture', as propounded by the Thatcher government, and high unemployment levels.

Financial services providers have been alert to these changes in the labour force and specially tailored product offerings have included flexible pension plans and small business loans.

North–South divide

The concept of a North–South divide has existed for several hundred years and can be seen quite clearly with respect to political differences and income and employment differences. For example, as at January 1990 the unemployment rate in the South East stood at 3.8%, while in the North of England the rate was 9.1% and in Northern Ireland it was 14.4%. Home ownership and house price differences are also well known, for example over 70% of homes in the South East are owner occupied, whereas in Scotland the ratio stands at about 40%.

The north–south divide is, therefore, likely to continue to be of significance to financial services organisations because of the opportunities presented for targeting. Geographic segmentation of markets can be combined with other segmentation areas, such as psychographic area, to provide a more sophisticated approach. Suitable examples here could, perhaps, include the Midland Bank's Meridian, Vector and Orchard accounts which, though not wholly successful, sought be match account features to lifestyle.

Financial literacy

The increase in home and share ownership encouraged by the Thatcher government in the 1980s, coupled with increases in disposable income obtained by income tax reductions, meant that more people have become financially aware and sophisticated. Hard data to substantiate this situation is difficult to obtain, but pointers do exist. For example, Barclays introduced an annual fee for Barclaycard holders in 1990 in an attempt to increase revenue to counteract customers who took advantage of interest free credit time periods.

Other evidence to support the trend towards increased financial sophistication includes the growth in media coverage of financial matters. For example, the *Daily Mail* has a financial advice column called 'Money Mail'. Other examples include Radio 4's 'Money Box' and the financial section of Ceefax and Oracle (the latter services being particularly well equipped to present Budget Day special coverage).

8. Marketing decisions

This short section attempts to provide a brief overview of the strategic marketing decisions which can be related to the environmental changes noted above. In brief, these responses have centred around increased advertising expenditure, new product innovations and the development of new distribution channels.

Advertising

In recent times the contribution of mass-media advertising to the marketing mix of financial services organisations has increased very significantly. For example, according to Media Expenditure Analysis Ltd (MEAL), the highest spending advertiser in 1990 was the Halifax Building Society, with an estimated spend of over £27 million. Table 10.5 gives details of the top 10 advertisers for 1990 and, as can be seen, Nationwide and Abbey National Building Societies and the National Westminster Bank all feature in the table.

Other prominent financial advertisers include Barclays Bank with £12.4 million, Alliance & Leicester Building Society with £11.4 million, Girobank with £10.9 million, Lloyds Bank with £10.2 million, and Sun Alliance with £9.0 million. These figures provide clear evidence that many financial services providers now outspend traditional heavy advertisers in the fast moving consumer goods sector.

A strong contributory factor in the increased significance of media advertising has been the need for organisations to establish a clear corporate identity or brand in order to differentiate themselves from their competitors. This is particularly the case for building societies who, up to the early 1980s, used to operate a price cartel where all societies charged the same mortgage and offered the same savings accounts rates. However, the future of such corporate branding is now becoming questionable. According to a commentary in *Marketing Week* (12 April 1991):

Table 10.5   Top 10 brands, 1990, by advertising spend

Rank	Brand	Total spend (£ million)
1	Halifax Building Society	27.6
2	Tesco	24.3
3	British Sky Broadcasting	23.7
4	McDonalds	19.9
5	Nationwide Building Society	19.0
6	Electricity Board Floatation	18.1
7	National Westminster Bank (personal accounts)	17.8
8	Woolworth	16.9
9	MFI	16.8
10	Abbey National	15.3

Source: Media Expenditure Analysis Ltd.

the position of building societies as brands is becoming increasingly anomalous as they increase their range of services rapidly to compete with the High Street banks.

Widened product portfolios

Financial services providers have broadened their product portfolios. This process of new product introduction, which appears to be taking place without a corresponding amount of 'old' product deletion, can, perhaps, be most clearly illustrated by reference to the building society sector.

The Building Societies Act 1986, which came into effect on 1 January 1987, provided a new legislative framework. It permitted a progressive deregulation of the products which societies could offer and the range of activities which they could undertake. Building societies are now empowered to provide:

- Lending services, e.g. unsecured loans
- Investment services, e.g. unit trust management
- Insurance services, e.g. acting as a broker or agent
- Trusteeship, e.g. family and personal fund trusts
- Executorship, e.g. acting as an executor for wills
- Land services, e.g. estate agents.

As might be expected, this legislation has had a profound effect on the sector, with many building societies becoming more like banks and offering cheque books, overdrafts, interest paying current account, ATM cards, and credit cards. Indeed, one society, the Abbey National, converted to plc status, and, in effect, became a bank (see Chapter 3 for a more detailed discussion of this).

More examples of increased product innovations can be found in other legislation. For example, Personal Equity Plans (PEPs) and Tax Exempt Special Savings Accounts (TESSAs) have their origins in Finance Acts, and the Social Security Act 1986 created the market for personal pensions.

Distribution

Traditionally, financial services providers have each used one distribution channel to reach their customers. Banks and building societies have utilised their very extensive High Street branch networks, while insurers have tended to develop direct sales or broker outlets. However, competitive pressures have encouraged suppliers to form joint ventures and alliances and to adopt multichannel distribution methods. Currently, distribution channels include:

- Direct mail
- Direct response advertising
- Estate agency
- Setting up tied agencies
- Setting up direct sales forces
- Automatic teller machines
- Home banking systems
- Joint ventures

The impact of the Financial Services Act 1986 has led to almost all major banks and building societies forming tied agency arrangements with insurance providers.

Indeed, banks and building societies have now become major retailers of insurance and pension products and have succeeded in securing advantageous commission deals from underwriters who do not wish to be excluded from this important channel.

The full service bank branch system has been effective for collecting and delivering retail banking services. However, such extensive networks are under threat from various pressures such as increased costs and alternative distribution outlets, for example, home banking. A trend towards branch closures (and staff redundancies) and the introduction of the so-called 'Hub and Spoke' system of branch organisation is already evident.

Most financial services suppliers have started to utilise direct mail and other direct marketing techniques. Customer databases are increasingly being developed in order to permit the sophisticated targeting of various market segments.

9. Conclusions

Determinants of corporate and marketing strategy are clearly formed by the complexity of the mixture of micro and macro forces that financial institutions face in their environment. We have seen, in this chapter, that these forces include demographic and social, economic and competitive as well as political and legal forces. We have also seen, in this chapter, that the pace of change quickened in the 1980s, and has continued to do so in the 1990s. We believe that, to be successful, financial institutions must be aware of, and anticipate, these changes in the forces that have been outlined above. They can then formulate the 'best' strategy for successful growth and diversification in the late 1990s.

Strategic competition still remains focused on non-price methods of competition. The limited amount of price competition supports a kinked demand analysis of oligopolistic competition. Developments in competition in the 1980s have forced the banks to respond with new products and to develop more direct selling methods. Expansion of demand for advances was sufficient in the 1980s to maintain growth in services for both building societies and banks. However, it now seems likely that any growth in the market will be severely restricted, and with increased competition for financial services it seems that there is over-capacity. A period of rationalization seems inevitable, particularly for the number of High Street retail branches. Innovation has enabled the providers to diversify, but it has also meant that the large overheads carried by the banks in the form of excess capacity are no longer necessary. It is noticeable that the banks are already curtailing recruitment. If expansion of the sector is to continue, then it seems that providers will have to turn to Europe.

Notes

1. Causal evidence is sometimes cited on the importance of sales or growth as managerial objectives, which may include expenditures on advertising, investment, or R&D which are different from optimal levels. The oligopolistic models used in this chapter to provide a framework for financial institutions rely on profit maximisation as the firms' objective. Alternative models have been developed that use alternative managerial objectives to explain firms' behaviour; the best known of these are Baumol's sales revenue maximisation model and the Marris growth model. The interested reader will find a good discussion of these 'managerial models' in Koutsoyiannis (1985) or Ricketts (1987).
2. As with any economic model, a number of simplifying assumptions are made; these include the provision of homogeneous products (no differentiation strategy by firms), symmetrical firms, including identical costs (in the original form the model assumes no costs), and normally, there is an assumption of linear demand. One of the attractions of the Cournot model is that these assumptions can be relaxed without affecting the significance of the predictions of the model.

Further reading

Ansoff, I., *Corporate Strategy : an analytical approach to business policy for growth and expansion* (McGraw-Hill, 1965).
Channon, D.F., *Bank Strategic Management and Marketing* (John Wiley, 1986).
Drake, L., *The Building Society Industry in Transition* (Macmillan, 1989).
Goodhart, C.A.E., 'The Conduct of Monetary Policy', *Economic Journal*, 99(396) (June 1989), pp. 293–346.
Grieve-Smith, J., *Business Strategy : an introduction* (Basil Blackwell, 1985).
Hardwick, P., 'Economies of Scale in Building Societies', *Applied Economics*, 21 (1989), pp. 1291-1304.
IBI, *1992 : Planning for Financial Services and Insurance* (Butterworths, 1990).
Johnson, G. and Scholes, K., *Exploring Corporate Strategy : text and cases* (Prentice-Hall, 1989).
Koutsoyiannis, A., *Modern Microeconomics* (Macmillan, 1985).
Laidler, D. and Estrin, S., *Introduction to Microeconomics* (Philip Allan, 1989).
Luck, D., *Marketing Strategy and Plans*, 3rd edn (Prentice-Hall, 1989).
Maycock, J., *Financial Conglomerates: The New Phenomenon* (Gower, 1986).
Porter, M.E., *Competitive Strategy: Techniques for Analysing Industries and Competitors* (Collier Macmillan, 1980).
Richardson, L., *Banks in the Selling Role* (John Wiley, 1981).
Ricketts, M., *The Economics of Business Enterprise* (Wheatsheaf, 1987).
Rothbert, R. (ed.), *Corporate Strategy and Product Innovation*, 2nd edn (Free Press, 1981).
RSA, Tomorrow's Company: 'The role of business in a changing world'. Interim Report (RSA, 1994).
Schelling, T.C., The Strategy of Conflict (Harvard University Press, 1960).
Scherer, F.M., *Industrial Market Structure and Economic Performance (Rand McNally, 1980).*
Shapiro, C., 'Static Oligopoly Theory', in Schmalensce, R. and Willing, R. (eds), *Handbook of Industrial Organisation*, vol. 1 (North-Holland, 1989).

CHAPTER 11

A Unified European Market for Financial Services

Diane Walker

1. Introduction

The free movement of goods, services, capital and people within the European Community was a clearly defined goal of the 1957 Treaty of Rome. The achievement of this aim is, however, dependent upon there being a financial Common Market; deregulation within banking and credit, brokerage and insurance would be insufficient to liberalise the market. It is vital that capital is free to move across the borders of the various member states.

2. Free movement of capital

Article 57 of the Treaty of Rome provides for this freedom, but adoption of the principle throughout the Market has been slow. Controls were removed in the UK in 1979 and others abolished restrictions in July 1990. Newer members of the Community, with weaker financial services industries, have been granted transitional arrangements to delay adoption until the late 1990s.

3. The single licence

The road to the granting of a single licence is proving a difficult one for the financial services industry, and there are two aspects to be considered in the evolutionary process necessary to achieve the goal; harmonisation and liberalisation.

The granting of a single licence, or 'passport', allowing institutions to operate throughout the Community under a single licence, granted in the State where a company's Head Office is located, is a prime objective of the Treaty of Rome. Members would then be free to operate in other community states, control being vested in the parent company and its home country. The Single Market, which since 1 January 1995 has included Austria, Sweden and Finland, will include other countries, members of the European Economic Area, currently Iceland and Norway, with the inclusion of Lichtenstein anticipated.

Harmonisation

The nature of long-term and investment business makes customers of the financial services industry particularly vulnerable. For this reason, governments feel an especial need to protect consumers. The industry is therefore heavily supervised. There is a natural governmental reluctance to relinquish control, as in the event of failure by a supplier, the burden of financial support is most likely to fall back to the State. The need to legislate to harmonise the regulations imposed by the disparate states to allow for differences in the degree of protection afforded is therefore hampered by a natural and well-founded caution.

Elsewhere in Europe, in countries such as Germany, markets are heavily regulated and because of the reluctance by some members to see deregulation in their markets, agreement of directives for the insurance sphere has lagged behind banking and investment services. In the UK, however, reliance is placed upon self-regulation in banking, insurance and investment industries (see Chapters 2 and 3). The institutions themselves jealously guard this privilege, but recent events seem likely to resurrect the question of its adequacy. London's prestige as the primary financial services centre has been damaged by the Barlow Clowes and Robert Maxwell cases. The financial services industry relies on confidence, and that confidence is being thoroughly shaken.

The areas typically affected by regulations and controls are accounting practices, annual reporting, solvency ratios and public disclosures, and ultimate responsibility can lie with the 'home' or 'host' country. A 'home' country is the state within which an organisation's Head Office is based, a 'host' country is the state within which the organisation is operating. Home country control is the eventual goal in the free market.

In the event of an inability to harmonise regulations, there must at least be a mutual recognition of member states' controls in order to advance to liberalisation.

Liberalisation

The freedom to operate in other Community states is approached in two ways; the freedom of *establishment* and the freedom of *services*.

Freedom of establishment

Some members allow other States to operate within their boundaries only with the use of indigenous companies. If they do permit companies to establish their own operation, the host country often retains the right to monitor and regulate it, sometimes requiring systematic prior notification of product details.

A basic right of establishment already exists, however, in the European Community for providers of financial services. In general, firms from one member State can compete on equal terms with domestic firms in other member States, provided that they establish local offices and conform with national rules and regulations and obtain authorisation from each host State.

Freedom of services

This enables companies to offer their product in other community States, without the establishment of an outlet, with home country control and without prior approval of products or systematic notification. There have been some successes in the attainment of this ultimate goal, but disputes remain.

4. Achievements towards harmonisation

The First Banking Co-ordination Directive (1977) required all member States to establish systems for authorising and supervising credit institutions, and created a basic right of establishment, as noted above (freedom of establishment).

The Second Banking Co-ordination Directive (1989), together with the harmonising effect of the Own Funds and Solvency Ratio Directives, were adopted in 1989 (see chapter 2), and establish a legislative framework for the creation of a single market in banking from January 1993. Securities trading by credit institutions is included and the concept of a single banking licence is introduced. This single authorisation and subsequent supervision by the home authorities allows banks to set up branches and operate freely through-. out the Community. Since October 1989 it has also been possible to sell unit trusts and similar services across Community borders without hindrance.

The Second Non-Life (Services) Directive (effective from July 1990), provides for freedom of services, with home country control, in large risk insurance business. The Second Life Directive allows proposers for most types of life assurance, acting on their own initiative, to purchase contracts across borders, without the intervention or control of the proposer's own country. The key issue in this case is that pursuit of the business originates with the proposer, not the life office. Freedom of services for other non-life mass risks and other life insurances exists, but with host country control. There is not much advantage, therefore, if they are a highly regulated state, as in such an environment many barriers to entry would exist.

The Third Non-Life Directive (agreed in December 1991 and in force from July 1994), allows the purchase of insurance from companies licensed by any one member state. This removes the problem of the Second Directive, where initiative for purchase had to be with the proposer. Life offices can now pursue business across borders. Most members have until 1994/5 to implement the legislation, but again newer members are being given until later in the 1990s to comply.

From July 1994, the Third Life Directive has enabled any EC member to provide policies to another member state on the basis of home country authorisation, but some restrictions have been imposed. There will, for instance, be a limited system of prior notification of premium rates and the setting up of new composites, companies which transact more than one class of insurance business, has been banned. The Insurance Accounts Directive 1991, which required appropriate laws to be passed by 1 January 1994, has also now been approved.

These Directives will, of course, have a much greater impact in highly regulated countries which, until these changes, had much greater controls over their industries. Although the perception in such countries would be that such control provided greater consumer protection, to organisations wishing to operate within their boundaries, the same controls would be viewed as barriers to entry, if not protectionism. The UK enjoys a very deregulated, innovative and competitive industry and can expect a favourable response from those more restrictive countries, at least in the first instance.

5. Problem areas

Investment Services Directive

The *Investment Services Directive* (ISD) would give investment firms a similar home country authorisation passport to that provided for banks. It will define which types of investment business will qualify for the single operating licence. For those organisations involved in this area of the industry, and therefore affected by the Directive, a minimum level of business capital will be required. Unfortunately, the types of investment businesses to be affected have yet to be decided, but the failure to agree the ISD has not stopped the passing (in June 1992) of the Capital Adequacy Directive. This has caused great concern amongst intermediaries offering investment advice.

Capital Adequacy Directive

The *Capital Adequacy Directive* aims to set minimum capital requirements for all non-bank investment firms in the European Community, including insurance brokers and independent financial advisers wishing to trade across borders.

By agreeing this area before the Investment Services Directive, many companies may find themselves financially burdened when their business activities are not appropriate to the levels of capitalisation demanded. A high requirement could wipe out smaller brokers when, unless they are handling a client's money, such financing should not be necessary.

Reciprocal arrangements

The size of the new European Community market will attract outside suppliers. To protect itself, the European Community has intimated that reciprocal agreements may be sought with third countries (non-members) to ensure fair access and equal treatment. The Second Banking Co-ordination Directive includes such a reciprocity provision. If the European Community insists on equal rights of establishment and national treatment, some non-member countries could retaliate and restrict the operation in their markets. A fierce application of *reciprocity* could affect the UK enormously, as London gains more business from third countries than any other EC member. Some foreign countries, unable to reciprocate because of national laws, could experience unfavourable treatment of their own companies, and may retaliate in a way detrimental to the London insurance market.

Harmonisation in taxation

The most recent (Third) Life and Non-Life Directives make the 'single passport' in insurance an imminent reality, but where tax regulations differ throughout the Community, the development of cross-border sales opportunities could be limited.

The harmonisation of *taxation* laws is proving one of the most difficult areas for member states to resolve. Currently the UK is heavily penalised in relation to its fellow Community members; investment income and capital gains on life assurance policies sold across borders to people residing outside the UK are taxed in the UK.

UK insurance companies meet corporation tax demands on their general reserves for claims equalisation and catastrophes and their non-life claims reserves have to be discounted. On the life side, only pension business enjoys a regime similar in some ways to the European approach. Other life funds are taxed, with a reduction for running expenses. All other countries tax life companies on their profit allocation to shareholders, with deductions for closing reserves. Initial expenses for attracting new business is also deductible. This inequality severely affects the relative size and power of UK companies in relation to fellow EC members and, progressively more importantly, non-members such as the USA and Japan. They are more vulnerable to hostile takeovers and catastrophe claims.

The fundamental weakness in the concept of the free movement of services and financial products has been exposed by the case of a Belgian national, Hans-Martin Bachmann. In February 1992 the European Court of Justice supported the Belgian court in their refusal to allow tax relief against several life assurance policies taken out by M. Bachmann with German Companies. The decision was based on the principle that deductibility could only be permitted where the issuing insurer was established in Belgium, despite M. Bachmann receiving the support of the European Commission in his appeal.

In an effort to ensure fiscal balance, national authorities are maintaining a major barrier to the free movement of labour within the Community.

Linguistic and cultural barriers

The differences in *language, culture* and *customs* are likely to be a barrier to the movement of domestic business across borders, at least with regard to an influx to the UK. The British broker network is already making use of other countries' insurance products for the larger risks, but traditions are deeply embedded and although it is widely accepted that the average domestic client is unaware of the identity of their insurer, doubt is being expressed about there being a major use of foreign insurers for the smaller risks. In many States, insurers without local establishments will be at a severe competitive disadvantage because they may not be able to offer the same type of service as a domestic insurer with local networks. Legislation has so far concentrated on the freedom to sell products, but the consumer is dependent upon the willingness of suppliers to sell. This is a form of discrimination against the customer: what about their freedom to buy?

Not least of the traditions to be considered is the choice of payment mode. Consumers in France, Italy and UK are heavy users of cheques for non-cash payments and low users of bank transfer. Dutch and German customers use bank transfers for over half their non-cash payments. There are 180 Automated Banking machines per million population in UK, France and Spain, between 84 and 62 per million in Belgium, Ireland, Germany and Italy, and under 40 per million in Portugal, Netherlands and Greece. The UK has 35 million bank and retailer credit cards in issue, whilst Germany has under 1 million. Fixed rate interest loans are the norm for house purchase in

France, Germany, Italy and the Netherlands, whereas variable rate loans predominate in the UK.

Successfully selling in a unified market involves the alteration of some very fundamental business strategies.

6. Reactions to a unified market

Mergers

In response to the threats of takeovers, *mergers* have been seen amongst UK insurers in an attempt to enlarge their capital base. Other less defensive strategies have been to participate in cross-shareholdings to gain immediate access to new markets. Co-operation agreements will provide a wider geographic service.

Choice of domicile

Companies with a European-wide presence will be able to select which regulatory environment is the most advantageous to them, so there will be an increasing emphasis on the choice of Head Office location. The repercussions will affect employment, taxation income and balances of trade.

Merchant banks

Merchant banks see the advent of the single market as bringing an increased number of mergers and acquisitions work from European companies and are building infrastructures of joint ventures with European partners in anticipation.

Joint ventures

European banks are combining with insurers in co-operative and joint ventures, although this progress towards 'one stop shopping' is not without difficulty. The ability to buy insurance products when other financial decisions are being taken is attractive to both consumer and salesman, but banks and insurers have different sales cultures. Bank staff resent being measured on sales targets, and even when specialist sales teams are trained to follow up the warm leads passed to them via the data-sharing activities of their organisation, how will they react when forced to move into the area of cold selling?

When the public are offered an entire range of financial service products from one source, will they prefer to use an independent financial adviser and lose faith in the banks' counselling? Most significantly, when insurance claims disputes inevitably arise, will the banks lose their lending and borrowing customers because of dissatisfaction in totally separate areas?

Much of the exponential growth in the sales of life insurance products, however, is at the expense of the banks' own retail deposits, and this form of cannibalisation is difficult to compensate. Moving into the insurance field by banks is not an answer to poor banking performance.

The progress towards disaggregation of financial services, and the resultant creation of larger financial groups, will pose another problem in the area of supervision.

Reinsurance

Reinsurers are merging or crossing shares with direct insurers. A true single market has existed in the reinsurance industry since 1964, and there will, on balance, be an increased demand for reinsurance in a unified market for financial services.

Alternatives to insurance

Improved risk management programmes will widen commercial enterprises' use of self-insurance and captive companies. This will reduce demand in the direct market and more use will be made of the competitive reinsurance rates on offer.

Insurance companies, as a result of a reduction in the direct cover requirement and because of increased capacity arising from mergers and acquisitions, will require less proportional reinsurance, but their needs for non-proportional and catastrophe covers will increase.

Venture capital

British *venture capital* institutions recognise that Europe presents an exciting opportunity as funds will be required by entrepreneurs. The European Commission has acknowledged that buy-outs are a significant feature of activity, and provides several incentive schemes for venture capital investment in transnational seed and start-up companies.

Cost control

A key element, although not the basis, for success in the new market will be cost control. The development of *direct selling* by both banks and insurers has been an attempt, and so far a very successful one, to increase market share at minimal cost. The concept of branchless banking illustrated by First Direct has proved the envy of Midland Bank's rivals, and many insurance companies have opened a direct selling network. True freedom of services in the European Community will allow companies to take full advantage of these arrangements.

Distribution channels

Another important element, recognised and being developed by institutions, is the *distribution channel*. The UK's network of intermediaries is well established and will initially give home insurers an edge in the free market. That network, however, is already being used by non-UK companies. Is this the time to be alienating the broker world with aggressive direct selling and sometimes below-standard service? Brokers, pressed by the direct marketing tactics of their principals, are driven to concentrate on niche markets, innovation and quality service.

In Europe, with more regulated markets and a smaller variety of products, consumers have less need for advice on the relative merits of competing goods and therefore brokers abroad have had, traditionally, a more limited role. This is most likely to change dramatically.

7.   UK strengths and weaknesses

The UK, particularly London, has a reputation as the leading financial services centre. It is renowned for its product innovation, contract and pricing flexibility, technical skills and risk selection techniques. It has experience over a long period of time of operating in a deregulated price market and this will, initially, give the UK an advantage in a liberalised market. Many EC companies, however, have British subsidiaries and have therefore been gaining the same experience. The new Directives discussed above will also limit the divergence between national supervisory laws.

Britain has a reputation for offering innovative products. As demand increases, there will be a greater need for them. European companies, however, have become much more innovative in the past decade and no longer rely as heavily on the British market for placing specialist risks. Britain's vast experience of operating overseas, and its dependency upon such experience in the insurance field, should maintain its superior position with third countries. This is threatened by a possible application of reciprocity and retaliation.

The often quoted Cecchini Report (*The European Challenge 1992. The Benefits of a Single Market*, 1988) indicates the price differences for banking, insurance and brokerage across the European Community. It hypothesises that as business moves to the lowest priced market, average prices will decline. The market will expand because it will attract more new business by virtue of the lower prices, and with an expanded market there will be more employment and an increase in GDP. As the demand for financial service products is income elastic, a higher GDP will enhance the demand, particularly for life and savings products. The expected lower inflation rate of the single market will also increase employment and disposable income, again increasing demand for protection and investment.

The report states that as Britain's prices for many financial services products are lower than other EC states, it will benefit from an integrated market. The report does not, however, indicate profitability. It is recognised that opening up previously protected markets to competition will pressure prices and companies. The resulting lower prices and greater choice is seen to be for the benefit of consumers.

In a market where many prices have been kept at uneconomic levels in the past, however, is it not in the best interests of those consumers to ensure a stable, albeit higher priced, market in which to invest and arrange protection? A destructive pursuit of market share will result in over-capacity, uneconomic pricing and instability.

If the industry sets its prices based on calculations for profitability, not market share, we could ultimately see increases, not reductions. Experience from other countries' sources may differ and require increased rates.

The European insurance market was worth $375 billion in 1989, equal to 31% of the world's total insurance premiums. Europe also experienced a 7% growth rate in 1989, but it is unlikely that the rate would be sustained through the 1990s because of the maturity of many of the member States' markets. Developing markets in Southern Europe, however, show the greatest potential with estimated 20–30% growth over the next five years.

The UK has a low penetration into the European Community. Some forays into Europe have proved unsuccessful and withdrawals have been made in recent months. Abroad, however, Continental companies have been pursuing a policy of merger and acquisition for some years, and the availability of suitable parties for British companies to acquire is diminishing. The emphasis seems now to be one of consolidation of European networks.

The UK strategy appears to be one of achieving critical mass to avoid takeover by other expansionist companies, and forming co-operation agreements with foreign partners. Sun Alliance are in agreement with a Swiss firm to work on multinational risks. Eureko has been formed by a number of EC companies as a jointly owned European holding company, pooling subsidiaries outside their home market. UK insurers are in a relatively weak position compared with some of their overseas competitors, because of their unfavourable taxation treatment. They are perhaps also the only market in the world where a hostile bid for an insurer is met with minimal regulatory problems. Britain's linguistic weakness is well publicised. We are at an immediate disadvantage, both practically and psychologically, when negotiating abroad.

UK publicly quoted companies are under constant scrutiny, and therefore managers, it has been argued, concentrate on short-term performance. The long-term business nature of the financial services industry is at odds with short-term planning, and creates major problems in the event of catastrophe claims on insurance policies.

8. Conclusions

Financial service institutions appear to be occupied with preserving the core domestic operations which became over-extended during the late 1980s. They are now suffering the ill-effects of a widespread recession, severe lending losses and catastrophe claims. In order to survive the expected competition in the coming years, companies are having to concentrate on increasing efficiency and effectiveness.

In the past, many operations have been used to subsidise other areas of business; the banks used personal customers' deposits to fund lending, insurers used domestic insurance premiums to subsidise commercial accounts. Now banks have been forced, to retain market share, to offer interest on current accounts, and insurers have sustained tremendous losses on their personal lines business. In an attempt to deal with these losses, the industry has seen the worst cuts ever in it labour force, with little prospect of an early recovery.

The approaching Single Market is ill-timed for the UK industry. The survivors will be those companies who are able to improve their management and financial controls, not merely cut costs, and concentrate on profitability rather than market share. The competitive advantage will be with those companies having a quality workforce, able to sustain a services orientated approach to satisfy their customers' expectations.

Further reading

Ceccini, P., *The European Challenge 1992: The Benefits of a Single Market* (Gower, 1988).
Cranston, R., *1992: The Legal Implications for Banking* (CIB Bankers Books, 1989).
Dixon, R., *Banking in Europe: The Single Market* (Routledge, 1991).
Ellis, T.H., *European Integration and Insurance* (Witherby, 1990).
Jackson, S. (ed.), *The Banking and Securities Industry 1992* (Ivanhoe, 1991).
Owen, R. and Dynes, M., *The Times Guide to 1992* (Times Books, 1990).
Quelch, J.A. *et al.*, *The Marketing Challenge of 1992* (Addison-Wesley, 1990).

Journals and publications

Chartered Insurance Institute, *CII Journal*.
Department of Trade and Industry, *Europe Open for Business* series.
Financial Times.

Index

Abbey Members Against Flotation (AMAF), 41
Abbey National, 8, 145, 148, 166, 173
accounting standards, 112, 151–2
accrued income scheme, 81
accumulation and maintenance trusts, 88
activity-based costing, 151, 153–5
advertising, 173–4
advice, financial, 6, 24
ageing populations, 171
Alliance & Leicester Building Society, 173
Altman, E.I., 134, 137
arbitrage, 10
artificial intelligence, 71–3
Association of Investment Trust Companies, 116
Association of Unit Trusts and Investment Funds, 115
Atlantic Computers, 13
Australia, 54
Automated Teller Machines (ATMs), 69, 74, 183

Bachmann, Hans-Martin, 183
backlog problem, 73
BACS (Bankers Automated Clearing System), 68
balance of payments, 53
Bank of Credit and Commerce International (BCCI), 13, 27
Bank of England, 16, 27, 28, 35, 41, 57, 64, 111–12
Bank of Scotland, 68, 148, 167
Banking Act (1987), 31, 36, 163
Banking Directives, 35, 180
banks, 4
    corporate finance and, 11, 57–8; credit analysis for, 122–40
    corporate strategy for, 158, 161–8
    cost structure of, 142–56, 185–6

credit creation by, 4–6, 143
crises in, 5–6, 13–14, 20
diversification by, 7–8, 55, 99, 144, 165
European Union and, 31, 35–6, 168, 178–88
information technology and, 68, 69–70, 71, 72, 73–4
insurance and, 11–12, 99, 165, 184–5
interest rates and, 58–64
regulation of, 7–8, 20, 27, 28, 31–6, 57
retail, 9, 57, 58, 142–56, 167, 175
taxation and, 80, 89
Barclaycard, 72, 173
Barclays Bank, 123, 148, 152, 173
Barlow Clowes, 13, 25, 27, 179
Basle Accord, 31, 33–6
Beaver, W.H., 134
Belgium, 183
Beveridge, Lord, 50
'Big Bang', 7
'Black Wednesday', 54
Blue Arrow, 25
bond washing, 80
branchless banking, 9, 68, 69, 147, 185–6
Bretton Woods system, 49, 53
British American Tobacco (BAT), 8
British and Commonwealth Bank, 13
British Telecom, 69
brokers, 106, 186
budget constraint, 51–2
building societies, 4, 99, 145, 148–50
    conversion of, 8, 41, 174–5
    corporate strategy for, 158, 162, 166, 167
    interest rates and, 58–64
    mergers of, 40, 41, 162, 166
    regulation of, 7, 8, 20, 23, 28, 36–41
    taxation and, 80, 89

Building Societies Act (1874), 36
Building Societies Act (1986), 7, 17, 28, 36, 37, 38, 39, 41, 144, 163, 174
Building Societies Association (BSA), 38, 39, 162, 169
Building Societies Commission (BSC), 28, 36, 37, 38–9, 40, 41
Building Societies Investor Protection Fund, 40
business cycles, 48, 58
business ethics, 168
Business Expansion Scheme (BES), 89
BZW, 108–9, 119, 120

capital adequacy, 182
   in banking, 32–4, 35, 36
   in building societies, 37, 38–9
   in insurance, 42–3, 45–6
Capital Adequacy Directive, 182
Capital Asset Pricing Model (CAPM), 103–4, 107, 120
capital flows, 53, 178
capital gains tax, 84, 85, 87, 88
cash, 69
Cecchini Report, 186–7
Cheltenham & Gloucester Building Society, 37
Citibank, 72
Clucas Report (1992), 26, 27
community charge, 82
Companies Act (1967), 42
Companies Act (1980), 116
competition, corporate strategy and, 157–68
Competition and Credit Control (CCC), 57
concentration risk, 35
Conley, J.M., 105
Consumers' Association, 24
conversion of building societies, 8, 41, 174–5
Co-operative Bank, 148, 168
corporate financial services, 10–11, 57–8
   credit analysis in, 122–40
corporate strategy, 157–68
cost structures of financial services, 142–56, 185–6
costs of regulation, 17, 18
Cournot duopoly model, 160–61
Courtis, J.K., 133–4, 138
Craven v. *White* (1989), 93
credit (loans)
   analysis of risk in, 122–40

creation of, 4–6, 143
   growth of, 142–3
credit cards, 72
credit scoring, 72
Criminal Justice Act (1993), 17, 27
cultural barriers, 183–4
customs duties, 82

database technology, 70, 74, 75–8, 175
debit cards, 69
debt securitisation, 10
decision-making aids, 70–73
demand
   management of, 49, 55
   for services, 2
demographic changes, 171
Department of Trade and Industry (DTI), 15, 16, 17, 23, 26, 42, 43–5
deregulation, 7–9, 23, 52, 57, 119, 144, 162, 163
derivatives, financial, 9
derived products, 144, 145
development land tax, 89
Direct Line, 70
direct taxation, 81, 82
Director of Public Prosecutions (DPP), 26
discretionary trusts, 87–8
disintermediation, 10–11
diversification
   by banks, 7–8, 55, 99, 144, 165
   investment, 98–9
duopoly, 160–61

Eastern Europe, 54
EFTPoS (Electronic Funds Transfer at Point of Sale), 68, 69
employment, 2, 172
   in financial services, 3, 55, 68
endowment effect, 60, 62, 64
endowment life assurance, 6, 24, 99, 112
entry barriers, 9, 19
equity (shares), 69, 89–90, 96, 107–18, 170–1
estate agency, 8
ethical issues, 168
Eureko, 187
European Monetary System (EMS), 54, 110
European Union (EC, EU), 31
   exchange rates and, 54
   financial services and, 31, 35–6, 43, 44, 168, 178–88
   monetary integration of, 54, 110

Exchange Rate Mechanism (ERM), 54, 110
exchange rates, 49, 53
exchange risk, 35
exit barriers, 9
expert systems, 71–3

Finance Act (1989), 98
Finance Act (1990), 90
financial advice, 6, 24
financial derivatives, 9
financial disintermediation, 10–11
financial innovation, 57, 164
  information technology, 67–79
Financial Intermediaries Managers and Brokers Regulatory Association (FIMBRA), 16, 17, 20, 26, 27
financial intermediation process, 3–4, 145
financial literacy, 172–3
financial markets trading, 72
financial products, 6–7, 144, 145
  development of, 69–70, 164, 165, 174–5
financial ratios, 133–40
financial services, 1
  changing nature of, 7–12, 55–6
  corporate strategy in, 157–68
  cost structure of, 142–56, 185–6
  deregulation of, 7–9, 23, 52, 57, 119, 144,162, 163
  economic significance of, 1, 2–7, 55–6
  European Union and, 31, 35–6, 43, 44, 168, 178–88
  growth of, 1, 2–3, 56–7
  information technology in, 67–79
  macroeconomic environment of, 48–65
  marketing in, 70, 99–100, 152, 154–5, 168–75
  regulation of, 7–9, 13–26, 31–46, 57, 163, 178–88; recommended changes to, 26–30
  structure of, 7–9, 55–6
  taxation and, 80, 81, 89–93
Financial Services Act (FSA, 1986), 7, 11, 16, 17, 23, 24, 28, 37, 99, 115, 144, 163
Fire Auto and Marine Insurance, 42
First Direct, 9, 68, 79, 147, 150, 167, 186
fiscal neutrality, 83, 88
Fogler, R. H., 118

Ford, 144
France, 54, 183, 184
fraud, 1 3, 25–6, 72
free resources test, 34
Friedman, Milton, 51
Friendly Societies Act (1992), 17
fund managers, 99, 104
Furniss v. Dawson, (1984), 93

gearing test, 34
General Motors, 144, 151
Germany, 54, 179, 183, 184
Girobank, 173
globalisation, 9–10
Goodhart, C.A.E., 60–1, 163, 164
government (state)
  borrowing by, 51–2
  economic management by, 6, 49–55
  financial regulation by, 7–9, 13–30, 31–46
  taxation and, 52, 80–93, 97–8, 112, 182–3
government securities, 96, 107–20
Gower, Jim, 28
Gower Report (1982), 24
Grays Building Society, 13
Greece, 183
growth, economic, 50, 52, 53, 58
Guinness, 25

Halifax Building Society, 166, 167, 173
Haugen, R.A., 103–4
hearth tax, 82
hedging, 39–40
home banking, 9, 68, 69, 147, 185– 6
Hong Kong & Shanghai Banking Corporation (HSBC), 165, 166
household structure, 171–2
housing, 91–2, 97, 98, 169–70
  mortgages and, 6, 7–8, 20, 91, 99, 165, 169
Howe, Geoffrey, 88

IBM, 73
Income and Corporation Taxes Act (1988), 116–17
income tax, 82, 84–5, 87, 88, 89
index tracker funds, 104, 107, 115–16
indirect taxation, 81, 82, 83
inflation, 49–50, 53, 54
information technology, 67–79
inheritance tax, 85–7
innovation, *see* financial innovation

insider dealing, 16–17, 26, 27
institutional investment, 95–120
insurance, 4, 70, 72
    banks and, 11–12, 99, 165, 184–5
    European Union and, 43, 44, 168,
        180–1, 182–3, 184, 185, 186, 187
    institutional investment and, 95, 105,
        107, 112–14
    investor compensation and, 20
    regulation of, 41–6, 180–81
    taxation and, 98, 182–3
Insurance Companies Act (1974), 43
Insurance Companies Act (1982), 17, 42,
    43–5, 112
Insurance Directives, 180–81
interest
    rates of, 51, 53, 54, 58–64
    taxation and, 80–1, 84, 89, 90
intermediation, financial, 3–4, 145
International Monetary Fund (IMF), 54–5
International Securities Market
    Association (ISMA), 28
internationalisation, 9–10
investment, 3–4
    institutional, 95–120
    taxation and, 80–81, 83, 85, 97–8, 112
Investment Management Regulatory
    Organisation (IMRO), 16, 17, 21,
    23, 26, 27
Investment Services Directive, 181
investment trusts, 95, 116–18
investor protection regulation, 14–15,
    20–6, 31, 40
Investors Compensation Scheme, 20, 22
Ireland, 183
Irish Life, 15
Italy, 183, 184

James Capel Tiger Index Fund, 107
joint ventures, 167, 184–5

Keasey, K., 139, 140
Keynes, John Maynard, 49, 58
kinked demand model, 159–60

language barriers, 183
Laurent, C.R., 136
law of one price, 59, 61
lending, *see* credit
Life Assurance Companies Act (1870), 41
Life Assurance and Unit Trust Regulatory
    Organisation (LAUTRO), 15, 16,
    17, 20, 21, 26, 27

liquidity, 32, 35, 39
literacy, financial, 172–3
Lloyds Abbey Life, 144
Lloyds Bank, 72, 144, 148, 166, 173
Lloyd's of London, 23–4, 28, 123, 151
Lloyd's of London Act (1982), 17, 24
London Stock Exchange, 16, 17, 22–3,
    26, 108, 117

McGuinness, P., 139, 140
macroeconomic environment, 48–65
management information systems, 40
manufacturing sector, 2, 55, 151–2,
    153–4
market failure, 13
market trading, 72
marketing, 70, 99–100, 152, 154–5,
    168–75
Markowitz, Harry, 100–2
Marks & Spencer plc, 8, 68, 144
Maxwell, Robert, 13, 23, 27, 179
Mehra, R., 109
merchant banks, 184
mergers, 40, 41, 162, 165–6, 184
Midland Bank, 9, 123, 146, 147, 148,
    150, 152, 154, 164, 165, 166, 167,
    172, 186
Modern Portfolio Theory, 100–10, 120
Modern Quantity Theory, 51
Mondex, 69
monetary theory, 50–51
money supply, 5, 6, 48, 51, 163–4
Monopolies and Mergers Commission,
    165, 166
moral hazard, 21–2
Morse, Sir Jeremy, 24, 28
mortgages, 6, 7–8, 20, 91, 99, 165,
    169
multinational corporations, 9–10

Nation Life, 43
National Westminster Bank, 27, 69, 123,
    148, 173
Nationwide Anglia, 166, 173
Netherlands, 183, 184
neutrality, fiscal, 83, 88
New Zealand, 54
non-financial institutions, 8, 68, 144
Norwich Union, 15
Nottingham Building Society, 68

O'Barr, W.M., 105
off-balance sheet risks, 33

oligopoly theory, 157, 158–61
Own Funds Directive, 31, 35, 36, 180

passport, banking, 35, 178–9
Peckham Building Society, 37
pension schemes, 6, 100
  institutional investment and, 95, 105,
    107, 110–12
  taxation and, 89, 91, 98
Personal Equity Plans (PEPs), 89–90,
  116, 171
Personal Investment Authority (PIA),
  16, 25, 26–7
Personal Pension Plans (PPPs), 100
Phillips curve, 50
Pinches, G. E., 136, 139
Pitt, William, 82
polarisation principle, 11, 25
poll tax, 82
Policyholders Protection Act (1975), 43
population changes, 171
Porter, M. E., 153, 155
portfolio investment, 98–9
portfolio theory, 100–10, 120
Portugal, 183
Premium Life, 15
Prescott, E., 109
price discrimination, 166
privatisation, 52, 72, 171
products, *see* financial products
Proffitt, D.L., 118, 119–20
progressive taxation, 81, 82
property, 97
  see also housing
Prudential, 27
prudential regulation, 14, 31–46

quantity theory of money, 51

Ramsay v. *IRC* (1981), 93
ratios, financial, 133–40
reciprocal agreements, 182
regional differences, 172
regressive taxation, 81, 82
regulation, *see under* financial services
reinsurance, 185
relational databases, 70, 75–8
reporting requirements, 40
reserves, banking, 5, 6
Restrictive Practices Court, 23
retail financial services, 9, 11–12, 167,
  175
  cost structure of, 142–56

risk appraisal, 122–40
risk aversion, 100
risk weighting, 33, 35, 38–9
Royal Bank of Scotland, 148

saving, 3–4, 83
Schumpeter, Joseph, 48
Scott Report (1973), 43
Securities and Exchange Commission
  (US), 26
Securities and Futures Authority (SFA),
  16, 17, 21, 23, 26, 27
Securities and Investment Board (SIB),
  15, 16, 21, 23, 24, 38, 99, 114
segmental marketing, 152, 154–5, 172
self-employment, 172
self-insurance, 185
self-regulation, 22–4, 179
self-regulatory organisations (SROs), 15,
  16, 20, 23, 28, 38, 99
Sephton, T., 154
Serious Fraud Office (SFO), 25–6
service sector employment, 2
shares, 69, 89–90, 96, 107–18, 170–1
Sharpe, William F., 102–3
Siegel, J.J., 109–10
single licence, 35, 178–9
Smith, R.K., 118, 119–20
Social Security Act (1986), 100, 171
social structure, 12, 169–73
Solvency Ratio Directive, 1, 35, 36, 180
Spain, 183
Standard Industrial Classification (SIC),
  1
standardisation, 2
state *see* government
State Earnings Related Pension Scheme
  (SERPS), 100
Stephens, A. A., 118, 119–20
structural regulation, 7–8, 14, 23, 31
Sun Alliance, 173, 187
supply-side economics, 52, 55, 57
system risk, 15

Taffler, R.J., 134, 136
Takeover Panel, 26
takeovers, 165–6
  see also mergers
Tax Exempt Special Savings Accounts
  (TESSAs), 80, 89, 90
taxation, 52, 80–93, 97–8, 112, 182–3
Taxes Act (1988), 80
technology, information, 67–79

196   *Index*

'tracker' funds, 104, 107, 116–17
Treasury, 15, 16, 38
Trustee Investments Act (1961), 110
trusts, 87–8
TSB Bank, 123, 148, 165

unemployment, 49–50, 53
Unfair Contract Terms Act (1977), 42
unit trusts, 95, 114–16
United States of America, 26, 54, 107, 112

value added tax (VAT), 81, 83, 88
value chain analysis, 155
Vehicle and General Insurance
    Company, 13, 43

venture capital, 185

Walker, Sir David, 24
Ward, T., 154
White, Stuart, 154–5
Wilson Report (1980), 36
window tax, 82
withholding taxes, 82
women, financial independence of, 12, 172
Woolwich Building Society, 166
World Bank, 54–5

Yorkshire Bank, 148

Zavgren, C.V., 139